SIGN CARVING

BY GARRIT D. LYDECKER

TAB BOOKS Inc.
BLUE RIDGE SUMMIT, PA. 17214

3/29/85 Main Line $12.95

FIRST EDITION

FIRST PRINTING

Copyright © 1983 by TAB BOOKS Inc.

Printed in the United States of America

Library of Congress Cataloging in Publication Data

Lydecker, Garrit D.
Sign carving.

Bibliography: p.
Includes index.
1. Wood-carving. 2. Signs and signboards. I. Title.
TT199.7.L93   1983   674′.88   83-4926
ISBN 0-8306-0101-5
ISBN 0-8306-0601-7 (pbk.)

Contents

Preface

The driving force of our age is technology. The population equivalent of many rural communities can be found housed in a single, immense building. The accoutrements of our daily lives are produced in mass by tireless machines. This has produced a quality of life unparalleled in history. The conveniences and opportunities available are so abundant as to be taken for granted by all but a few.

Within this society, however, there is a growing number of men and women who no longer feel comfortable with the new, the quick, and the cheap. Many are nostalgic for a time and place they never knew. They seek comfort in the past when our artifacts possessed a simple beauty and sense of permanence. These people, whose numbers increase daily, form the basis for today's resurgence of crafts. They are both the producers and consumers of products that at least give the appearance of patient and careful work. Work created by the intangibles of human mind and hand makes each piece in some way special.

One sign of the times is indeed the signs of the times. Signs often reflect—in advance—the directions a society will take. Flashing signs reflect a flashy economy, tasteful signs connote stable values.

In the past several years there has been a slow but steady growth in the use of handcrafted wooden signs. The styles range from aboriginal funk to urbane slick; but their message is clear.

Many people are no longer content to identify their homes, possessions, businesses or products by use of mass produced plastic items. Such sentiments form a strong base for sign carving businesses.

It is unfortunate that history has left us so few details of the artisanal methods of the past. Most written works from a century or two ago presume so much prior knowledge on the part of the reader as to render them all but meaningless to all but a handful of today's students. Where detailed information is given, many of the products and materials cited have passed into oblivion. Many jealously guarded secrets of the master craftsmen of the past died silently with them; there were no apprentices to continue the handicraft. Thus the increasing desire to own handcrafted wooden signs, together with the lack of currently usable information, has once again created the mystique of the master craftsman.

There is no reason that the average craftsman should suffer from the lack of technical information. While it is true that no amount of technical skill can compensate for a lack of artistic ability, all the ability in the world cannot adequately function without technical information.

Whether you are a weekend craftsman wanting to put your name on the mailbox or a person searching for an entirely new business and way of life, this book will help you. Old techniques have been updated. New skills requiring power tools are explained. New materials that are readily available are cited throughout, and sources for uncommon materials are included.

There are few opportunities outside the fine arts that offer as many possibilities to exercise creative talents as sign carving. All phases of the craft are stimulating. Because each product is a new one—calling for new thoughts and new expression—the craft is seldom, if ever, boring. It is genuine fun!

The manual work is easy; it allows you to channel most of your energy into the creative processes. At the start, the financial outlay can be kept to a minimum. This will allow you to get a really good taste of the enjoyment without making a serious financial commitment. Good tools appreciate in value, and they can be considered a good investment.

The beginning sign crafter should start a notebook at the earliest possible moment. While every effort has been made to make this book as comprehensive as possible in a single volume, new ideas and information constantly present themselves. It is best to get into the habit of recording them immediately. Your memory is not as good as a pencil and paper. An inexpensive three-ring binder—filled with blank, lined paper and graph paper—and a supply of colored pencils are all that is needed. As the notebook fills, it will be necessary to organize the information. The chapter headings of this book can be used or new headings might suggest themselves.

It has been my good fortune to teach various woodworking skills to children. To adult readers trying woodworking for the first time, I have these few words of caution: Think like a child. Children know that perfection is slow coming and never achieved on the first try. Do not be afraid to learn and do not be afraid to fail. Failures are temporary and much is learned from them. And most childlike of all, enjoy yourself.

The work of the sign crafter—like the work of any artisan—is intensely personal. Each artisan develops methods and techniques that work well for him. While every effort has been made to give unbiased coverage to all methods and techniques, I suppose it is only natural that a certain number of my personal preferences (prejudices?) have found their way into this book. If they are helpful, well and good. In those instances where my preferences may clash with yours, I have tried to give the reasons behind my choices in the hope that my line of reasoning will help.

Introduction

This book is intended as a comprehensive instructional guide to the craft of sign carving. Very little step by step "fold tab A into slot B" directions are given. This book is organized according to the sequences generally followed in sign carving. Under sequential headings are found various methods of accomplishing the job at hand. It would be best to read this book through from cover to cover, as though it were a novel, before beginning any projects.

There are several methods that can be used to accomplish a particular operation in the crafting of a sign. If the craftsman becomes familiar with all of them, a method consistent with the final objective can be selected.

For example, the joining of two or more boards to form a sign blank can be accomplished in several different ways. It might be desirable that the joints show in the finished sign; perhaps even a slight space between the boards. Alternatively, it might be desirable to have the sign blank a smooth, unblemished surface. The choice of methods might be governed by the final placement of the sign. Interior or exterior environments will require the selection of different methods of joinery or adhesives. Therefore several methods of joinery are given together with the values and limitations of each method. Many adhesives are discussed as well. The bibliography lists books that treat the subjects of joinery and adhesives in greater detail. The sign crafter should make every effort to acquire the broadest possible knowledge of the many disciplines which make this one of the most demanding and rewarding of all crafts.

At the end of each section, there is a list of all the tools and materials covered in that section. They are organized by the operation to be performed. This will help the beginner to ensure that no tools or materials are forgotten until the crucial moment arrives. There is no situation quite like the one experienced when the gold size has reached the perfect stage of drying and the supply of gold leaf is far smaller than anticipated.

Just as there are few step-by-step directions given in this book, so too there are very few basic designs given. The reason for this is to encourage originality. There are simply far too many design possibilities; a single volume could not possibly hope to contain them all. If it did contain many designs, most would be useless because the artistic preferences of most individuals fall into a fairly narrow portion of the available spectrum. A portion of your notebook should be devoted to design ideas that appeal to you.

Art books, magazines, and newspapers are all good sources of design ideas. Your eye will soon become trained to see shapes, relationships, and unusual typefaces that appeal to you. There are very few creative geniuses in any field. Most truly good sign crafting work will be done by people talented in observing, modifying, and adapting the work of others. Adaptation is a legitimate artistic endeavor. Out and out copying or plagiarism, of course, is not.

The beginner will soon sense the elements of design or "style" that appeal most to him. It might come as somewhat of a shock to realize that the style most appreciated might not be the style in which the individual works best. An artist might have many of his own paintings in his studio, but the walls of his *home* might be decorated with the paintings of other artists. This is true also of the sign crafter. He might truly admire the works of others, even secretly wish he could do the same, but actually work in an entirely different style. It is therefore imperative for the beginner to experiment as much as possible, and to try to free himself as much as possible from preconceived ideas. Success as a sign crafter comes from developing a personal style and then praying very hard that the style becomes popular.

The beginner should expose himself as early as possible to the styles and work of others. This can be done by keeping a notebook (and perhaps a camera) in your car even on local trips. Another way to see the work of others is to subscribe to trade magazines listed in this book. At least write and ask to purchase a single copy. This is an economical way to see if the magazine is worth the subscription price. The advertisements in these magazines are also educational.

1
Overview

T he need to communicate information in a graphic form is as
old as mankind. The term *sign language* denotes an ancient
method of communicating information directly across tribal and
language barriers (Fig. 1-1). They are still sometimes used to
communicate information. Signs were also used to communicate
indirectly. A scout or hunter could leave information that would be
needed by those who followed. Histories could be left to other
generations by the use of signs (Fig. 1-2). Religious information and
practice can be communicated by the signs of totem and taboo (Fig.
1-3). It is interesting to note the continuing use of ancient signs
today (Fig. 1-4) and the adaptation of ancient forms to present-day
use (Fig. 1-5).

Many of the preceding examples served nomads and hunters in
the past and they continue to serve their contemporaries today. But
with the establishment of population centers, different and more
complex signs soon were needed.

One difference soon felt was the need for permanence. Bent
twigs and berry juice stains were no longer sufficient. The art of the
sign crafter was born right along with the alchemical mysteries of
substrate, vehicle, and pigment that continue to this day.

Permanence was only one necessary factor. The need for
detailed information quickly became apparent. Traveling directions

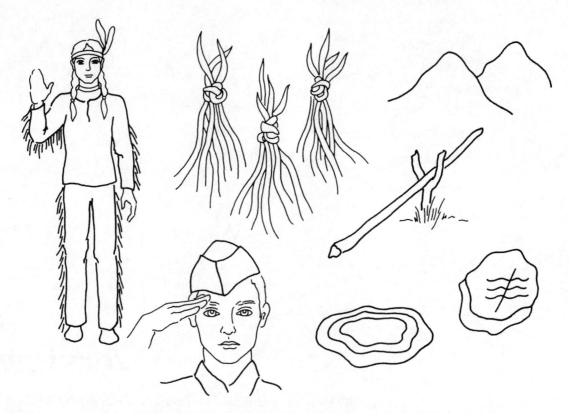

(Fig. 1-6) and trade signs (Fig. 1-7) were quickly developed. As competition quickened, the advertising sign was born (Fig. 1-8).

Fig. 1-1. Sign language.

THE PHILOSOPHY OF SIGNAGE

Although a profitable business can be based on a wide variety of signs, the usual money-maker for most sign crafters is the advertising or trade sign. The principles discussed can be adapted to all forms of signage.

The first thing that all signs *must* do is provide information. That is the function of a sign. In its most rudimentary form the sign provides specific information. As in Fig. 1-9, it enables someone seeking a specific house to eliminate hundreds of other houses on the street. Think of the problems, not to mention tragedies, that are averted by the simple house number. It creates order in a system that would be chaotic without it.

Notice how the information provided by the sign becomes more and more specific as more and more information is added to it (Fig. 1-10). The principle at work here is *exclusion*; that is the exclusion of all the unwanted names, addresses and vocations on the street. This works only up to a point.

Figure 1-11 shows what happens when the inclusion of specific

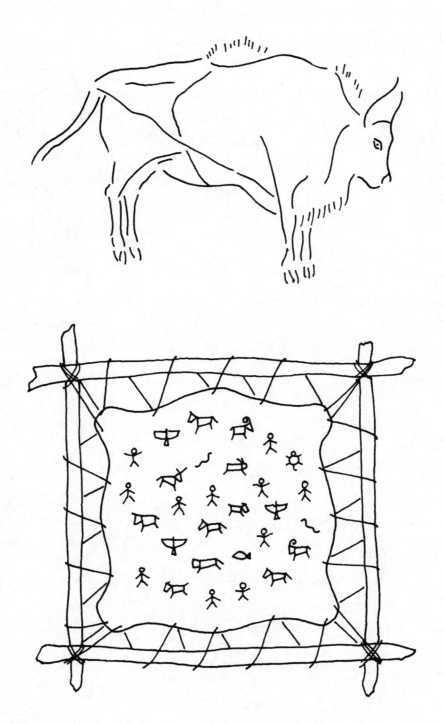

Fig. 1-2. Signs that are messages.

Fig. 1-3. Informative signs.

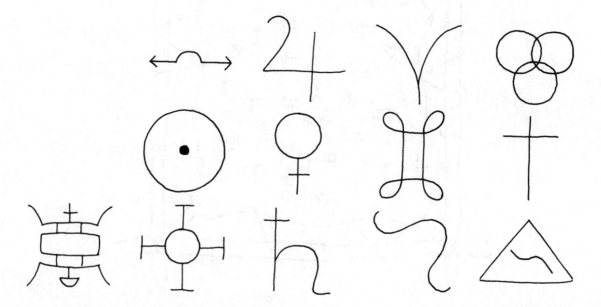

Fig. 1-4. Examples of ancient signs.

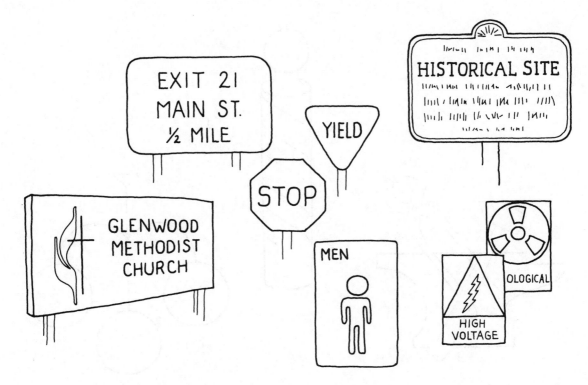

Fig. 1-5. Present-day signs are sometimes adaptions of ancient signs.

Fig. 1-6. Directional signs.

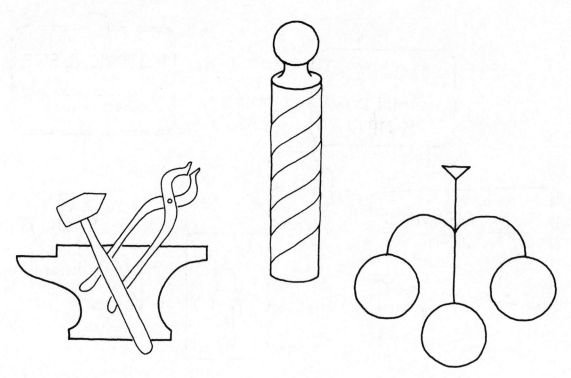

Fig. 1-7. Trade signs.

Fig. 1-8. Advertising.

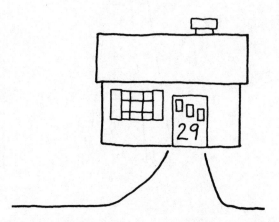

Fig. 1-9. A sign provides specific information.

Fig. 1-10. Examples of exclusion.

information and the principle of exclusion rise up to do battle with one another. We have very nearly reached the borders of chaos.

RULES

Less Is More. An important principle is that the maker of a sign assumes that the person reading it already has some information. In comparing C of Fig. 1-10 to Fig. 1-11, the sign shown in C of Fig. 1-10 is the better sign. It assumes that the reader knows the function of an attorney. To a person who does not know the function of an attorney, the additional information on the sign in Fig. 1-11 can be presumed to be meaningless as well.

It might be objected that the sign in Fig. 1-11 carries certain useful information relevant to the specific areas of expertise of attorney Jones. The argument is not relevant because a carefully

Fig. 1-11. Inclusion versus exclusion.

executed and costly hand-carved wooden sign cannot be turned into a billboard any more than a mouse can be enlarged to become a cat. A sign crafter approached to execute a sign such as shown in Fig. 1-11 will do both himself and attorney Jones a favor by referring Jones to a billboard painter.

Form Follows Function. A good sign provokes action. *Any* good sign does this, but there are different types of good signs, different provocations, and different actions.

An acre of flashing lights on Times Square provokes action by both enticement and intimidation. A hand carved sign provokes action by restraint and charm. A painted paper banner proclaims limited time bargains. A hand carved sign invokes feelings of timeless prestige. All these signs provoke action, but the means of provocation are inherent in the media. The means of provocation are *not* interchangeable.

Messages. The medium contains its own message.

2

Carvable Materials

I t is doubtful whether there exists a carvable material that has not been carved into a sign. Wood, stone, glass, masonry, shells, jewel stones, and more have been used. Of the commonly available materials, wood and wood products are by far the most common material for carving.

WOOD

Like anything else derived from nature, wood is subject to a wide variety of virtues and faults. No two trees are the same and no two boards are the same even though cut from the same tree. Each board has an individual character with some interesting problems for the sign carver. Weight, rot resistance, tendency to warp or shrink, strength, brittleness, and defects all combine to challenge a carver's knowledge and resourcefulness. In making selections of both lumber species and individual *boards*, some knowledge of lumber science and technology will be helpful.

Once the brushwood, leaves, and fine roots are removed, a tree can be thought of as having three parts: the root, the bole or trunk, and the crown. See Fig. 2-1.

The root is the toughest, densest, and most rot-resistant part of the tree. The curving grain of the root makes this section desirable for curved timbers used in boat and furniture building. Pieces of

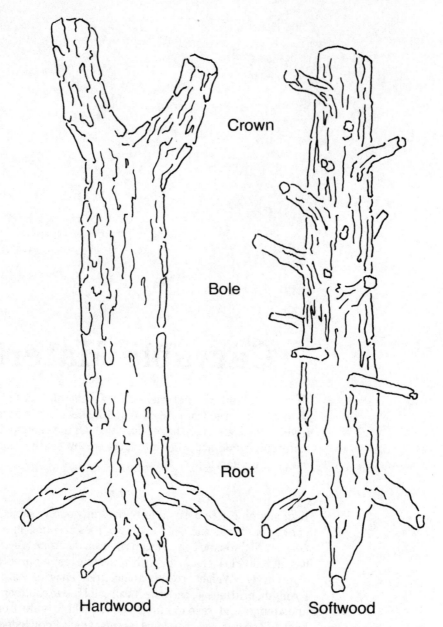

Crown

Bole

Root

Hardwood   Softwood

Fig. 2-1. Tree parts.

the root section are often called *knees* or *hackmatack*. Their use is limited and the supply is generally quite scarce.

The crown also provides some knees and small dimension lumber, but the dominance of sapwood tends to make the lumber of poor quality in all but the largest branches. Larger branches are often used in making other lumber-related products such as flakeboards. The environmentally conscious will be glad to know that very little of the tree is wasted.

The grain in the crotch sections tends to be quite wild and well figured. This section is generally reserved for the manufacture of veneers for marquetry work.

Virtually all lumber commonly available in lumberyards comes from the bole of the tree. Within the bole of the tree are two types of spongy tissue; sapwood and heartwood (Fig. 2-2). Sapwood is the area of wood directly under the bark (represented by fine lines in Fig. 2-2). The spongelike cells are open and they conduct the flow of sap from the roots to the leaves. Directly below the sapwood is the heartwood (drawn in heavy lines in Fig. 2-2). This wood, once sapwood, forms the bulk of the bole of the mature tree. The cells of heartwood are filled with resins and pigments that strengthen the cells and give support to the tree.

The boards shown in Fig. 2-3 reveal the relationship of

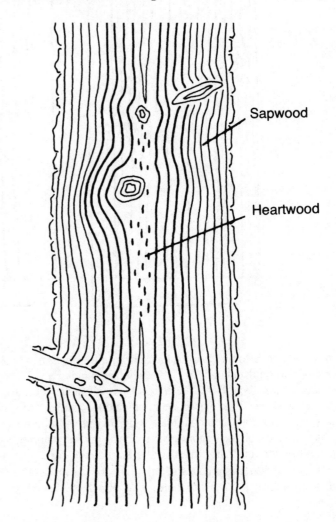

Sapwood

Heartwood

Fig. 2-2. Types of tree tissue.

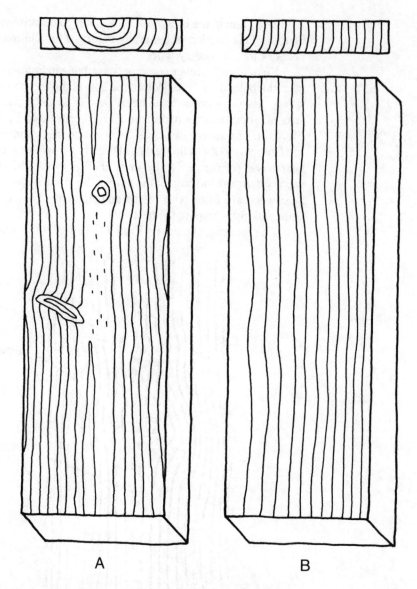

A   B

heartwood to sapwood. Board A has a far greater portion of spongy, coarse sapwood than board B. When you are making a selection at the lumberyard, boards that are mostly or all heartwood are the better choice. The tissue is more stable and less subject to shrinkage, warping or cracks, and yields a superior sign. Problems occur in that in some of the vigorous softwoods grown commercially, sapwood might constitute most of the bole of the tree.

Figure 2-4 shows a cross section of a tree trunk and the way boards may be cut from the bole. The effect of shrinkage—the

Fig. 2-3. Sapwood (A) and heartwood (B).

evaporation of moisture from the wood—are represented more graphically than will actually occur. The upper two boards are tangentially cut or slash sawn. The lower two boards are radially cut. When selecting boards, the radially cut boards are the better choice. Shrinkage will produce far less warping than tangentially cut boards.

Because the radially cut board is generally an "accident" of the slash sawing process, both types will generally be found in the same pile at the lumberyard. Selecting boards can therefore be a long and laborious process.

Find a large lumberyard that will let you pick through the piles. Be sure to leave the piles at least as neat as you found them or you will soon be looking for a new yard.

DEFECTS IN LUMBER

Figure 2-5 shows two common defects found in logs. *Checks* result from differential drying of the log; the outer layers dry more quickly than the center. *Shakes* are caused by high winds. The wind load from a storm occasionally develops torsional stresses in the trunk of the tree that twists layers of wood apart along an annual growth ring. Shakes in sapwood are generally hollow voids. Shakes in heartwood are generally filled with resins and pitch that form a pitch pocket.

Figure 2-6 shows the many sizes and types of knots found in boards. In softwoods, knots have no connection with the living tree. They are the remains of broken branches that have been incorpo-

Fig. 2-4. A tree trunk cross section.

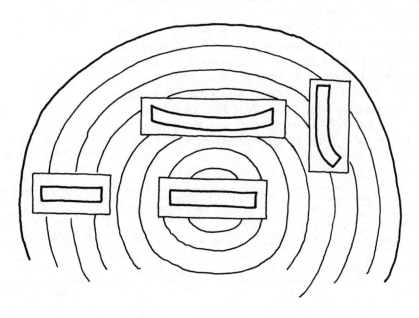

13

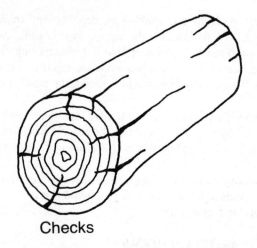

Checks

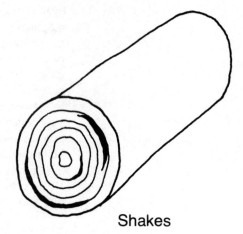

Shakes

Fig. 2-5. Common defects.

rated within the living tissue of the tree. The difference in density and seasoning time account for the extreme hardness of knots. Because knots are extremely hard to work with in carving, it is best to choose "clear" or "select" stock for sign use.

Figure 2-7 shows bark pockets and pitch pockets. These common defects should be avoided when selecting lumber for sign use. Problems occur when these types of defects are concealed within a board and then are revealed by carving. While it is possible to correct these defects, the extra work is difficult. It is better to reject a suspect board.

Figure 2-8 shows a *wane* that occurs when a check or shake is near the edge of the board and the small segment is separated from the plank during the milling process.

Figure 2-9 shows the various effects caused by warping. Warping occurs when stresses built up in the living tree are released by the milling process. Warping can also occur, for the same reason, when a board is resawn to smaller dimensions.

Figure 2-10 shows a piece of lumber with a *pith* center. This defect generally occurs in wide boards (see Fig. 2-2). Pith—the original sapling of the tree—is softer and more brittle than the surrounding tissue and it tends to split out easily. Reject boards with a pith center.

Fig. 2-6. Knot sizes and shapes.

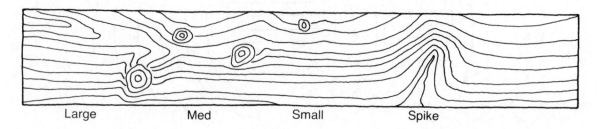

Large   Med   Small   Spike

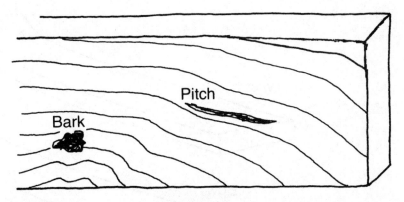

Fig. 2-7. Common defects.

GRAIN IN LUMBER

Grain is the annular growth rings of the tree revealed during the milling process. A small experiment will help you to visualize the milling process and the grain created by it. The layers of an onion are created in much the same way as the layers of growth in a tree. If an onion is sliced along the grain (opposite of the way you do for cooking), the slabs of tissue will represent boards. The exposed layers represent the grain. Slicing several onions and experimenting will show you how strengths can be used and weaknesses can be avoided.

Board B shown in Fig. 2-3 will be easier to carve and less apt to warp than board A. The upper sides of both boards also will be easier to carve than the lower sides.

The term *with the grain* is used extensively throughout this

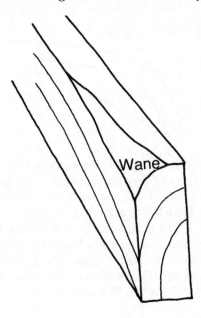

Fig. 2-8. A wane results when a check or shake is near the edge of the board.

15

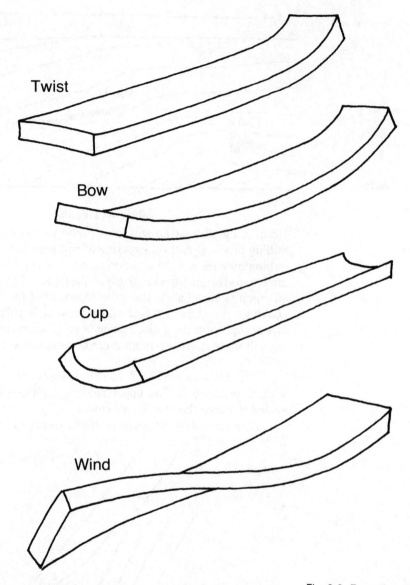

Twist

Bow

Cup

Wind

Fig. 2-9. Examples of warping.

book. The term can be explained in various ways that usually mean "in the general direction." For our purposes, with the grain means *in the direction the grain leaves the surface of the board.* The two boards shown in Fig. 2-11 are examples of boards ripped from the same slab. Note how the grain flows from one board into the next. This flow is the meaning of the term "with the grain."

Looking at one of the boards in section, you will notice that with the grain means from the center outward on one side, and from the edges inward on the other. Because boards have grain in both

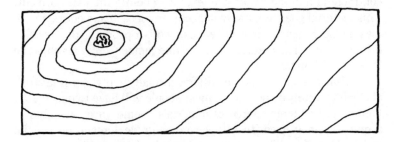

Fig. 2-10. Lumber with a pith center. (end view).

directions, working with the grain means working so that tools take the best possible advantage of *both* directions of grain.

LUMBER GRADES AND SPECIFICATIONS

Those who have had the experience of renovating an old house know that the quality of lumber is quite different today than in the past. The long, thick, perfectly straight grained and blemish free lumber of the past is almost nonexistent today. European and Asian interests have invested heavily in both American and Canadian lumber production, and those interests tend to skim the cream of the crop for themselves. The small supply of prime lumber that remains is

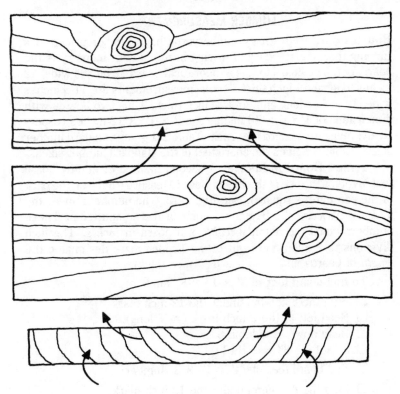

Fig. 2-11. With the grain.

17

contracted for at the wholesale level long before the trees are cut. This material goes to large manufacturers of sash and doors, moldings, ladders, pencils, and a great many other products that require prime lumber. The result is that this fine lumber never reaches the local retail lumberyard.

While a few artisans can still find a small supply of prime stock at small privately owned mills, most people will have to use a retail lumberyard as their source of materials. Some yards are able to acquire a small quantity of appearance-grade lumber on special order. This "small" quantity would probably be sufficient to last most artisans several lifetimes.

Most yards stock only the *factory select* grade; this is a downgrading of the former *clear* specification, and it allows a certain number of blemishes and defects. Lumber is graded only on one face. The back and sides of the board may be of poorer quality (while remaining "select"). Therefore it is best to ask for directions to the select pile and pick through the pile yourself.

To acquire the best lumber, become a "regular" at the yard. Visit at off hours when contractors are not there. Become friendly with the foreman who might begin to put special pieces away for you. You could bring coffee and a tip during the right season.

LUMBER MEASUREMENT

Board Foot. While many lumberyards have lumber priced at a running foot, the standard of pricing in the lumber industry is the board foot. The board foot is a theoretical board 12 inches wide, 12 inches long, and 1 inch thick. Actual measurements are 11½ inches wide, 12 inches long and ¾ of an inch thick. Thus two boards with dimensions of 1 × 6 × 48 inches and 2 × 12 × 12 inches respectively, measure 2 board feet each. Table 2-1 gives standard lumber sizes. Table 2-2 gives the board feet of the standard lumber sizes.

Essex Board Measure. A second method of finding board feet involves the use of the Essex Board Measure (found on the back of the carpenter's square). See Fig. 2-12. The numbers under the 12-inch mark are the beginning point of the computation. These numbers equal the nominal *width* of a board in *inches*. The inch divisions to the left and right of the 12-inch mark designated the *length* of boards in *feet* (of boards 1 inch thick).

To find board feet of 3'-×-1"-×-8" lumber:

☐ Find the 8 column under the 12-inch mark.
☐ Read left to the 3-inch mark (= 3' long).
☐ Read down to column 8.
☐ 3' × 1" × 8" = 2 Bd Ft.

To find board feet of 14'-×-1"-×-8" lumber:

☐ Find the 8 column under the 12-inch mark.

Table 2-1. Standard Lumber Sizes.

Lumber	Thickness		Face width	
	Nominal	Finished	Nominal	Finished
Boards	1″ 1 1/4″ or 5/4″ 1 1/2″ or 6/4″	3/4″ 1″ 1 ¼″	2″ 3″ 4″ 6″ 8″ 10″ 12″	1 1/2″ 2 1/2″ 3 1/2′ 5 1/2″ 7 1/4″ 9 1/4″ 11 1/4″
Dimension	2″ or 8/4″ 3″ 4″	1 1/2″ 2 1/2″ 3 1/2″	2″ 3″ 4″ 6″ 8″ 10″ 12″	1 1/2″ 2 1/2″ 3 1/2″ 5 1/2″ 7 1/4″ 9 1/4″ 11 1/4″

☐ Read right to the 14-inch mark (= 14′).
☐ Read down to column 8.
☐ 14′ × 1″ × 8″ = 94 or 9 and 4/12 Bd Ft.

To find board feet of 9′-×-1″-×-3″ lumber:

☐ 3″ lumber is not there.
☐ Find 9 under the 12-inch mark.
☐ Find 9′ 9″ lumber = 69 or 6 and 9/12 Bd Ft.
☐ 6¾ Bd Ft ÷ 3 = 2¼ Bd Ft.

To find 7′ × 2″ × 4″

☐ Read for 7′ × 1″ × 8″

To find 9′ × 2″ × 8″

☐ Read for 18′ × 1″ × 8″

LUMBER SPECIES

Lumber species is determined by the tree from which it is cut. The species are divided into two categories: softwood is derived from evergreens, and hardwood is derived from decidous trees.

To make matters more complicated, the terms soft and hard have very little to do with the true hardness of the wood. The terms refer to the hardness of the tree (more or less). For example, yellow pine, a "softwood," is so hard that it can't be carved and balsa, a "hardwood," is so soft it can't be carved. Of the species commonly available in lumberyards (in the Northeast), there are very few that are of interest to the sign carver.

Softwoods

The California sugar pine (*Pinus lambetriana*) is the softwood of choice. This tall, stately tree yields stock that carves with ease, is not damaging to tools, and finishes beautifully. Where available, it is common to find 2-inch, 3-inch and even 4-inch stock. Supplies are fair to good.

White pine (*Pinus strobus*) is the second choice. It comes in two varieties: northern white pine—that is excellent for carving and slightly more durable than sugar pine—and western white pine that is slightly more fiberous and grainy than the northern variety. Supplies vary.

Table 2-2. Board Foot Measures.

SIZE	LENGTH IN FEET					
	1	4	8	12	16	20
	BOARD (Square) FEET					
1 × 2	.01	.03	1.33	2	2.66	3.33
1 × 3	.25	.50	2	3	4	5
1 × 4	.19	.75	2.66	4	5.33	6.66
1 × 6	.50	2	4	6	8	10
1 × 8	.75	2.66	5.33	8	10.66	13.33
1 × 10	.83	3.33	6.66	10	13.66	16.66
1 × 12	1	4	8	12	16	20
2 × 3	.50	2	4	6	8	10
2 × 4	.33	2.66	5.33	8	10.66	13.33
2 × 6	1	4	8	12	16	20
2 × 8	1.50	5.33	10.66	16	21.33	26.66
2 × 10	1.66	6.66	13.33	20	26.66	33.33
2 × 12	2	8	16	24	32	40

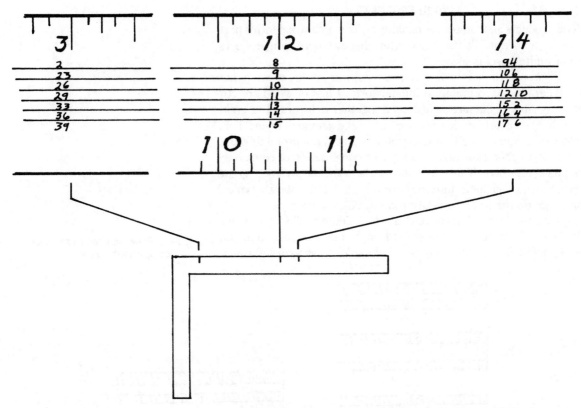

Fig. 2-12. Essex Board Measure.

Redwood (*Sequoia sempervirens*) is stringy and hard to carve with hand tools. It carves well with power tools. The wood is brittle and does not finish well. Best for rustic signs with bold carving and no finish. Surface can be abraided with a wire brush for interesting textures. Supplies are fair.

Hardwoods

Oak, American white (*Quercus alba* et al.) is easy to carve and is quite durable. Excellent for staining and clear finishes, the supply is fair to good.

Mahogany, Honduran (*Swietenia marcophylla*), and African (*Khaya ivorensis*) are easy to work with and they finish beautifully. Very expensive and prone to rot the supplies are generally poor.

Phillippine "mahoganies" (Luan and Tanguile) are not true mahoganies. They are poor working, but supplies are excellent.

Teak (*Tectona grandis*) carves well, but it quickly dulls tools. It is hard to finish well because resins prevent finishes from adhering. The finish is generally oiled. Teak is excellent for use around water, as on boats, but it is extremely expensive. Supplies are generally fair at some yards near coastal areas.

21

WOOD PRODUCTS

Wood products are composition materials in which wood forms part of the composition. To the sign crafter, these composition products are of limited usefulness.

Plywood is a sheet material made of lower grades of wood that are generally unacceptable in lumber form. Plies of wood are cut into long ribbons that are sandwiched together in layers. The grain in each layer is oriented at 90 degrees to the previous layer. This produces a dimensionally stable material that is not prone to warp. Figure 2-13 shows the size and interior composition of commonly available plywood. Table 2-3 shows the various plywood grade designations and their intended use. Figure 2-14 shows typical markings on the face of the plywood to designate grade.

Due to the wild grain and the tool-dulling adhesives used, plywood is of limited usefulness to the sign crafter. As a medium for hand carving it is useless, but as a backing for a hand-carved sign it

Fig. 2-13. Plywood sizes and interior composition (full size).

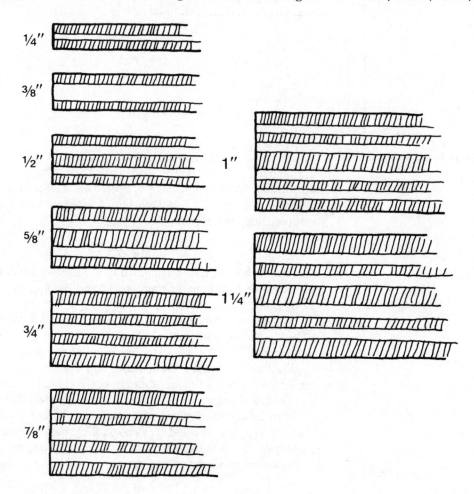

¼″

⅜″

½″   1″

⅝″

¾″   1¼″

⅞″

Table 2-3. Plywood Markings.

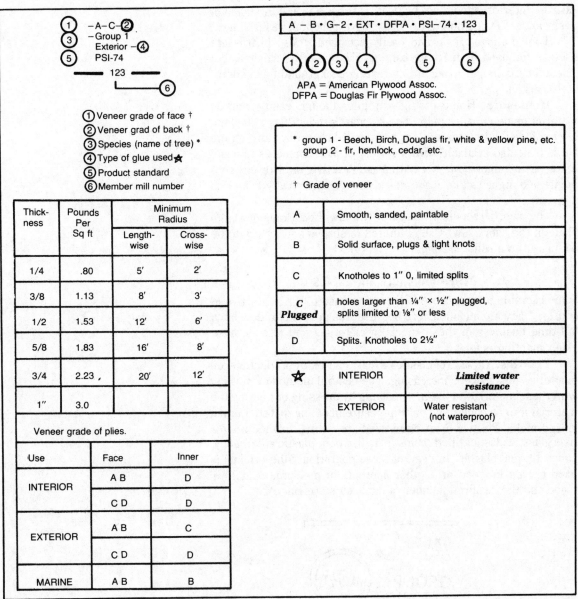

Thick-ness	Pounds Per Sq ft	Minimum Radius	
		Length-wise	Cross-wise
1/4	.80	5'	2'
3/8	1.13	8'	3'
1/2	1.53	12'	6'
5/8	1.83	16'	8'
3/4	2.23	20'	12'
1″	3.0		

Veneer grade of plies.

Use	Face	Inner
INTERIOR	A B	D
	C D	D
EXTERIOR	A B	C
	C D	D
MARINE	A B	B

① Veneer grade of face †
② Veneer grad of back †
③ Species (name of tree) *
④ Type of glue used ☆
⑤ Product standard
⑥ Member mill number

APA = American Plywood Assoc.
DFPA = Douglas Fir Plywood Assoc.

* group 1 - Beech, Birch, Douglas fir, white & yellow pine, etc. group 2 - fir, hemlock, cedar, etc.	
† Grade of veneer	
A	Smooth, sanded, paintable
B	Solid surface, plugs & tight knots
C	Knotholes to 1″ 0, limited splits
C Plugged	holes larger than ¼″ × ½″ plugged, splits limited to ⅛″ or less
D	Splits. Knotholes to 2½″

☆	INTERIOR	*Limited water resistance*
	EXTERIOR	Water resistant (not waterproof)

has value. As a medium for hard-edged machine carving, the marine grade is excellent.

Particle Board. This material is composed of scraps resulting from other manufacturing processes. The wood is chipped into small pieces. The smallest size of particle board is chipboard, and it does not look like wood at all. Larger particles are used to make flakeboard, and in this material the look of wood is preserved. The pieces of wood are compressed into a resinous binder. Type 1 boards (interior) should not be used as it has a urea-formaldehyde resin binder. Type 2 boards (exterior) have a phenolic resin binder.

Tool dulling, brittle and easily damaged, these boards are useless for hand or machine carving. They can be sandblasted. These boards might make an interesting background for modern-style carved signs.

Homosote. Homosote is a fragile, though easily worked material made of paper pulp. The standard product has a medium grey color with fine texture on the face and coarse texture on the back. It is also available with a variety of face laminates in many textures and colors. Many exciting and dramatic interior environments and signs can be made quickly and economically from this material.

The material should not be cut with a saw. Use a knife or a knife blade in the sabre saw. Use is limited to shapes and letters to be laminated to a solid backing.

OTHER CARVABLE MATERIALS

Some carvable materials are of little or no use to the average sign crafter. They are included here because it is possible to develop a full-time business in these specialty materials and also because experimenting is fun.

Plastics. The use of plastics to cast one-off or production-run quantities of signage is increasing. The general method of working with these materials is *negative molding* by pressing or pouring the material into an open mold or by pressure injecting material into a closed mold. Plastics most often used are resins, foamed resins, fiberglass, Celastic, filled resins (plastic wood, plastic steel, etc.), concrete, and plaster. In most of these operations, the original is hand carved in wood or another appropriate medium. A mold is made and the required number of duplicates are run off.

Fig. 2-14. Plywood grade designations.

Foamed Plastic Sheet. Due to the light weight, reasonable cost, and ease of working, foamed plastics are finding increased use in the manufacturing of signs. Large props and display pieces as well as very ornate signs can be made of these materials. The material can be worked with sharp hand tools following typical wood-carving methods, or it can be carved with electrically heated knives, hot wires, etc. The material is chemically sensitive however, and great care must be taken to select compatible adhesives and paints. Water-based materials are generally safe but not acceptable for exterior use. The finished product is dimensionally stable, but very easily damaged.

Stone. Concrete, stone, cast stone, and plaster are all carvable materials. Carving these materials is extremely labor intensive. The materials are unforgiving of mistakes in execution.

Glass. Glass, mirrors, and cast plastic sheets are all carvable with specialty tools. The result can be highly dramatic signage. Large panels can be individually carved or smaller panels can be carved and joined rather like leaded glass windows. Especially handsome signage can be created by combining both carved wood and carved plastic sheets in a single unit that can simultaneously lit from both front and back.

3
Design

In this chapter the rules of good sign design are explained. The development of a personal style is *not* covered. The rules of good design are analogous to a mathematical formula: $X + Y = Z$. Your personal style can be injected into the formula as would be arithmetic values. Thus $1 + 2 = 3$ and $7 + 3 = 10$ are the results of personal style and choice, while the original formula, $X + Y = Z$, remains constant. This approach should result in both the maximum number of "good" signs, and the widest variety of personal expression.

It is often said that rules are made to be broken, and the most successful artists are the ones who break the most rules. This is true in *part*. The second part (seldom stated) is that the most successful artists *never* arbitrarily break the rules! There is always an inherently sound reason that causes the rule in question to be invalid in a particular case.

The most iconoclastic artists of the past (good ones that is) knew what the rules were and why the rules were there in the first place. Seen in this light, these artists never really broke the rules. They used the rules in a new way and elevated them, perhaps, to a higher form of expression. In this chapter adhere to established rules. Once understood, you break then at your peril, and, I hope, to your advantage.

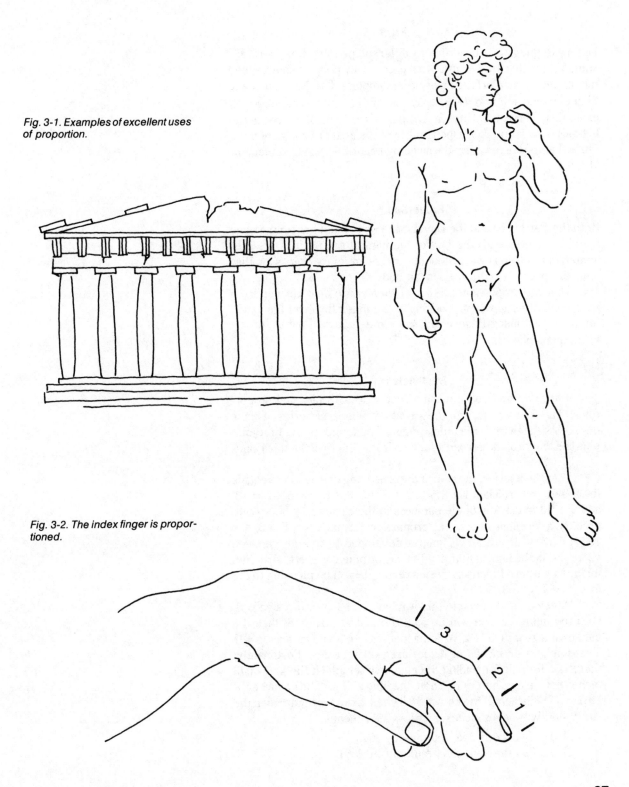

Fig. 3-1. Examples of excellent uses of proportion.

Fig. 3-2. The index finger is proportioned.

27

APPEARANCE

Different things are beautiful to different people. But there are some things that are beautiful to a great many people; snowcapped mountains or a colorful sunset are examples. The Parthenon and Michelangelo's David (Fig. 3-1) are universally recognized as examples of great beauty. If beauty is really in the eye of the beholder, then it is the responsibility of the artist to put something there that most eyes perceive as being beautiful. The first element of beauty is proportion.

Proportion

Both the Parthenon and the David make use of familiar proportions found in nature. With the David, the natural proportions are presented in an obvious way. Most observers are more or less familiar with the proportions of the human body.

That the proportions of the Parthenon are also derived from nature is not so apparent. Looking at the index finger of the David (or your own index finger) will show the "natural" nature of the Parthenon. See Fig. 3-2.

Rectangles

There are two ways of drawing a rectangle with pleasing proportions. The first way is with the so-called Fibonacci Series. This is the series taken from the index finger. The length of the first joint plus the length of the second joint equals the length of the third joint: $1 + 2 = 3$.

To make a series, the sum of the preceding two numbers equals the third number. Thus $1 + 2 = 3$, $2 + 3 = 5$, $3 + 5 = 8$, $5 + 8 = 13$, and $8 + 13 = 21$. Any of the numbers in the series may be used to produce a rectangle of pleasing proportions. Thus 3×5, 5×8, 8×13, and 13×21 are all rectangles developed from a progression observed in the human figure, a flower, or pine cone, etc. Any sign included within a Fibonacci Series rectangle will be pleasing to the eye. See Fig. 3-3.

Developing a rectangle this way is easy. If a known size is 3, then the unknown size will be 5. If the known size is 8, then the unknown size will be 13. What happens when a known size is 48? The numbers 48 inches or 4 feet are not in series. Fortunately, there is a formula for finding the unknown length. If the known 48 inches equals the short dimension, the long side will be 48 inches × 1.61 = 77¼ inches. If the known 48 inches is the long side, then the short side will be 48 inches × .61 = 29¼ inches.

☐ To find short side, multiply by .61.
☐ To find the long side, multiply by 1.61.

Fig. 3-3. Fibonacci Series rectangles.

A second method for drawing a pleasing rectangle is by use of the golden rectangle of the ancient Greeks: the proportions of the Parthenon. An unknown long side can be found by using a known short side. In addition, the procedure may be reversed to find an unknown short side from a known long side.

A square equal to the length of the short side is drawn. A compass is then set off to the length of the diagonal, and the arc is swept to the baseline. The rectangle is then completed as shown in Fig. 3-4.

If the arc is extended from both sides of the square, a second rectangle is developed. It is different in proportion than the first, but based on the same rule and thus still pleasing. See Fig. 3-5.

Other rectangles can be generated by extending the rule—each in a different proportion, but all related—and all based on the same natural progression (Fig. 3-6).

There are very few signs that a sign carver will be called upon to execute that will not fit into a rectangle. The first step toward creating beauty in the eye of the beholder is to use a beautiful rectangle. A very strong second step is symmetry.

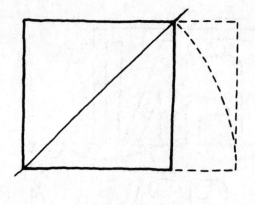

Fig. 3-4. Note the baseline arc.

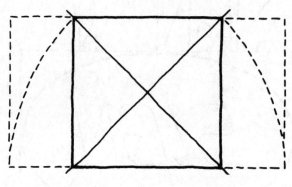

Fig. 3-5. The arc is extended.

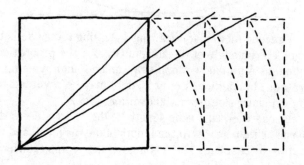

Fig. 3-6. Extending the rectangle.

Symmetry

Symmetry is a principle found in nature. It involves the balance of the individual parts as well as the balance of the parts within the whole. Simple bilateral symmetry, in which one part is the mirror image of the other (Fig. 3-7), is only one type of symmetry. There are 17 kinds of symmetry thus far discovered in nature.

Static symmetry and dynamic symmetry (Fig. 3-8) are two other forms used to achieve an overall pleasing effect. Both are natural forms that are familiar to the eye.

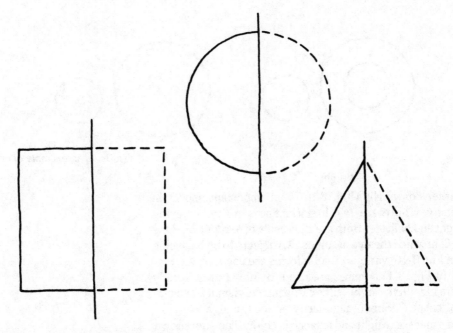

Fig. 3-7. An example of simple bilateral symmetry.

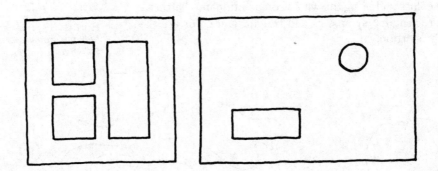

Fig. 3-8. Static and dynamic symmetry.

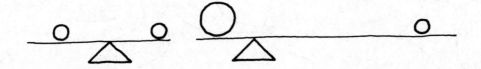

Fig. 3-9. An example of perceived
weight.

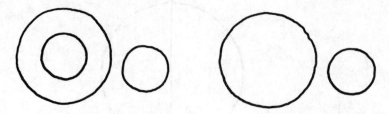

Fig. 3-10. An example of visual weight.

Weight

Visual or perceived weight (Fig. 3-9) is an important aspect in achieving beauty. There are two important aspects in achieving pleasing weight and balance. Both are the result of perception. One is *visual weight* in which the eye assumes two objects to be balancing each other. In Fig. 3-10, various circular forms are used to illustrate this balance. In Fig. 3-11, figures are used to show how naturally occurring items familiar can be either in balance visually or completely out of balance. Simple familiarity is not the key.

A second aspect of weight and balance is color. The sign shown in Fig. 3-12 is drawn in black and white. The balance is poor because of the lack of color weight. If you take a watercolor set and paint the circle a brilliant red/orange and the letters a pale blue/green, the weight of the colors will bring the whole composition into balance.

Related rectangles, symmetry and weight, and color are the elements of proportion.

Fig. 3-11. Figures can be in or out of balance. Familiarity is not the key to balance.

Fig. 3-12. Color would enhance the balance of this sign.

COMPOSITION

Composition is the structural basis of the overall design. For an artist who paints pictures, the elements of composition all fall within the borders of the canvas, and the artist has control over them all. For the sign crafter, many of the elements of the composition are outside the sign itself.

The color and texture of a wall or the architectural style of a building are elements over which the sign crafter has no control, but nevertheless must use well. People see the building and the sign together. They must both form a pleasing composition in the beholder's eye. A beautiful jewel out of character with a beautiful setting is not a piece of beautiful jewelry.

Composition of the sign concerns the placement of the various elements of the sign within the borders of the blank sign. This is different from the composition of the lettering itself (discussed in Chapter 5).

Space

A sculpture, a sign, or any other work of art occupies space. This space divided itself into two types: *Positive space* and *negative space*

Fig. 3-13. Examples of positive and negative space.

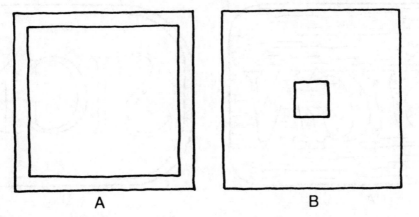

A   B

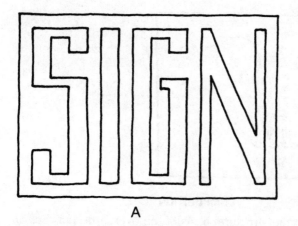

A

B

Fig. 3-14. Signs using positive and negative space.

(or *white space*). The wall on which the sign sets (or the empty space around a free-standing sign) is negative space. The sign itself is positive space. Within the sign itself, the blank is negative space, and the lettering and decoration are positive space.

Figure 3-13 shows two examples of positive and negative space. At A, the positive space overpowers the negative space (see also Fig. 1-11). At B, the use of negative space forces attention on the positive space.

Figure 3-14 shows two examples of the use of positive and negative space. In these examples, space is used to establish the mood of the signs or perhaps to enhance the moods. Using a piece of tracing paper, juxtapose the blanks and the lettering to obtain further examples of the correct and incorrect use of space. Notice also that what *appears* to be a rule in Fig. 3-13 is quite successfully "broken" in A of Fig. 3-14.

Positive and negative space can be further used to create beauty by varying the color weight and texture weight of both spaces. In A of Fig. 3-15, an abraded natural finish is used in the negative space to set off the slickly carved and gilded letters of the

Fig. 3-15. Weight and texture can be varied.

A

B

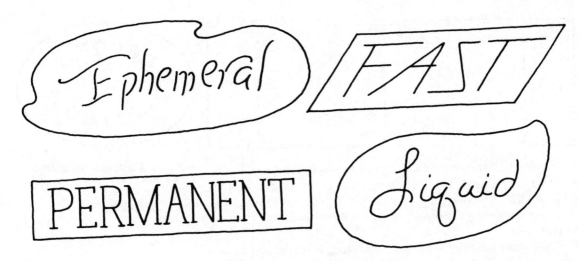

Fig. 3-16. Examples of flow.

positive space, this achieves a trendy "country" look. In B of Fig. 3-15, the smoothly painted white wood of the blank (negative space) forces attention to the highly faceted and gilded lettering. This gives a look of timelessness and tenderness. As trade signs for gift shops, these two signs would be for entirely different types of shop. One caters to the trendy young, while the other would cater to blue-haired collectors of plates and spoons. You have control over the positive and negative spaces. You should use them well.

Flow

If space is what establishes the identity of a piece, flow is what establishes character. If a sign has three dimensions, flow gives the fourth dimension: time. Simple examples of flow are shown in Fig. 3-16.

Flow is within the concept of focus. Major and minor elements, the positive and negative spaces, all converge to a point of focus which contains (or at least *should* contain) the major emphasis of the sign. This is the essence of the message.

Fig. 3-17. Note the point of focus.

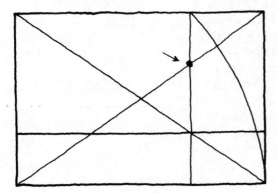

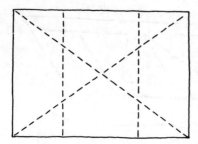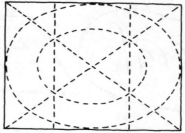

Figure 3-17 shows a simple sign that uses the major point of focus within a rectangle to project the essence of the message: Palm Isle is WARM. The eye is automatically drawn to this essence by the flow generated by the convergence of the two major axes within the rectangle.

By further subdividing the rectangle along its major and minor axes, you can further locate points of focus within the rectangle. You can then locate essential design elements on these points of focus as in Fig. 3-18.

If you did not take the time to draw rectangles with a compass, do it now. Refer to Fig. 3-4 and draw the golden rectangle. Then draw the axes in Fig. 3-17 and the axes in Fig. 3-18. Do it a few times because this is quite educational. Experiment. Where are the major points of focus for a rectangle based on the Fibonacci Series?

It will quickly become apparent that the golden rectangle is not the perfect solution for every problem. The restaurant signs shown in Fig. 3-19 are a case in point. The one named "The Wheel" allows the use of the Golden Rectangle as the basis of the sign. "Wagon Wheel" did not. The signs can be made to look good by experimenting with the golden rectangle. As shown in B of Fig. 3-19, the signs can be laid out simply to fit the lettering. This is a more customary approach among sign crafters. The results are not as pleasing nor as eye-catching as those shown on A of Fig. 3-19.

Fig. 3-18. Points of focus used to locate design elements.

Color

The sign crafter will do well to study color theory in some depth. Good color usage will very often offset problems of mediocre design much the same way a good cup of coffee will "save" a poorly prepared meal. Unfortunately, very few people seem to be able to make good coffee just by reading instructions. It takes time, experience, and experimentation. So does good color sense. The beginning sign crafter should actually do the experiments given here.

The Color Wheel. Begin by purchasing a set of inexpensive poster colors that are available in toy and stationery stores. At the same time purchase, two large sheets of white poster paper and an inexpensive compass if you don't already have one.

On a piece of poster paper, about 14 inches square, lay out a

Fig. 3-19. Golden Rectangles are not the solution to every problem.

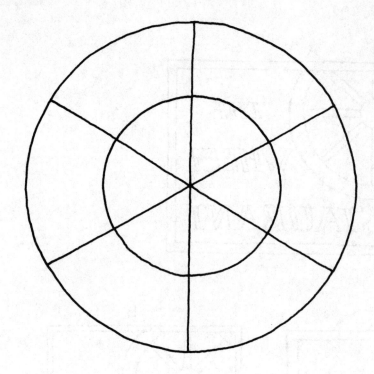

Fig. 3-20. A concentric circle.

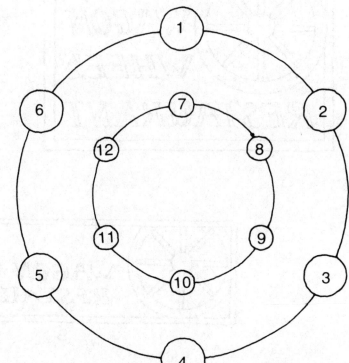

Fig. 3-21. Inner and outer rings.

circle with a radius of 6 inches. Lay out six points on the circle to form a hexagon. Connect all six points across the center of the circle. Draw a concentric circle with a 4-inch radius. At this point, the result should look like Fig. 3-20.

At each point of the two concentric hexagons, draw a circle. The outer ring of circles is to have a radius of 1 inch; and the inner ring is to have a radius of ½ inch. The result should now look like Fig. 3-21.

Each of the circles are to be painted as follows: #1 pure yellow, #3 pure blue, and #5 pure red. Allow the card to dry. While the card is drying, assemble the following materials: nine small pieces of the poster paper about 3 inches square, a jar of clear water, newspapers, a shallow pan about like an ice cube tray, and a wet rag.

Begin by dipping the brush into the water and brushing it out on the newspaper until almost all the water is absorbed. Dip the brush into the yellow paint and brush onto one of the 3-inch pieces. Brush most of the color remaining on the brush onto the newspaper and rinse in water. Brush out as above and dip an equal amount of the blue paint onto the brush. Immediately brush onto the wet yellow paint and mix to a green. Paint circle #2 green.

As soon as the circle is painted, place the card into the pan and cover with the wet rag to keep the paint moist. Repeat the proce-

Fig. 3-22. The color card.

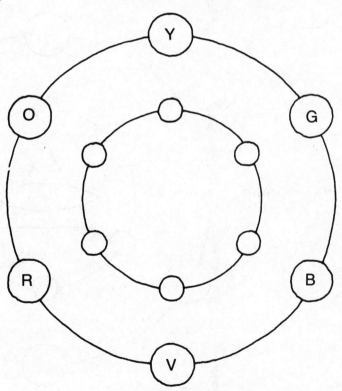

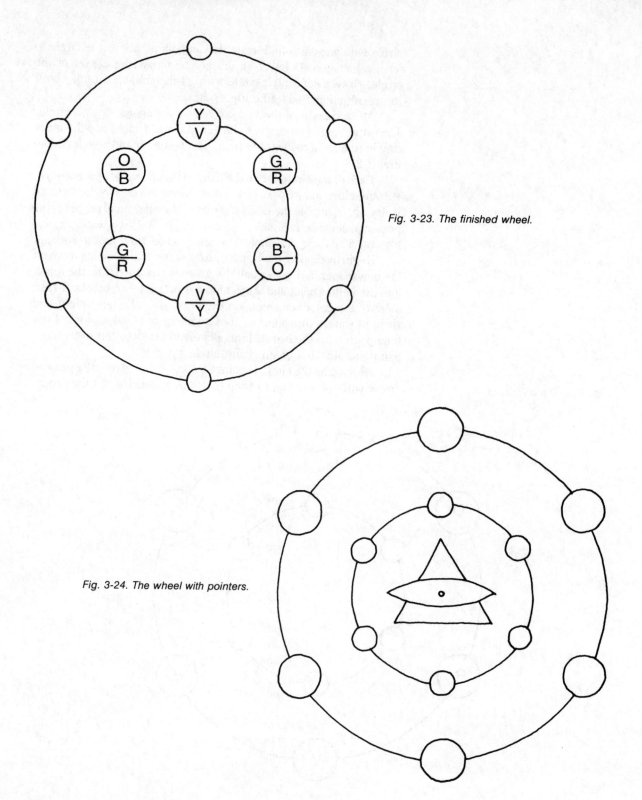

Fig. 3-23. The finished wheel.

Fig. 3-24. The wheel with pointers.

dure with blue and red to form a violet. Paint circle #4 violet and place the card in the pan. When the brush leaves traces of color on the newspaper after rinsing, fresh rinse water is needed.

Repeat the procedure with red and yellow to make orange. Paint circle #6 orange, and rinse the brush. You should now have the color card painted, as shown in Fig. 3-22, and three cards of moist paint in the tray.

Take out two clean 3- ×-3 cards and begin to mix colors for the inner circle (#7 through #12). Begin with circles #7 and #10. For circle #7, mix about 35 percent pure yellow with about 75 percent of the mixed violet in the pan. For circle #10, reverse the mixture using 75 percent yellow with 25 percent violet. After painting circles #7 and #10, it would be best to dispose of the three cards to avoid later confusion.

Repeat the procedure for circles #8 and #11 using pure red and mixed green. Remember to paint #8 the green dominant and #11 the red dominant.

Repeat the procedure again for circles #9 and #12. Figure it out. The finished wheel now looks like the one shown in Fig. 3-23, and you know a lot about poster paint.

To finish the wheel, two pointers are needed. The triangular one should be painted using a 50/50 mix of red and green to give a (?) color. For the two-ended pointer, mix an orange with the 50/50 mix used for the triangular pointer. This color is (?). When all is dry, mount the pointers to the center of the wheel using a thumb tack or brad. The results looks like the wheel shown in Fig. 3-24.

Using the Color Wheel. By having mixed all of the colors yourself and learning how to mix the colors for the pointers, you will remember how to obtain these colors. By turning the pointers, you will automatically select colors that go well together. In a two color scheme, the two-ended pointer is used. In a three-color scheme, the triangular pointer is used.

Making the color wheel and mixing all those colors is probably enough confusion for one day. Unfortunately, the color wheel in itself is not enough to get a thorough understanding of color usage. Therefore a second set of experiments is necessary.

The color wheel shows which colors go together, but it does not show *how* the colors interact. A proportional change occurs when one color is *dominant* (background) and a second is *recessive* (lettering).

To begin this experiment, you will need 12 3-inch squares of the poster paper and 12 1-inch squares. Two of these color chips in each size should be painted with the colors on the outer ring of the color wheel (circles #1 through #6). That is two 3-inch yellow, two 1-inch yellow, two 3-inch green, two 1-inch green, etc. After all these color chips are painted and dry, you are ready to begin the

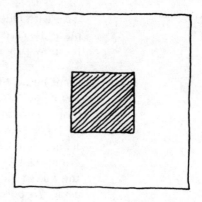

Fig. 3-25. Select one large and one small chip of color.

experiment. Yes, it *does* give you a chance to mix those colors again.

Begin by using the two-ended pointer. Select one large and one small chip of the colors indicated, and place them on a piece of white paper as shown in Fig. 3-25. Now you must become subjective. Notice how the colors change in relation to each other when used dominantly and recessively. Try to determine which combination is the more pleasing to you, and try to figure out *why* you feel that way about it.

Now use the triangular pointer to repeat the experiment. There will be two 3-inch chips of dominant color, and one 1-inch chip each of two recessive colors. Notice how the small chips tend to make the large chips change color (and vice versa). Notice also how the chips change when placed on a white background and when placed on one of the colors.

Now repeat the experiment with all the colors from #1 through #6. And if you really want to do it right, continue with colors #7 through #12.

You could go the library and get out a book on color theory that explains what is happening and why. But it is better to know with your eye *that* it happens than to know with your mind *why* it happens. After a few confusing hours with color chips, the whole business will begin to make sense to you. Then you will know color and a book on color theory will make sense to you. It really is like making good coffee. Practice helps.

Principles of good design are proportion, symmetry, weight, and composition. Principles of composition are space, flow, and color. With these principles of good design in mind, you can now turn to specific principles of different types of design.

PERIOD DESIGN

Period design does *not* mean copying examples of signs from a particular period of history. It does mean using the same principles of design or design trends that sign crafters of the period used in creating their works. The object is to call up in the mind of the viewer an image of the period. Historical accuracy is not as vital to success as are the feelings of the period.

A contemporary sign crafter working in the Colonial motif will be guided by the design principles of the period. His work will be original but faithful to the period. A sign crafter who merely adapts from existing examples of the period is neither faithful to the period nor original in his work. After all, the sign crafters of the period did not all copy examples from Colonial Williamsburg! It is in this area of the design process that true artistic skill shows itself.

There are many periods of history in which signs played an important role. Nevertheless, there are only two periods in history in which carved wood signs played an important part. These are the Colonial and the Victorian periods.

Colonial Design

A great many of the citizens and slaves of the period were illiterate. Many more were just barely literate in a day when spelling and grammar were not completely standardized. The first signs used in the colonies were simple pictographs (Fig. 3-26) designed to show the availability of goods and services. Among the more common were the blacksmith, the barber-cum-surgeon, the butcher, and the cobbler.

Fig. 3-26. Examples of colonial pictographs.

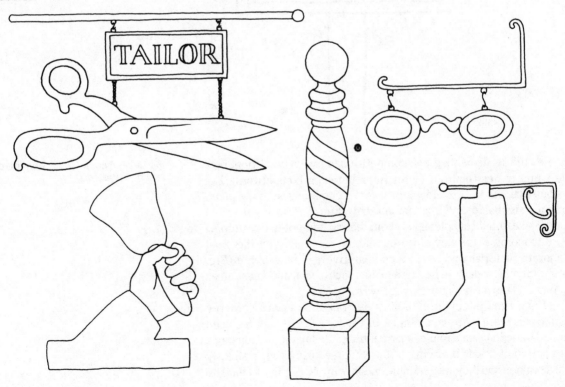

As the settlements grew, competition between practitioners of the same trades required distinctions between competitors. The second stage in the development was the combination of the pictographic signboard and the nameboard (Fig. 3-27). Figure 3-17 shows an example of colonial style in theory, but not in execution.

Economy is the key word in colonial design. Even the most elaborate pictorial was set in a comparatively simple frame (Fig. 3-28). Signs tended to be framed in much the same manner as pictures. They *were* pictures with words added.

Long runs of simple moldings surrounding square-cornered signboards were quite common (A of Fig. 3-29). Any curves used tended to be long and simple; a carpenter could lay them out using a thin batten of wood (B of Fig. 3-29). Reverse curves were slightly less common and they were simple and flowing (C of Fig. 3-29). The

Fig. 3-27. A combination signboard and nameboard.

ends of the curve would often form a button or fiddlehead where appropriate. The fiddlehead was derived from nature. Curling leaves or, more often, a growing fern was used as the source of the curve (D of Fig. 3-29).

Carving was more often used on the frame than on the sign itself. The reason was simple. The signboard was made by a carpenter and later painted by a painter. The two crafts were not often

Fig. 3-28. Colonial designs include using a simple frame.

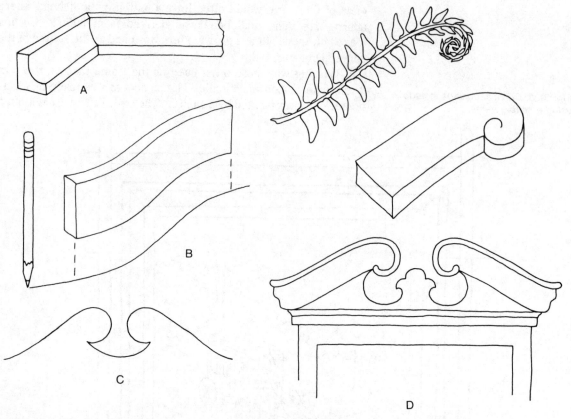

Fig. 3-29. Examples of long and simple curves.

done by the same person. Thus the architectural embellishments of the sign—the moldings, spindles, and decorative elements—were the work of the carpenter. The pictorial elements and the lettering were painted on the surface by a sign painter. Occasionally, the lettering and the major pictorial elements were outlined by a shallow V cut, presumably, to aid in future repainting (Fig. 3-30).

Gold leaf was mightily expensive then, as it is now, and it was generally limited to the estate boards of the gentry. Elaborate carving was generally limited to shields, crests, and other ornamental purposes, and it was quite often commissioned in England or Europe. See Fig. 3-31.

The keys to colonial design are simple carvings freely done without strict adherence to rules of symmetry and balance, simplified natural curves and forms; carving limited primarily to architectural aspects; and painting used extensively on the pictorial and lettering portions.

Colonial Colors. There are genuine problems in selecting colors for colonial signs. Our ideas of the colors used in colonial times are often quite far removed from historical fact. We look at the lovely white spired New England churches and conclude that they

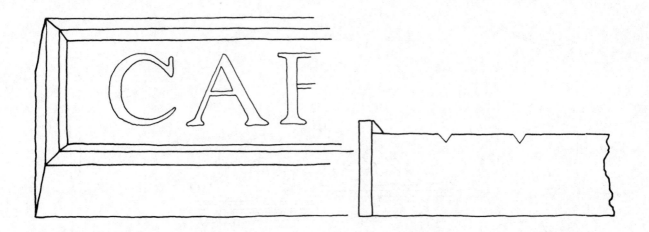

Fig. 3-30. The V cuts aid in repainting.

Fig. 3-31. Examples of elaborate carving.

Fig. 3-32. Historically accurate sign shapes.

were always white. These churches were often excessively colorful with horizontal bands of orange and chocolate for the building and yellow trim and red doors. It is hard to imagine these stately buildings painted in such a manner, yet records prove the case.

When executing a colonial sign, it is necessary to establish whether it will be in a historically accurate setting or not. If it must be accurate, be sure to consult an expert in local history for colors.

For general purposes, colonial signs should be painted with the dark and muted colors of the inner ring of the color wheel. There are many paint manufacturers who offer "Colonial Colors" in their product lines, and it is a good idea to use these colors wherever possible. After all, your customer has probably seen these color cards too.

When mixing your own colors, use a small amount of varnish to get a slippery and slightly transparent paint. When using standard sign painters' paints, mix in a small quantity of burnt umber or VanDyke brown with each color to "sadden" them. Matt or eggshell finishes are to be used in place of shiny finishes.

Figure 3-32 shows a variety of historically accurate sign shapes. They are not to be copied, but they can be freely adapted to serve specific purposes.

Victorian Design

Naturally there were quite a few intermediate stages in the evolution from the Colonial to the Victorian periods, but the average sign customer knows nothing of them—and probably cares less. Perhaps

Fig. 3-33. A comparison of styles.

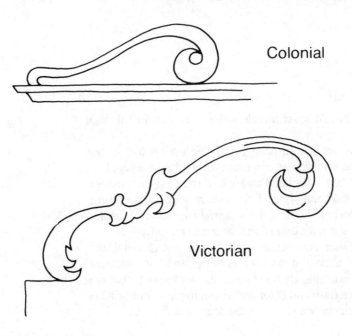

Colonial

Victorian

this is as it should be. At least it makes things easier for the sign crafter.

Fig. 3-34. Stylized leaf forms.

Victorian signs are based on naturally occurring forms, but rather than being simplifications of natural forms they are ideals of those forms (Fig. 3-33). The hand and eye of the designer are felt much more than in Colonial signs. Forms do not follow the limitations of natural materials. Instead the materials are cut and formed to follow the artist's conception of line and movement.

While much of Victorian ornament is simple and graceful, the term *Victorian* today almost always refers to the florid and baroque elements of Victorian usage. By this I mean those elements that are constructed to create flash and color and visual impact. Victorian is to Colonial as the circus wagon is to the stage coach.

Long, straight lines are anathema. Every line must be broken into curved sections with only a minimal concern for bilateral symmetry (Fig. 3-33). The natural curves of growing things are not translated into wooden moldings, but moldings are rendered as branched arabesques of stylized leaf forms (Fig. 3-34).

The simple V incisions around letters of the Colonial sign are replaced by deeply carved letters. High-relief figures replace the painted pictorials (Fig. 3-35). The tobacconist's pictograph of tobacco leaves to replaced by the cigar-store Indian. The use of gold leaf, so sparingly used on the Colonial sign, becomes almost excessive. Textures that were painted on flat surfaces in the Colonial period are now carved with great precision onto curved and reverse-curved surfaces.

It is important to realize that if the Victorian sign crafters

Fig. 3-35. A high-relief figure.

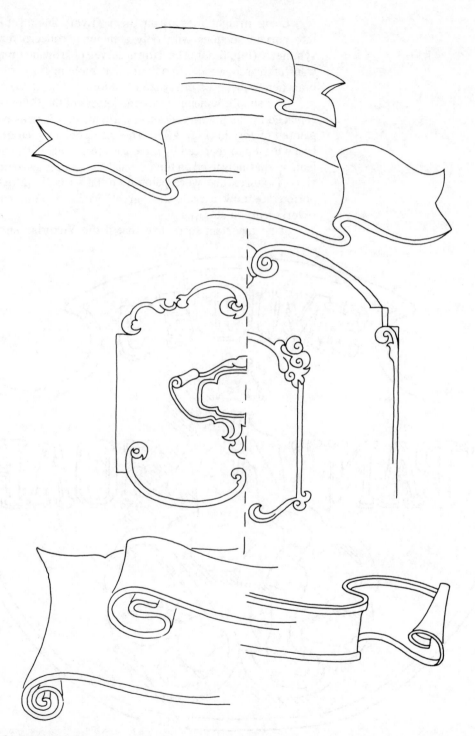

Fig. 3-36. Complex sign shapes.

could have had neon, they would have used it. The deep cuts and high reliefs and the curved surfaces gilded and burnished were all attempts to capture and use ambient light to sparkle, flash, and inpact.

Color. The constant search for brighter and more permanent paints made much stronger colors available. Highly refined earth pigments and pigments manufactured chemically were available in wide color ranges. Rapid drying vehicles made it possible to turn out more signs more quickly than before. Where mat finishes dominated the Colonial signs, full gloss finishes were now available, and they were preferred.

Figure 3-36 shows several sign shapes. You will note the complexity of some of them, and the greater variety of shapes. They are not to be copied, but they can be freely adapted to specific purposes.

Modern Design

In the carving of modern signs, modern design theories must be used with some restraint. Not every modern trend translates well into carved wood. The key here—as with Colonial signs—is simplicity. The tools and techniques now available make it very possible to "overcreate."

For example, the plastic laminates available for furniture manufacture simulate the very best examples of wood grain and finish. They sometimes tend to make furniture made of real wood look inferior by comparison. Furniture makers realize this and they execute different styles in different materials. Examples are Parson's tables in wood-grain plastics and Queen Anne tables in genuine wood. A flawlessly finished Parson's table in real wood would be very much more costly than it's plastic counterpart (and probably not look as good). So it is with modern signs.

Comparatively few modern designs translate well to carved wood. Of those that do, almost all make use of the natural color, grain, and texture of the wood as an important design feature as the dominate negative space or, less frequently, as the recessive positive space.

One of the modern design trends that translates extremely well to carved wood is the hard-edge graphic. This trend uses pure design as the major design element; that is, continuous line dominates. Pure (unshaded) colors and flat plane surfaces are used extensively. The origin of this design trend appears to be the printed electronic circuit board, and all successful hard-edge graphic signs appear to use this philosophy. Hard, perfectly straight and perfectly parallel lines dominate (Fig. 3-37).

The apparent simplicity of this style conceals the true difficulty of execution. Where there are so few lines to work with, every line

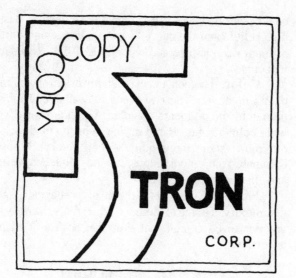

Fig. 3-37. Left: An example of a
modern design trend.

must be perfect. There is absolutely no latitude for mistakes and no
way to incorporate a tool slip into a "design feature." Free execution in the Colonial style adds charm, but free execution here spells
disaster. A slip of the chisel in the Victorian style might be an
opportunity to create a new flourish in the design. A slip of the
router here means starting all over with a new piece of wood.

Special tools and techniques are needed to do this work

Fig. 3-38. Simplicity of style.

54

Fig. 3-39. Simple hard-edged designs.

Fig. 3-40. The country look.

economically and well. The sign crafter should carefully examine the market potential for this type of sign before getting deeply committed in time and tools.

Colors in the hard-edge style tend to be strong and vibrant and smooth and shiny. Colored plastic sheet materials often can be substituted for paints or metal leaf.

Shapes are almost always dictated by a graphic arts designer. It is, in all likelihood, the symbol or "logo" of the company, and it must match the company letterhead, and business cards. A sign crafter called upon to execute an original design in the hard-edge style will do well to follow the simple rectangular format and limit the design to a single dominant element. See Fig. 3-38.

Simple Hard Edge. A second type of modern sign can be called the simple hard edge (as opposed to the hard-edged graphic). This style currently tends to dominate the carved sign market. This type of sign can be freely executed. By avoiding the precision ruled parallel lines as much as possible, minor mistakes can be tolerated. Actually a certain "funkiness" is preferable. See Fig. 3-39. The key here seems to be a bold but simple raised design, and a background relieved to a more-or-less uniform depth.

There seems to be no limitations on color choices. I recommend "strong" colors for male-interest establishments, and "cosmetic" colors for feminine-interest establishments. Finishes can range from matt to full gloss depending on the nature of the business.

Country. A third style of modern sign design can be called "country." The country look appears to be the coming thing in sign design. It is quite free and easy in execution, but it is somewhat structured in the design phase.

Fig. 3-41. Modern country designs.

To achieve the country look, it is necessary to get a general sort of unskilled folk-art look *without* leaping into recognized folk-art conventions such as Pennsylvania Dutch or Rosemaling. See Fig. 3-40.

Decorative elements tend to be simplified—as in the Colonial style—but realistic rather than interpreted. For example, a fiddlehead would be represented as a simplified fern rather than as a molding carved into a fiddlehead shape and ending in a button. See D of Fig. 3-29, and reverse the process. A curving sprig of wild flower might be used successfully, where a curving Acanthus leaf of the Victorian style would be out of place. The graphic look is out of place here and so is the hard-edge funkiness. The look to strive for seems to be pleasantly feminine but not excessively feminine. See Fig. 3-41.

Colonial colors do well on country-look signs, but the dominant colors seem to be taken from country-look fabrics such as gingham and calico. An excellent source for these colors is artists' acrylic paints. Eggshell finishes seem to be most popular, but only by a slight margin.

4
Layout of the Sign Blank

The sign blank, analogous to the artist's canvas, is the foundation on which the sign is constructed. In the case of carved signs, it is always made of a carvable material—usually wood. In the crafting of a period sign, the blank is generally made of separate planks fastened together, edge to edge, to give a solid blank of sufficient size for the completed sign. In cases requiring many laminations to achieve thickness, plywood can be used as the foundation on which to fasten successive layers.

The sign blank must be so constructed as to withstand the stresses generated by abrupt changes in temperature. The construction must be solidly glued to ensure that interior sections are not penetrated by water. Delamination, plank separation, and rot are generally caused by water seeping into poorly made glue joints. The surface must be sufficiently durable to resist the abrasive action of precipitation. These problems are fully discussed in the following chapters, but it is a good idea to be aware of construction methods during the design phase of the sign blank.

The shape of the sign blank is discussed in Chapter 3, but it is best to restate the overriding principle of design at this point: *simplify*.

The size of the sign blank is governed by the text and the style of lettering chosen. A sign reading:

will obviously require a blank of different proportions than a text reading:

J. G. SPANG

BROKER

For an example in this chapter, assume the sign crafter has been called by a real estate broker to execute a supplimental business sign to be placed on an older building. The sign is to read:

REAL ESTATE

SKETCHING

Sketching tools (Fig. 4-1 and Table 4-1) are taken to the site for the first meeting with the customer. Determine from the customer the location on the side of the building on which the sign is to be placed. A proportionately accurate freehand sketch should be made of the side of the building or at least a significant portion of it. This sketch will aid you in the design phase, and will stimulate your memory in the studio so that significant details can be recalled without a return trip to the site. Figure 4-2 shows an example of a portion of the subject building. Note the detail included.

If you have problems with freehand sketching, a most helpful book is *Thinking with a Pencil* by H. Nelms.

When discussing the sign with the customer, it is best not to ask him "What do you want?" Answers to such questions can stagger your imagination and overwhelm your ability (to say nothing of overwhelming the building). A far better approach is to make a series of quick sketches on the spot. Mention that they are in keeping with the architecture of the building and the feeling of the neighborhood, etc. Figure 4-3 shows three quick sketches; each of which would look good on the subject building.

Further discussions with the customer determined that the sign blank shown in B of Fig. 4-3 will be used. Text will be in Bookman bold italic with swash initials. An embellishment below will add appropriate character to the sign. A detailed discussion of type faces and layout are given in Chapter 5. At this point, a scale drawing of the sign should be made.

SCALE DRAWING

A bravura performance of technical finesse can add greatly to your

Fig. 4-1. Sketching tools.

Table 4-1. Sketching.

Tools	Materials	Miscellaneous
Pencils	Scratch paper	Second ladder
Pocket scale	Quadrille or Graph paper	Assistant to help measure
Clipboard or drawing board		Plumb bob
Measuring tape		Line level
Ladder		

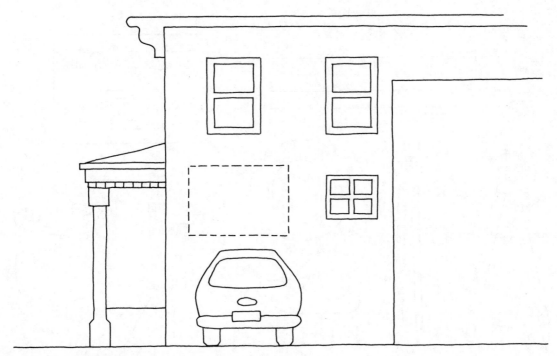

Fig. 4-2. The subject building.

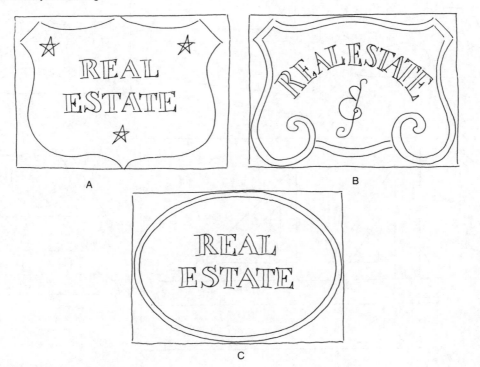

Fig. 4-3. Examples of quick sketches.

Fig. 4-4. Scale drawing tools and materials.

Table 4-2. Scale Drawing.

Tools	Materials	Miscellaneous
Pencils	Scratch paper	Stylus
Erasers, vinyl	Tracing paper	Masking tape
& kneaded	Drafting vellum or	Drafting tape
Architects	Bristol board	Thumb tacks
scale	Carbon paper	Push pins
Engineer's	Workable fixative	Dust brush
scale	Clear spray	Powdered eraser
Center-finding ruler	Quadrille paper	File folders
Drafting machine		Double-sided tape
or T-square		Dry stick glue
Triangles		Scissors
Straightedge		Razor blades
French curves		
Flexible ruler		
Pencil compass		

salesmanship. If you feel confident, a scale drawing and cost estimate can be executed on the spot. You might leave from the first visit with a commission and a check. I prefer to do the sketch and estimate at the studio, and to return with them at a future date. There is a risk of the customer getting cold feet, but I like to have the time to think things out. It is a matter of preference.

Scale drawings can be made on many surfaces and in many media. This is again a matter of choice. I prefer to work in pencil on tracing paper over a scline drawn on quadrille paper. This saves much time. Figure 4-4 and Table 4-2 show scale drawing tools and materials. You may choose to use other media or methods, but the general procedures given here will apply in most cases.

Note that graph paper has squares with the inch increments heavily ruled. Quadrille paper does not have the increments accented.

After the final rendering has been completed, the scale drawing, rendering, and a photograph of the completed sign are placed in the files for future reference.

Purpose of the Scale Drawing

The scale drawing serves many purposes. First, it can be traced over to create the final rendering (if one is needed) for presentation to the customer. Second, it can be used to determine the amount of material and time that a given sign will require. Third, it can be used as the original art for enlarging to final full size. It is therefore recommended that the scale drawing be carefully executed. Give full attention to accuracy and detail.

Scale Drawing Procedure

The scale selected should result in a finished drawing size that fits conveniently on the paper selected for final presentation to the customer.

There should be room for an attractive border. Render the border differently from the sign so that the customer is not confused by it and does not expect to see it included in the finished sign.

The approximate dimensions of a sign blank that will be in good proportion for the subject building are 3 feet high and 4 feet long. For the example in this chapter, 36″ × 1.61 = 57″ is too big for the area. You will have to try to get a golden rectangle into the sign another way. A convenient scale for an 8½-×-11-inch paper size is found to be 1½ inches equals 1 foot on the architect's scale. A scale rectangle is laid out in black marker on quadrille paper. Tracing paper is laid over the rectangle (Fig. 4-5) and a pencil sketch of the sign blank is made.

Drawing directly on the graph paper should be avoided even though it would seem easier. The grid lines tend to produce a subtle psychological effect in the draftsman, inhibiting free pencil work, and resulting in a "crabbed" style of drawing.

Sketching continues until a pleasing result is achieved (as in Fig. 4-6). The sketch is still a "rough" because it is neither centered nor symmetrical at this point.

Fig. 4-5. Lay tracing paper over the rectangle.

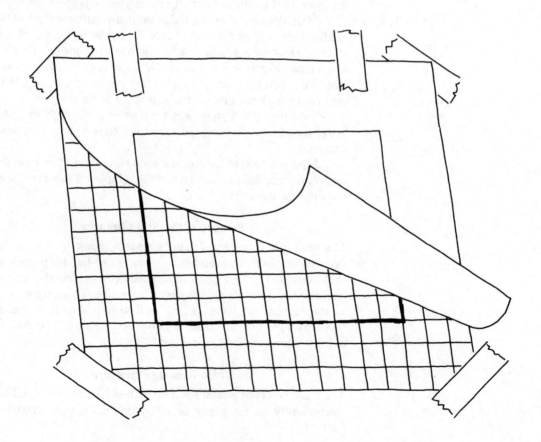

Fig. 4-6. A pleasing rough sketch.

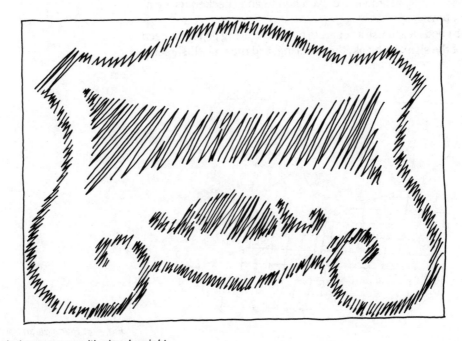

Fig. 4-7. Shaded areas vary with visual weight.

To quickly check whether the composition of the sign will be well balanced and pleasing to the eye, a chiaroscuro rendering of the rough sketch can be made. The areas of lettering, carving, and embellishment are blocked in with a pencil. These areas are shaded with a sketching pencil or carpenter's pencil according to the visual weight of the elements; some are darker than others. Figure 4-7 illustrates this check.

Returning to the rectangle on the graph paper, accurately establish horizontal and vertical center lines and diagonals. A clean piece of tracing paper is placed over the drawing (Fig. 4-8). Accurate registration is assured by hinging the top of the tracing paper with tape. Drafting tape is preferable to masking tape. The low-track adhesive separates cleanly (usually without tearing the paper).

The rough sketch is now inserted and the lines that are the most pleasing are traced on the top sheet. The rough is then withdrawn, flopped, repositioned, and redrawn on the other half. After the final tracing is completed, it may be carefully removed and folded along the central axis as a final check of symmetry (Fig. 4-9). At this point, the rough sketch should be discarded or clearly labeled to avoid later confusion.

The tracing should now be taped back on the quadrille paper (tape top and bottom). Additional pieces of tracing paper are laid over the finished drawing of the sign blank, and guide lines for the lettering and embellishment are sketched in and checked for symmetry as above.

It is a good idea to use a separate piece of tracing paper for each element of the sign: the blank, the lettering, and the embellishment.

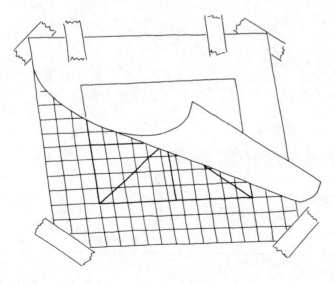

Fig. 4-8. Place clean tracing paper over the drawing.

Fig. 4-9. A final check for symmetry.

These elements can be repositioned for better composition, and a mistake in one element does not necessitate redrawing the entire sign.

At this point remove the entire tracing paper assembly from the drawing board and fasten it to a vertical wall. Walk around the room and view the composition from all angles. Lie on the floor if necessary.

A useful trick (and one I prefer to execute in the privacy of the studio) is to stand at some distance from the tracing—facing away from it. Bend far over and look at the tracing between spread legs. For some unknown reason, viewing from this ridiculous posture will often reveal awkward passages within the design. Why not turn the drawing upside down rather than stand on your head? I don't know why it doesn't work as well; it just doesn't.

If the design has passed muster, it may now be rendered, if necessary, for presentation to the customer.

RENDERING

At this point, the sign crafter has already invested a considerable amount of time and energy in creating the design. Whether the

Fig. 4-10. Rendering tools.

Table 4-3. Rendering.

Tools	Materials	Miscellaneous
Water color brushes	Water color paints	Water cups
Drawing pencils	Waterproof inks	Paper towels
Colored pencils	White acrylic artist's medium	Newspapers
Pens	Powdered graphite or sandpaper	
Indelible markers	to make your own	
Scale drawing tools		

additional time and effort required to produce a rendering is justified or not depends upon several considerations.

To the fledgling carver, a rendering should be done at least for the first large project. It is part of the design process, it is good experience, and it can aid you in selecting and mixing colors.

A customer you suspect will be hard to sell might be urged to complete the deal by a nicely presented rendering. Your first effort in a shopping area where you hope to get further business might be helped by a rendering. It is also a sales tool when talking to neighboring merchants: "Joe the tailor is ordering this one from me, and I couldn't help but notice that your sign . . ."

When dealing with architects or local government bodies such as town councils or architectural boards of review, a rendering is a must. Forcing yourself to execute your very first rendering under such do-or-die pressures is foolish. It is far better to do as many renderings as time permits in order to acquire the necessary skills at leisure.

Rendering Tools

Some of the many types of rendering tools are illustrated in Fig. 4-10, and listed in Table 4-3. Surfaces, media, skills, and final purpose of the rendering all play a part in the final choice. The following notes are my preferred methods. They will serve to point you in a general direction and help you set goals.

Rendering Methods

For all but the largest projects I prefer to do my renderings on a fairly heavy drafting vellum. It is quick, easy, and saves time because the line art can be traced directly from the scale drawing. The vellum is then "tipped" onto a heavy 8½-×-11-inch or 8½-×-14-inch bristol board. These sizes permit easy filing. A fixative spray and a filing folder keep the rendering clean.

If the rendering is to be done on a heavier translucent board, a light table can be used. See Chapter 5.

Heavy papers and boards can be made temporarily transparent by wetting the surface with alcohol. When dry, the paper returns to its original opacity, and rendering can be completed in the chosen medium.

For rendering on the heaviest boards, a nongreasy carbon paper with a very sharp 4H pencil or a small stylus must be used.

In lieu of carbon paper, the back of the scale drawing can be blackened with a medium-hard pencil. When traced over from the face, a light line is left on the board. A disadvantage of this method is that this makes the scale drawing difficult to read.

Colors and textures can be satisfactorily rendered in pencil, water colors, inks, or markers. The choice of media should be made with the final "feeling" of the finished sign clearly in mind. For example, a subtle sign in the Colonial style is well rendered in various hardnesses of pencil using powdered graphic and a water color brush for the delicate shading. A modern hard-edged graphic might be better rendered in vibrant indelible markers.

Fig. 4-11. The finished rendering.

Transparent or opaque water colors or colored inks may be used. I have found that a brand called Dr. Martin's Radiant to be quite satisfactory. It exhibits little tendency to "crawl" on drafting vellum.

Silver and gold inks are available from large craft and caligraphy suppliers. They are generally too flashy and they tend to overwhelm. Silver can be better rendered by a thin wash of a light blue/grey. Gold can be rendered by a transparent chrome yellow dark.

On occasion, it might be necessary to make a really flossy presentation on a black or colored board. Opaque white or colored ink is used for the line work. Areas of color are first underpainted in thinned white acrylic medium (Liquitex or Hyplar). Final colors are then overpainted in transparent watercolors.

Finish the presentation rendering by drawing a border or cutting a matt board as for a painting. The title block should include at least your name, address, and the date. When using a matt, the title block can be on either the art or the matt. The location on the art is customary. The rendering is now ready for presentation to the customer, Fig. 4-11.

A customer will often ask that the rendering be left for approval by someone not present. If the rendering has been paid for, as is the case with large jobs involving architects and committees, it must be left. If not it is a risk. The "someone else" might very well be a competitor.

5

Lettering

Lettering is probably the single most demanding aspect of sign crafting. As such it can be the most fun, but to beginners lettering is intimidating. Most people have poor handwriting. School teachers praise good penmanship in class, and further increase the self-doubt of the poor penmen. We all tend to stand in awe of the exceptional student who had good writing and could letter the class posters.

It should then come as a relief to most beginners to know that most professional sign painters have poor handwriting. Penmanship is not equatable to lettering skill. The good penman in school might have an easier time learning to create beautiful lettering, but that is the only advantage. *Anyone* who has the desire to become a sign crafter can learn to create beautiful lettering. The one thing necessary is quite simple. Cheat!

No one can draw a straight line without a ruler. No one can draw a circle without a compass. But by using a ruler and compass, anyone can make perfectly straight lines and round circles. Talent is limited to knowing about rulers and compasses. No more.

The following exercises are intended to illustrate how fast lettering skills can be acquired. A few tools (Table 5-1) are necessary. They are unlined paper, a ruler, a hard-lead pencil, a fine-point marker and a drawing board.

Begin with the marker. In block letters, write out the words

	Tools	Materials	Miscellaneous
Table 5-1. Lettering.	Ruler	Blank paper	Drawing board
	Fine marker		
	Pencil		

THE QUICK FOX freehand near the top of the sheet. It will look somewhat like Fig. 5-1.

With the ruler, mark out two parallel lines ⅜ of an inch apart. Letter the same text in the guidelines. Stop each vertical stroke exactly on the guideline. See Fig. 5-2. Notice that when all strokes are the same length, there is an improvement by at least one order of magnitude.

Now rule a second set of lines ⅜ of an inch apart. This time add a third line ¼ of an inch up from the bottom line. Repeat the text, but this time place all the central horizontal strokes on the middle line. See Fig. 5-3. Another improvement can be seen.

Now rule another set of lines. This time add serifs (these short little "tails" at the ends of the letters). The result is shown at Fig. 5-4. Notice how a uniformity has been introduced. It already gives the lettering a professional look. But this uniformity is almost too much. The letters have no individual character. They are boring.

Rule yet another set of guide lines. Letter the text again, but this time giving each letter some weight. The weight is created by the extra lines in each letter (Fig. 5-5).

Of course you can't add the weight just anywhere. There is a rule for adding the weight: *Always* picture the letter as being drawn in a single stroke *from left to right. Always* weight the *downward* strokes. This is clearly shown in Fig. 5-6.

As a final experiment, repeat the text using large, weighted uppercase letters for the initials and small, weighted uppercase letters for the remainder of the letters. Figure 5-7 shows the result.

Now compare your first attempt (Fig. 5-1 with your latest attempt (Fig. 5-7). You should notice a very great improvement. If there is *no* improvement try again. If there is *still* no improvement whatsoever, you had better rethink your decision to become a sign crafter.

☐ Guidelines are a must.
☐ Serifs help.
☐ Weight helps.
☐ *Always* weight the downstroke.

On a fresh piece of paper, lay out more guidelines as previously done. Carefully draw a weighted letter M and next to it draw a weighted N. Carefully draw vertical lines to enclose each letter as at the top of Fig. 5-8.

THE QUICK FOX

Fig. 5-1. Freehand block letters.

Fig. 5-2. Stop each vertical stroke exactly on the guideline.

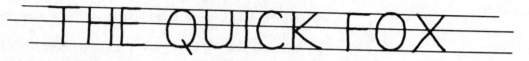

Fig. 5-3. Place all central horizontal strokes on the middle line.

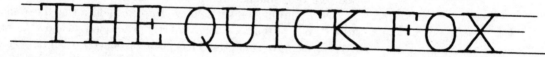

Fig. 5-4. Notice the uniformity.

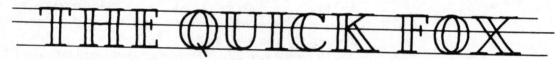

Fig. 5-5. Weight is created by extra lines in each letter.

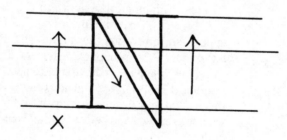

Fig. 5-6. Always weigh the downward strokes.

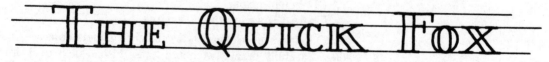

Fig. 5-7. Large, weighted uppercase letters for the initial letters, and small, weighted uppercase letters for the other letters.

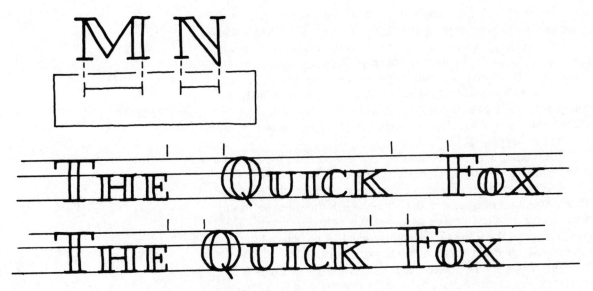

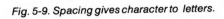

Fig. 5-8. Above: Spacing between letters is crucial.

Fig. 5-9. Spacing gives character to letters.

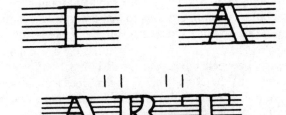

Fig. 5-10. Letter configurations.

Fig. 5-11. Letters must be balanced.

On a scrap of paper, mark off the horizontal space that each letter required. Now draw two sets of guidelines and reletter the text twice (once using the M space between the words, once using the N space). You will notice a difference between the randomly spaced words of your previous attempts and the evenly spaced words. You will also notice a difference in feeling between the texts with the two different spacing increments. The text with the M space seems complete. The text with the N space seems to be waiting for something.

The spacing between words is one of the most crucial elements in lettering. It is also one of the easiest elements to control.

Another crucial element is the spacing between the letters. This does not at first appear as easy to control as the space between words—and it isn't. A degree of subjectivity is involved here. The problem is that the letters have an individual shape and character. Like people, different characters interact differently.

The negative space within and around the letter gives it its character. The negative space for each letter is just as different from letter to letter as is the positive space of the letter itself. See Fig. 5-9.

Problems occur when the spaces in and around the letters are joined in different configurations to make words. As shown in Fig. 5-10, the word ART is used as an example. If the letters are given equal spacing, as they are on a typewriter, the word looks awkward. The weight between the A and the R is much different than the weight between the R and the T. When you add the same equal spacing to the different weights the difference becomes that much greater. The spacing between the letters must be altered so that the visual weight of the negative spaces appear to be about equal (as in the second example).

The spacing of the letters to achieve equal balance of the negative space weights has a direct effect on word length even when the same letters are used. See Fig. 5-11.

Spaces between words are of equal *size* spaces between letters are of equal *weight*.

On a fresh sheet of paper, rule three sets of ⅜-inch guidelines. Rule them one above the other with about 3/16 of an inch between (as in Fig. 5-12). Using weighted uppercase letters only, carefully render the following text:

THE QUICK BROWN
FOX JUMPS OVER
THE LAZY DOG

No, there is no illustration to show you what it "should" look

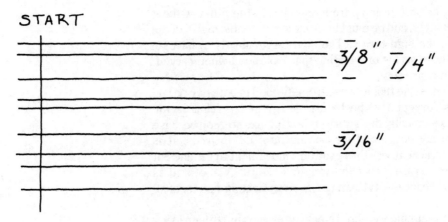

START

3/8″ 1/4″

3/16″

Fig. 5-12. Guidelines.

like. You have to do this one on your own. If you've been merely reading along, you're in trouble now. Stop here. Go back and *do* the exercises. The rest of us will wait for you.

You will have noticed that if you started all three lines flush left (on the START line) you had a problem on the right. Each line has a different number of individual letters while having the same number of words.

Rule the guidelines on a separate sheet and render the text once again. On line 1, use an N space between words. On line 2, use one N space and one M space. On line 3, use two M spaces. Compare the result with the previous attempt.

Does it seem that ruling all those guidelines is a hassle? Well it is and there is no way around it. Get used to the idea.

Examine your second attempt at rendering the text. There are almost certainly awkward spots such as letters too close or too far apart and letters that just won't flow. Circle these awkward spots and practice them on a separate sheet of paper. Yes, this *is* how the pros do it. When you get a combination that seems to work, redraw it in the margin.

Now when you think you have got it right, rule a third sheet and render the text again. Incorporate the improvements you have been practicing. You will now be fairly tired of the quick brown fox. Rest assured that you are not nearly as tired of the quick brown fox as a professional musician is of *do re mi*. In order to give a virtuoso performance of lettering, you must practice much more than you would like to. So take the time and render the quick brown fox . . . a few more times.

TYPEFACES

A sign *painter* needs to have a wide variety of alphabet styles or typefaces in his repertoire. The nature of sign painting demands this. He must be able to jump from one sign to the other without thinking about style, and he must be an expert in rendering all of the styles. Not so the sign *carver*. The sign carver needs to have an expertise in those styles of lettering that look good when carved. Fortunately they are few.

There is one style that looks extremely good in both period and modern signs (except for the hard-edged graphic). That is the Roman style (specifically the Trajan style). It looks so good because it was specifically developed for carving into flat surfaces. It is called Trajan because it was first used on a monument to the ancient Roman emperor Trajan. This lettering is universally accepted as one of the most beautiful styles, if not *the* most beautiful style, of all time.

Because the simple weighted block letters you have been using for practice are derived from the Roman style, you should have very little trouble mastering this style. The Trajan style, once mastered, will enable you to "knock out" sign after beautiful sign. You can fall back on this style of lettering for almost any sign you will ever have to produce, and you can have the utmost confidence in the result. And what is even better, you can cheat all the way through in mastering it.

Begin by securing a large package of paper ruled in ¼-inch squares and punched for a three-hole notebook. See Table 5-2. Because the smallest practical—and most common—size of signboard for a business is a 1-×-8-inch plank, this alphabet will be drawn to an approximate height of 4½ inches. This allows for a ¾-inch border, top and bottom, and a pleasing negative space within the border. For smaller and larger letter sizes, see Chapter 6 on enlargement.

Begin by finding the center of a sheet of graph paper. Using a pencil, accentuate the horizontal lines nine and 11 squares below center, and nine squares above center. The two nine square lines are the vertical limits or baselines of the letter. The 11 square line—which extends across the entire sheet—is the registration guide (explained later).

Start with the letter B; it is one of the most complex and least used of all letters (Fig. 5-13). The width of the B is 12 squares (or two-thirds the height).

Notice first the shape of the serif on the upper left of the staff.

Table 5-2. Typefaces.

Tools	Materials	Miscellaneous
Ruler	¼" quadrille or	Transparent adhesive tape
Fine marker	graph paper drilled	Drafting tape
Pencil	for 3-ring book	Dry transfer letters
Eraser		

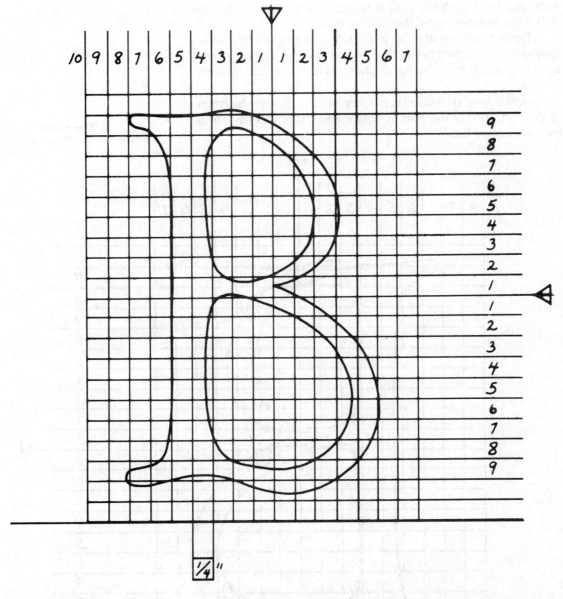

Fig. 5-13. The letter B is complex but seldom used.

The diameter of the top of the serif is very close to 3/16 of an inch and opens very quickly to ¼ of an inch. The reason for this is that the serifs will all be carved with a ¼-inch gouge or fluting tool. All the serifs on all the letters will follow this general pattern; some will start at a full ¼-inch, but none will start at less than 3/16 of an inch. Notice too that the serif starts beyond the sixth square, but not at the seventh square.

The left side of the staff is not a straight cut. The curve flows inward as it flows downward from the serif—quickly at first and then

79

more and more gradually until it reaches the thinnest part of the staff—two squares below the halfway point.

Turning to the serif at the lower left, it begins at a full ¼ of an inch wide, and slightly beyond the seventh square. The cut sweeps up in a complimentary, but not identical curve to meet the descending cut.

Lightly draw an identical curve (mirror image) for the beginning of the right side of the staff in square four. This will have to be partially erased later.

Fig. 5-14. These letters must be separated during tracing.

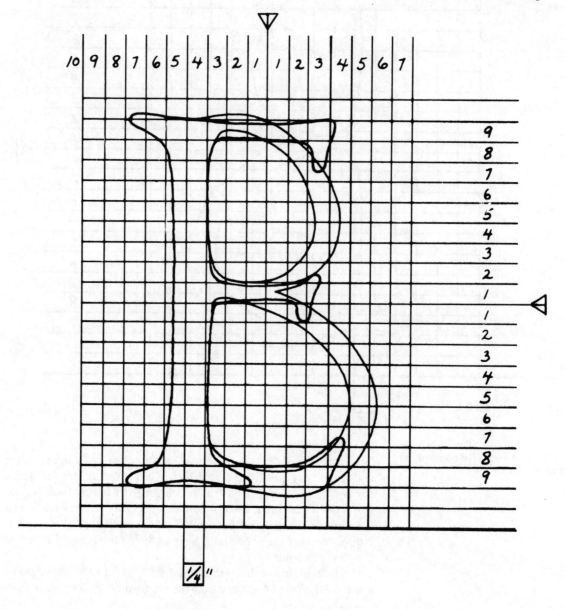

80

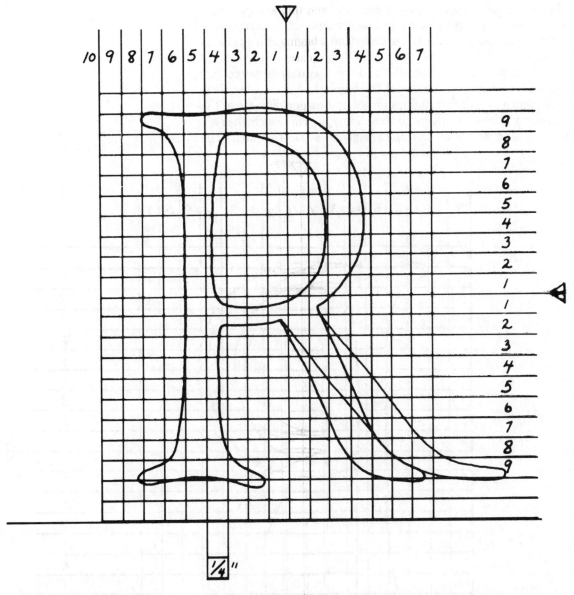

Fig. 5-15. The R is developed using the upper serif of the B and the lower serif of the F.

Now draw the upper and lower edges of the serifs. Notice that the serifs curve slightly inward from the horizontal before widening out into the upper and lower curved "limbs" of the B. This inward curvature is used in all the letters, but the curve is not identical for each letter. This gives a great deal of charm to the letters, while giving a certain "fudge factor" in case of a tool slip or a piece of contrary grain is encountered.

The upper limb of the B is narrower or less full than the lower limb. The thickest part of the upper limb is slightly above its center.

The lower limb is constructed in the same way as the upper limb, but is fuller and slightly heavier. The thickest part is correspondingly lower. This gives the letter a substantial feeling as it sits on its base.

Study the branch where the two limbs join. It is drawn correctly even if you don't think it is. The branch is above center of the letter, and it is ¼ of an inch thick for about the same distance as the upper serif. Notice too that where the limbs join the branch, they are both ¼ of an inch wide, and the result is *not* ½ of an inch. The

Fig. 5-16. The P can be traced and developed for the R.

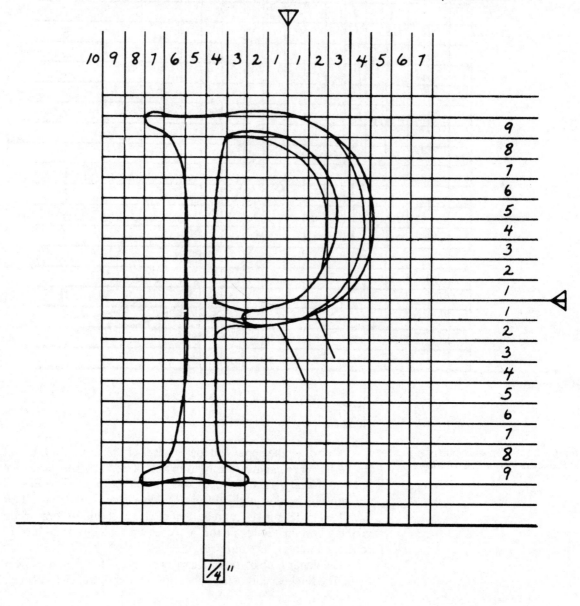

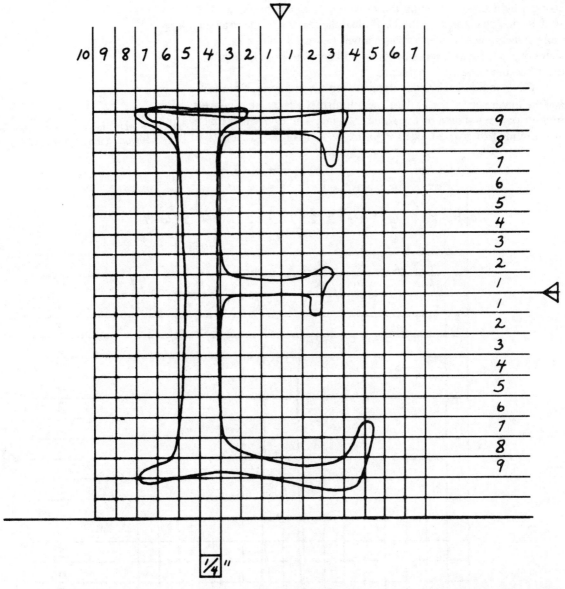

Fig. 5-17. To make an L, extend the E and reshape the upper serif.

approaching angles are different. The branch reaches its thinner part (¼ of an inch) *before* it reaches the staff, and widens out to meet the staff.

The inner edges of the staff are now redrawn from points slightly above center in each case to flow smoothly into the branch. When the letter is drawn to your satisfaction, ink in the line two squares below the base line. Leave the rest of the drawing in pencil for later correction.

Having now completed the letter B, begin the letters E and F.

Using a light table (or taping the drawings to a window) trace the staff, serifs, and branch of the B. Return the tracing to the drawing table and complete the letters as shown. Be sure to use a separate sheet of paper for each letter. Figure 5-14 contains both letters that must be separated during tracing.

The R in Fig. 5-15 is developed using the upper serif of the B and the lower serif of the F. The lower limb of the R can be rendered in the two ways shown on the same drawing. The two lower limbs are provided to give an extra measure of control to the negative

Fig. 5-18. The I, J, and T can be developed from the staff of any letter.

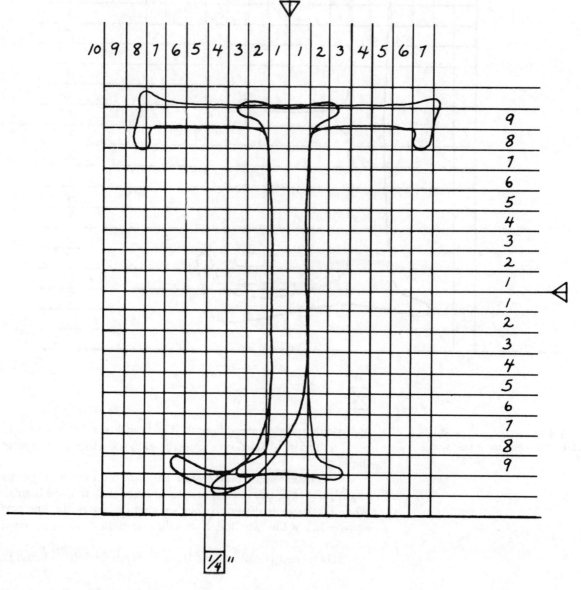

space between letters when making a layout. See Fig. 5-10.

Next the P is traced and developed from the R. See Fig. 5-16. Notice however that the branch of the P may be considerably lower than the branch of the R. The upper section of the limb of the P can be traced from the upper limb of the B, and the lower section from the lower limb of the B. Final fairing of the limb can be made on the drawing table. Notice also the two renderings of the branch of the P (included on the same drawing).

The L can be traced and developed from the E by extending the

Fig. 5-19. Development of the H and the U.

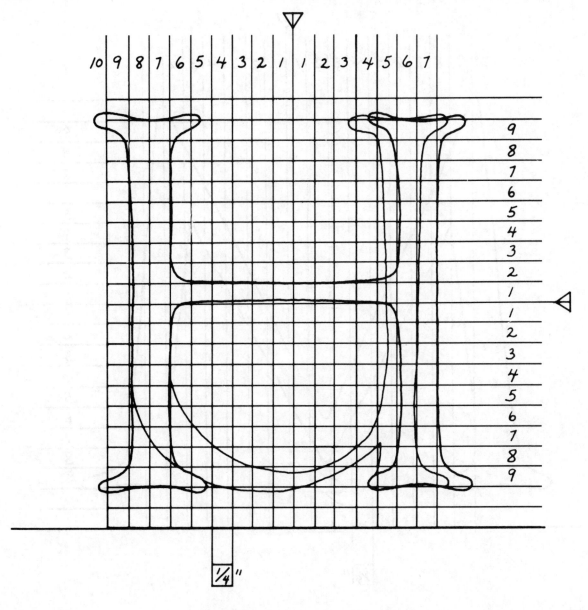

85

limb to the right and reshaping the upper serif as shown. See Fig. 5-17.

The I, the two forms of the J, and the T can be developed from the staff of any letter. See Fig. 5-18. And the H and the U can be developed from the staff of any letter. See Fig. 5-19.

The M should be carefully drawn first with a ruler, and the very slight curves should be added freehand with much erasing. The width without serifs is equal to the height. The middle point where the second and third strokes join falls exactly on center. The point

Fig. 5-20. Draw the M with a ruler.

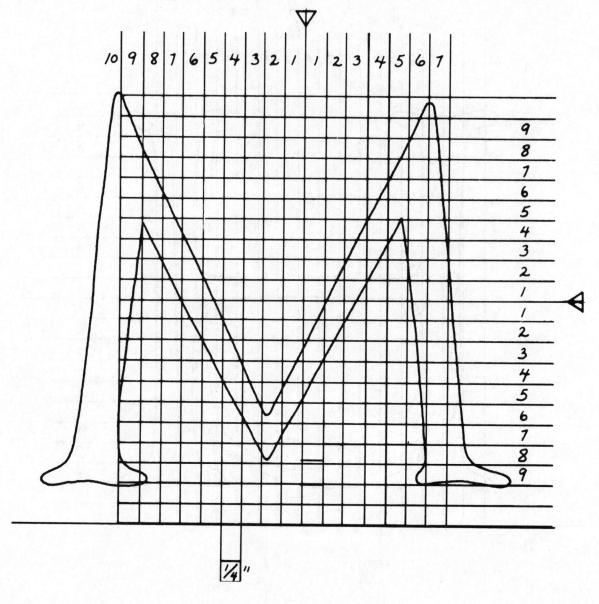

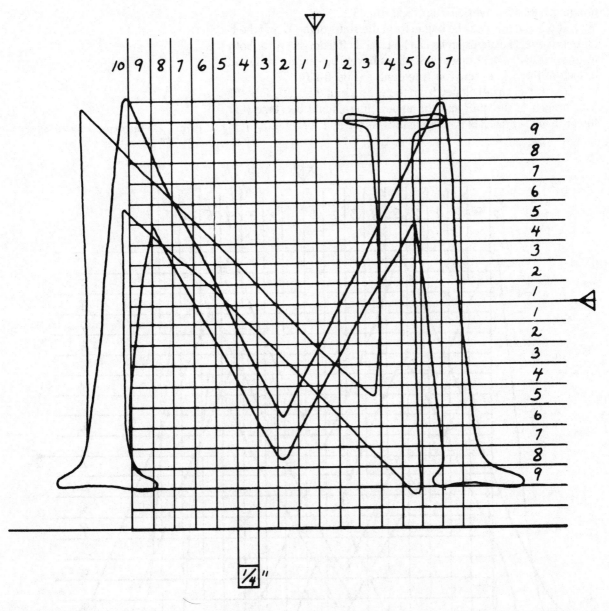

Fig. 5-21. Develop the N from tracings of the M.

may be on the baseline, but I feel it looks better slightly higher. See Fig. 5-20.

The N can be developed by tracings taken from the M. Notice the different widths and serif shapes. Notice too that the point of the N falls somewhat below the baseline. See Fig. 5-21.

The W is also developed from the M even though the letter is shaped quite differently. In this case, the points will extend slightly *above* the M. The registration line will have to be inked in when the drawing is turned right side up. See Fig. 5-22.

The X and the Y can be begun from the staffs of the W and the F respectively. The upper limbs can be traced off from the W for both letters. Note that the branch of the X is above true center, while the branch of the Y is exactly on true center (Fig. 5-23).

The K can be developed from the X by using the staff of the P. The branch of the staff and the upper limb should be somewhat lower than the branch of the P (making this letter an odd width). It is

Fig. 5-22. The registration line must be inked.

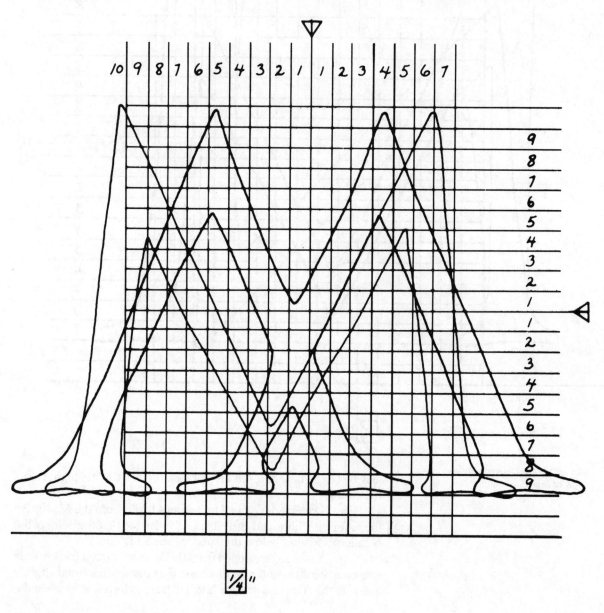

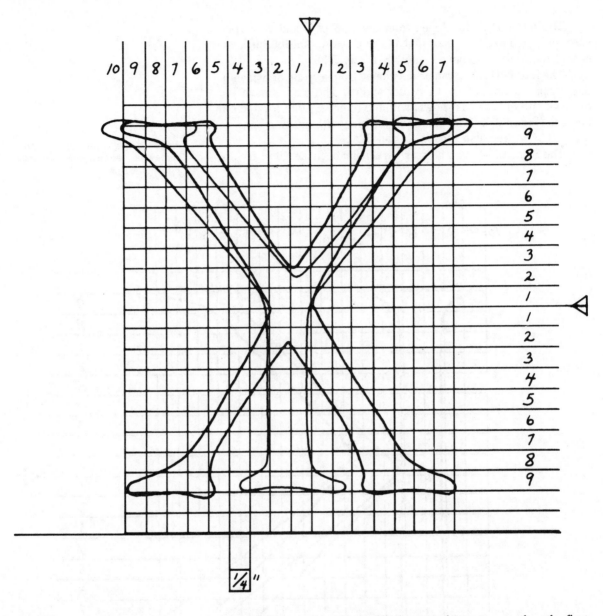

Fig. 5-23. The branch of the X is above true center and the branch of the Y is exactly on true center.

best to draw a second lower limb somewhat narrower than the first. See Fig. 5-10, 5-15, and Fig. 5-24.

The letter C is drawn next; there is nothing circular about it. It cannot be drawn mechanically, but must be redrawn and erased until it appears right. The thickest and thinnest parts are well off the vertical, shifting counterclockwise (Fig. 5-25).

The letter G is developed from the letter C. The staff *is* vertical. If you prefer, the serif top can be made somewhat smaller than the C and slant slightly more toward center. See Fig. 5-25.

The letter D is developed from the staff of P and a mirror-reversed tracing of the upper limb of the C. Note that the thickest part of the limb falls above center. See Fig. 5-26.

The letters O and Q can be developed from a circle drawn with the compass point set on the center shown. The circles must be redrawn into ellipses, as shown, with the thinnest point located on the axis (Fig. 5-27). Trial-and-error drawing with much erasing is the only way. See also Figs. 6-28 and 6-29.

The S and the Z must be drawn freehand because there are no

Fig. 5-24. Draw the second limb somewhat narrower than the first.

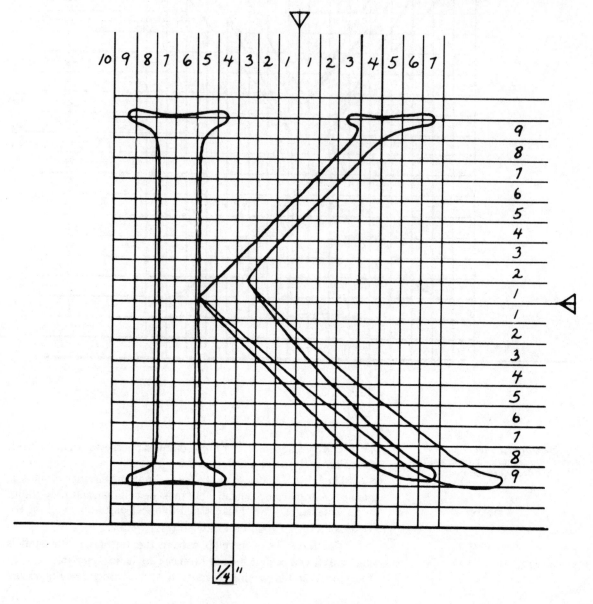

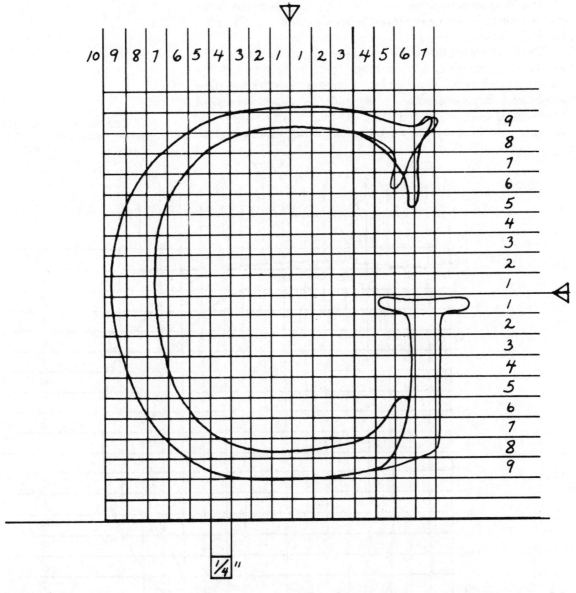

Fig. 5-25. Thick and thin parts are well off the vertical.

letters from which to develop them. The upper limb of the S is smaller, but thicker than the lower. Yes, it does look awkward, but it is right. The Z can be drawn out with a ruler, and the curves can be faired in by eye. Notice the simple curve of the upper limb and the slight reverse curve in the lower limb (Fig. 5-28).

The letters A and V can be drawn first with a ruler, and then faired slightly. The A and the V extend above or below the guidelines as shown.

All the letters should be drawn in pencil; they should *not* be inked in. The horizontal line two squares below the base line of the letters should be accurately inked in across the full width of the page.

You will notice that there are many heights of letters. The lettering exercise (Fig. 5-2) establishes uniform heights by using guidelines to start and stop the vertical strokes. The Trajan letters extend variously above and below the guidelines simply because of the negative space around and within the letters. The letter O, for example, would appear to be too small if set exactly on the

Fig. 5-26. *The thickest part of the limb falls above center.*

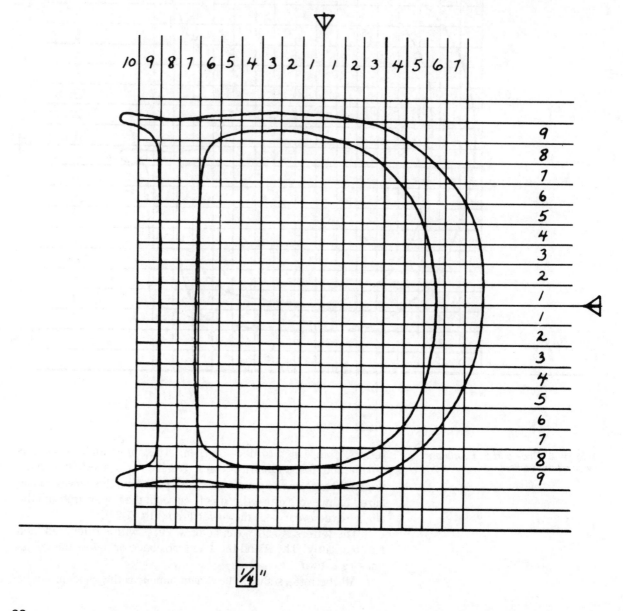

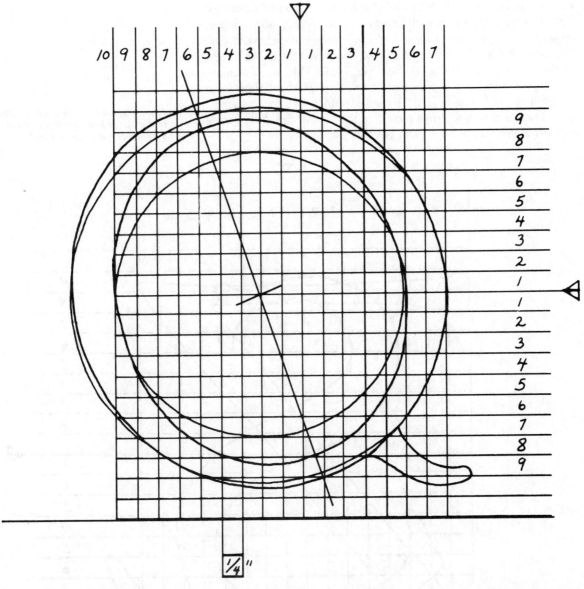

Fig. 5-27. Circles must be redrawn into ellipses.

guidelines. By drawing the letter slightly too tall, the finished appearance is that of an O drawn exactly on the guideline.

The Trajan alphabet will do very nicely for about 75 percent of all signs a carver is likely to be called on to execute. This can be extended about another 10 percent where its use is merely adequate. The remaining signs must be executed in other forms of lettering, but it is easy to "get by" on this one typeface by simply turning down the two signs in 10 that require another typeface.

Carving a long text for something like a historical monument is easy to do if one simple rule is followed. Use the larger uppercase Trajan letters for the initial letters of each word, and smaller, uppercase Trajan letters for the remaining letters in each word. See Fig. 5-7. The smaller letters should be about two-thirds the height of the letters just developed. See Fig. 5-29. This is a fortunate occurrence because this size just happens to be about right for a 1-×-6-inch plank, that is just the right size for most house signs.

There are no lowercase letters in the Trajan alphabet. That's one problem gone before it can get started.

Fig. 5-28A. Notice the simple curve of the upper limb and the slight reverse curve in the lower limb.

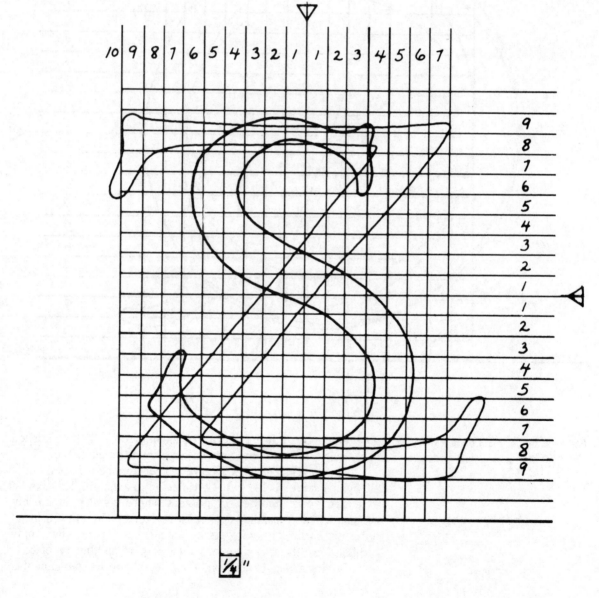

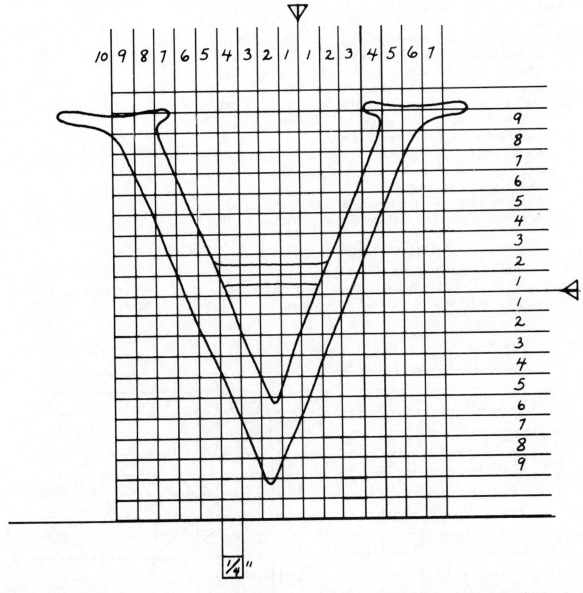

Fig. 5-28B. The letters A and V can be drawn first with a ruler.

Virtually *any* typeface can be carved in wood. The question is whether or not the final appearance is worth the effort. There are two typefaces that are worthwhile adding to your catalog. They are Bookman bold italic with swash characters (Fig. 5-30) and a script such as palace script (Fig. 5-31). A very flossy look can be achieved by using the Trajan lettering for body type, and using a manuscript capital (Fig. 5-32).

A very difficult problem sometimes occurs with some customers. They want an Old English, wedding text, or nothing specific.

When this happens, try to sell the customer on a Lombardic text such as shown in Fig. 5-33. If that won't do, try to find the simplest Old English sample you can or simply turn down the commission. Old English looks great in pen and ink and awful when carved.

The easiest way to use an oddball type style is to buy a sheet of the largest size dry transfer lettering available in that style. Examples are Letraset, PressType, and ChartPak. If the type can be obtained in white or a color, so much the better. Use the dry transfer letters in one of the following ways:

☐ Transfer the lettering to graph paper and rule over the grid in white, colored ink, or marker. Enlarge the individual letters by the graph method (see Chapter 6).

☐ Set the whole text, line by line, as it will finally appear. Be sure to work to exact scale. Enlarge optically (see Chapter 6).

LETTERING LAYOUT

Assuming that the sign blank layout (see also Chapter 6) is nearing completion, the lettering layout must begin. To begin this section as an example I will use a very simple but common layout. More

Fig. 5-29. There are no lowercase letters in the Trajan alphabet.

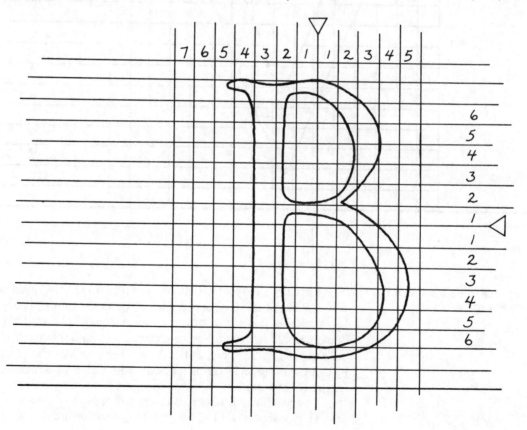

Fig. 5-30. Bookman bold italic with swash characters.

Fig. 5-30. Bookman bold italic with swash characters.

Fig. 5-31. Palace script.

complex signs involving larger texts are dealt with at the end of this section.

One of the first signs a fledgling carver should execute is a quarterboard style with his or her own name on it. This is good for drumming up business in the neighborhood.

The quarterboard should be of 1-×-8-inch lumber with ornate ends and the carver's name SMITH carved in the large Trajan. By the simple ruling of two parallel lines, the signblank is laid out. The text SMITH is laid out in the following manner.

A roll of paper 8 inches wide is used for the lettering. See Table 5-3. If a light table is available, the 36-inch-wide rolls of cheap bond paper used by sign painters for window banners is used. If no light table is available, a roll of the more expensive tracing paper can be used. The roll is cut 8 inches from the end (Fig. 5-34). Because the letters are 4½ inches high, and we know that the widest letters are 5 inches wide, the text SMITH will fit on a piece of paper 30 inches long (5 letters times 5 inches, plus some for luck.)

The straight edge of the paper is used for the guideline for the lettering. The S page is removed from the three-ring book and slid

Table 5-3. Lettering Layout.

Tools	Materials	Miscellaneous
Light table	Rolls of bond or	Dusting brush
Ruler	tracing paper	Light cardboard
Fine marker	Single-edged razor blades	Colored pencils
Pencil		
Eraser		

CARVED LETTERING

GOOD

Old English

BAD

Wedding

Lombardic

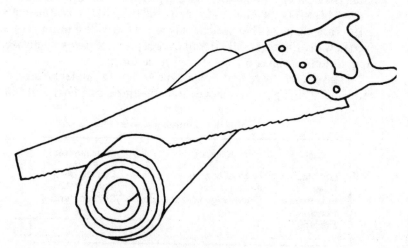

Fig. 5-34. Cut the tracing paper 8 inches from the end.

Fig. 5-32. Left (top): Trajan lettering with manuscript capitals.

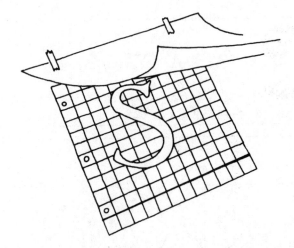

Fig. 5-35. Right: Align the layout paper.

Fig. 5-33. Left (center): Typefaces; Lombardic is best.

under the layout paper. The guideline that has been ruled in ink two squares below the letter is carefully aligned with the bottom of the layout paper (Fig. 5-35). The S is then carefully traced over in pencil, and the page is returned to the three-ring book.

The M page is removed and aligned with the layout paper. The M is slid left and right until a pleasing weight of negative space is found; it is then traced (Fig. 5-36). The process is continued until SMITH is traced on the layout paper.

Corrections in letter spacing are always needed. Make them with a razor blade and transparent adhesive tape rather than retracing (Fig. 5-37). The layout paper is cut down through the offending space, and the edge is overlapped or separated until the correct balance is reached. The assembly is juggled until correct and then taped on the back for strength.

After the layout is completed, it is removed and placed on the light table and taped in place on the blank layout. For larger signs, this step is not necessary with the quarterboard, because the blank and the text are on the same layout.

The preceding method works on virtually all signs. The only

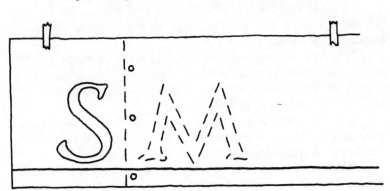

Fig. 5-36. Position and trace the M.

Fig. 5-37. Making corrections.

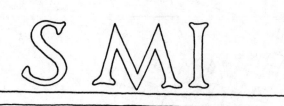

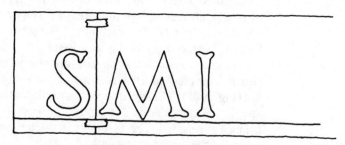

variation is in the complexity of the elements and the number of separate tracings necessary.

For long texts, the words can be laid out individually. The spacing of the words can be laid out on the sign blank later (Fig. 5-38).

For more than one line of text, the individual lines can be laid out and spaced, one above the other, until a pleasing layout is reached (Fig. 5-39).

To justify two or more lines of text, the longest line can be compressed by cutting and taping to the shortest pleasing line. The other lines can be laid out over it, cut apart, and lengthened to match (Fig. 5-40). See also Fig. 5-8.

When justifying lines is not possible, the lines of text can be measured to find the middle, and all the centers can be lined up down the center of the blank (Fig. 5-41).

When curved guidelines must be followed, the text is first laid out on a straight line. The letters are cut apart and individually taped

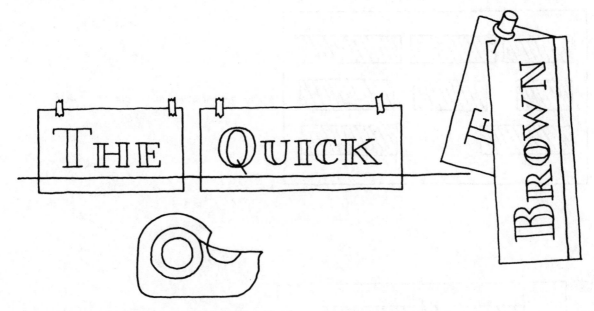

Fig. 5-38. For long texts, words can be individually laid out.

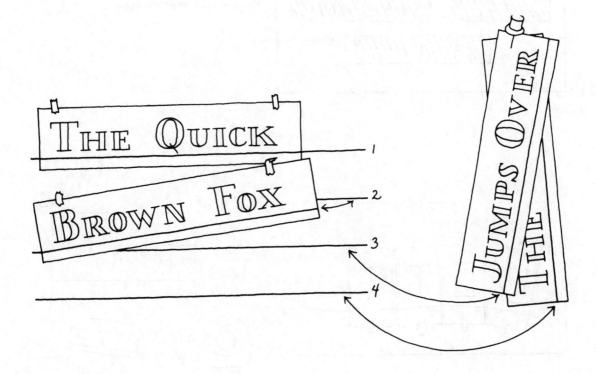

Fig. 5-39. Text layout.

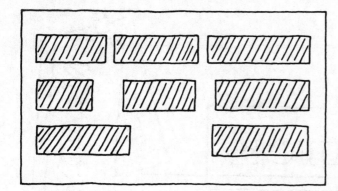

Fig. 5-40. Justified text layout.

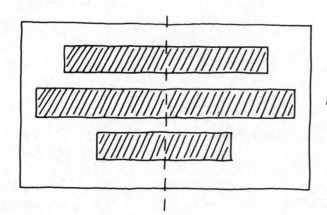

Fig. 5-41. Centered text layout.

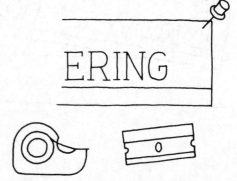

Fig. 5-42. An example of a curved guideline.

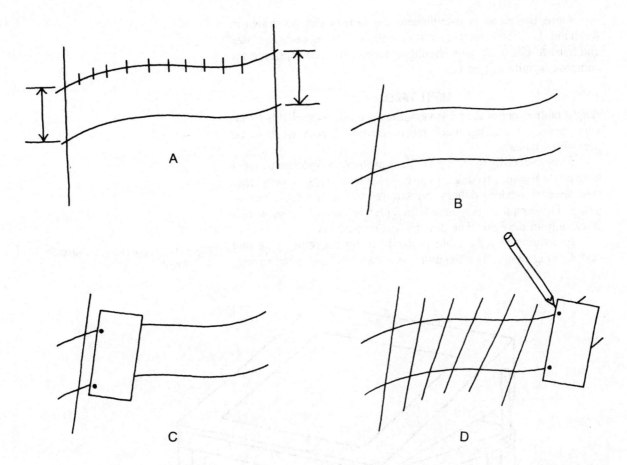

A

B

C

D

Fig. 5-43. Parallel guidelines.

down over the curved guideline (Fig. 5-42). If the curve is very slight, you might get away with it. Obviously in Fig. 5-42 we did not.

If you haven't got away with it, you will have to redraw *each letter*, using the first layout as a guide, until the letters along the curve are well balanced. This is best done by designing a sort of bastard Trajan italic letter on the spot.

Begin by drawing out the required curve with true verticals drawn at each end of the line (See A of Fig. 5-43). On a separate piece of paper, trace the first curve. Slide the tracing up along the end verticals until the right space is found. This will ensure that both curved lines are exactly parallel.

After the guidelines are drawn in parallel, a letter slope is drawn in that looks pleasing (see B of Fig. 5-43). A scrap of heavy paper or light cardboard is laid along the slope, and the ends transferred, making a gauge (see C of Fig. 5-43). When the tic marks on the gauge are intersecting the curved guidelines, all letter heights will be the same, and the slope will be correct (see D of Fig. 5-43).

Once the slope is established, the letters can be drawn in freehand. Use the original layout as a guide. This sounds complex and hard to do. It is. This should serve to curb your appetite for complex layouts and curves.

LIGHT TABLE

A light table is one of the most versatile accessories available to the sign carver. It enables much more accurate layout work to be performed quickly.

A commercially made light table is probably wonderful to use; I have never had the privilege. Figure 5-44 shows a type of model that cost several hundred dollars. Substitutes for such a table can be found. The simplest technique is to tape tracings to a window and work only in daylight. The drawbacks are obvious.

A homemade light table is available by recycling junk and castoffs (Fig. 5-45). The top must be translucent and quite strong.

Fig. 5-44. A light table is a versatile accessory.

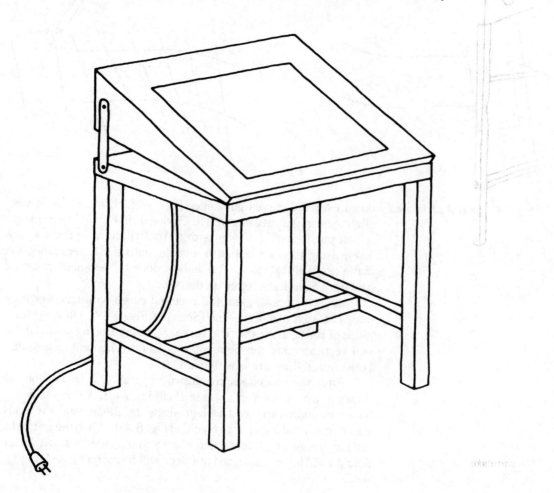

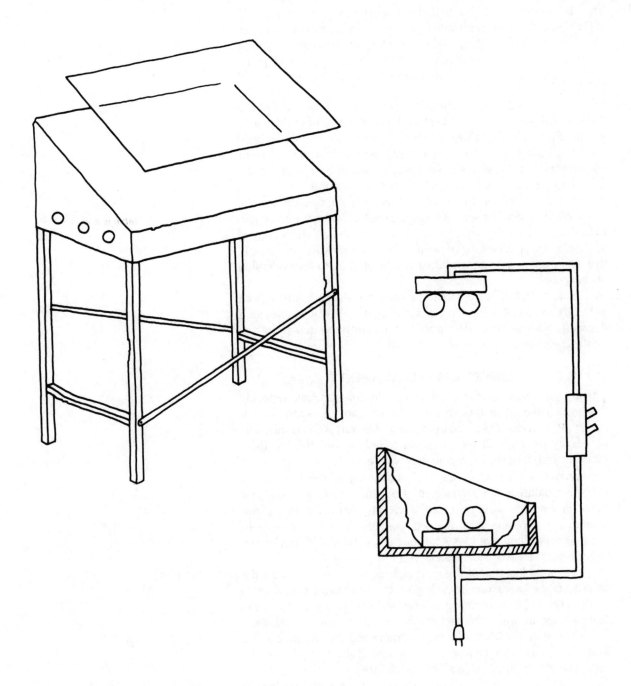

Fig. 5-45. You can make a light table from recycled junk.

The larger the better. A large piece of plate glass will do quite well. The ideal solution would be to find a sliding patio door, glass intact, at the dump. Even better would be a frosted glass shower door. For some reason, large, old plate-glass mirrors with damaged silvering are often much less expensive to buy than a comparably sized piece of plate glass. Some work with a razor blade will remove the old silvering.

Once the glass top of the light table is found, the rest of the table is built around it. The top should be set at a comfortable angle and height to work at while standing. The interior should be lined with aluminum foil to reflect more light. Wrinkled foil works better so don't try to get it smooth. Vent holes should be cut in the ends. Install as large a fluorescent light fixture as possible.

The inside of the top must be frosted to further diffuse the light. Window frosting spray was once popular; it might be possible to find some in an old variety store. If unavailable, a light coating of shellac and a light dusting of talcum powder will work, or you can use a mixture of flat beer and Epsom salts applied to the underside of the glass.

A large light fixture should be hung above the table. If both lights are switched in the same box, the light table can be used for a drawing table as well. Being able to instantly switch from one lighting source to another is very helpful.

Fig. 5-46. Simple borders.

BORDERS AND EMBELLISHMENTS

The design of the sign blank is described in Chapter 3 and lettering design is covered in this chapter. These two elements are not sufficient to create a sign that is a thing of beauty. To do this, it is necessary to bring all the elements together, and to bind them together into a unified and complete whole.

Borders. The first aspect of unification is the border. An unframed painting can certainly be beautiful. Putting a matt and frame around the painting in no way adds to the beauty of the painting. But to the eye of the beholder, the frame means something. It sets a limit that says "the beauty is within." The perimeter helps keep the eye concentrated within the frame.

A second function of the matt and the frame is to isolate the painting from the surroundings. It gives the eye a margin in which to work. The eye does not have to seek and constantly adjust to the razor's edge between the background and the unframed canvas.

On a sign, the border forms the frame and the negative space forms the matt. This concentrates the eye of the beholder on the lettering that is the "subject" of the picture.

Unlike the frame of a painting, a sign can have a frame or border that varies wildly from a simple rectangle and still be effective. Custom and usage have trained the eye of the beholder to tolerate

Fig. 5-47. Curved borders.

and even expect different and unusual shapes for signs. Indeed, part of the fun of signs *is* the variety of shapes.

Simple Border. The simplest border is a strip of contrasting color(s) painted around the perimeter (See A of Fig. 5-46). A strip of lumber, with or without a molding, can be added and painted to give visual depth and interest (See B of Fig. 5-46).

Carved Border. The carved border adds a great deal of interest to carved signs. The simplest router cut made along the perimeter—painted or gilded for contrast—will work extremely well (Fig. 5-47).

It is generally not a good idea to settle for a complete router cut. The ends are either poorly shaped or too mechanically precise. It is a better idea to stop the router cut short and work in an interesting end cut by hand.

A very complex border must be carved entirely by hand (Fig. 5-48). Such borders are beautiful indeed, and everybody wants one—until they hear the price.

Complex borders should be kept as simple as possible. For example, rather than carve entirely by hand establish two or more levels with the router. Then run the levels together by handcarving (Fig. 5-49).

Use simplified shapes wherever possible in order to cut time and costs. See Fig. 5-50.

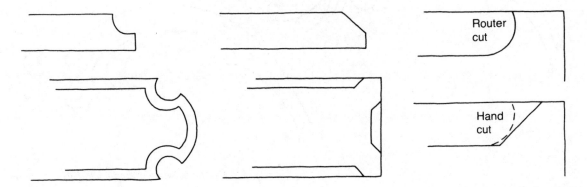

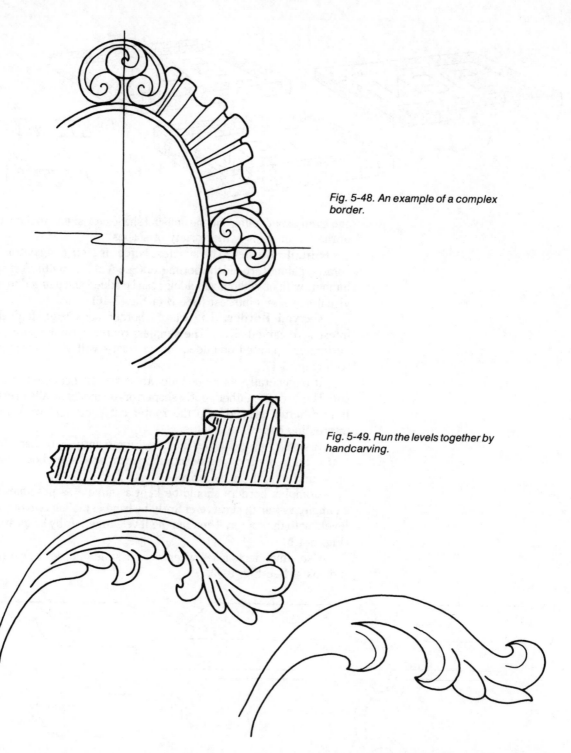

Fig. 5-48. An example of a complex border.

Fig. 5-49. Run the levels together by handcarving.

Fig. 5-50. When possible, simplify the shape.

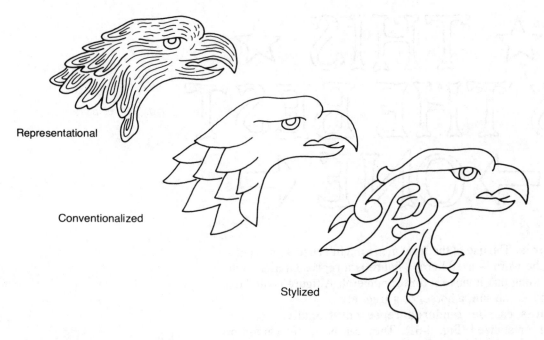

Representational

Conventionalized

Stylized

Fig. 5-51. Figures can be rendered
in three forms.

Fig. 5-52. Figures can be part of the sign or part of the border.

Fig. 5-53. Embellishments.

Figures. The use of the term *figure* might cause some confusion. As the word is used here, a figure is a representation of an objective thing that is not a letter or numeral. A figure could be a human figure, the sun, a horse, or a tree, etc.

Figures can be rendered representationally, conventionalized, or stylized (Fig. 5-51). They can be either carved or painted as either part of the sign or part of the border (Fig. 5-52).

Embellishments. As the term is used here, *embellishments* are nonrepresentation or nonobjective decorative elements. Where figures are used to convey part of the message of the lettering (Figs. 1-6, 3-34, 9-26, and 12-7), embellishments are generally used to take up space and balance otherwise awkward designs (Fig. 5-53). See also Fig. 4-6.

Fig. 5-54. This example of Victorian style is poorly thought out.

An exception to this is the Victorian style where embellishments were multiplied—often to the point of obscuring the message—simply for the artist's sheer joy in rendering embellishments (Fig. 5-54).

In designing borders, frames, figures and embellishments, it is necessary to observe the rules outlined in Chapter 3. Space, color, weight, and symmetry all play important parts.

Trial and Error. By now you will have come to the conclusion, quite correctly, that the sign is a highly complex entity. The readability and legibility of the text and lettering; the style; the color, weight and balance of the elements; and the space around and within the sign all make it complex.

When all these elements are in near perfect balance a sign is almost a living thing. It calls, invites, and welcomes with two voices. One voice should sing the melody; that is the message the sign is intended to convey. But it should also sing harmony in a second voice saying, "Look at me. I am beautiful."

To achieve this, a great deal of trial and error is involved. To simplify this trial-and-error process, follow the rules of good design. Break as few of the rules as possible. Use a light table for tracing. Tracing is *so* much easier than redrawing. Cut tracings apart and tape them together again and again. Look about you. What signs are beautiful? Why? Analyze.

6

Cartoon, Enlargement, and Transfer

The design work having been completed it is now necessary to transfer the design to the material to be carved. Of course, this must be the final full size.

CARTOON

The completed design on paper is called the *cartoon*; there is nothing humorous about it. Drawing a cartoon for a large elaborate sign is hard work.

For a small sign, such as the quarterboard lettered SMITH, you will probably draw the cartoon full size on the light table. For a large sign, the work will probably have been done to scale and then enlarged. Because several of the enlargement processes overlap the drawing of the cartoon, some of the processes in the following description will overlap as well.

Worktable

To begin with, you will need a drawing table/worktable at least as big as the largest sign you intend to carve. See Table 6-1. Limits are set by the available workspace, door size, transportation available to the site, and the man or machine power available to mount the sign. For a one-man shop, a 4- ×-8-foot worktable should be suffi-

Table 6-1. Cartoon.

Tools	Materials	Miscellaneous
Tape measure	Stick charcoal	Pencils
Chalk line	Craft paper roll,	Colored pencils
Triangle & T-square	Butcher's paper,	Chalk
Straightedge	Tracing paper roll, or	Masking tape
	Paper bags	Drafting tape
		Pushpins
		String or fish line

cient. A hobbyist can adapt the table described in the section to smaller proportions.

The table should be made of sheet material (plywood is best) with a stiffening framework backing it up. It is best to add a smooth, but slightly resilient surface covering such as lineoleum. A detachable lip on the bottom edge will keep tools and pencils from rolling off. Figure 6-1 shows a simple table.

In the interest of saving space, you can construct a combination drawing table and painting easel, with storage cabinet. Figure 6-2 shows such a table. Hinges placed at the arrows allow the leg to be folded under the table top, and the whole to fold flush to the cabinet front. So folded, it is out of the way, and may also be used with a projector set on the floor. The legs may be adjusted to different heights by nailing cleats to the floor.

Lighting

Lighting for the worktable should be as omnidirectional and free of

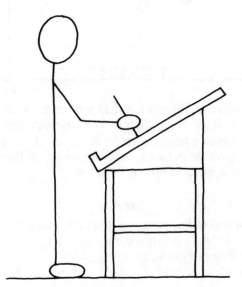

Fig. 6-1. A simple table.

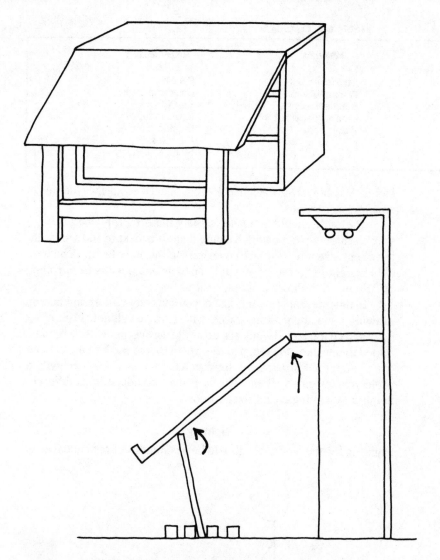

glare as possible. A fluorescent light will keep the shadow of the hands off the lines being drawn. But research has shown that fluorescent lighting tends to make people nervous and grumpy. That's not good for artwork. A combination of fluorescent and incandescent lighting seems to work best.

Fig. 6-2. A combination table.

Drawing

Layout of nicely flowing curves and perfectly straight lines is essential for a first-class job. This in turn calls for first-class (but not necessarily expensive) tools.

Layout paper should be strong and tough. It will have to

114

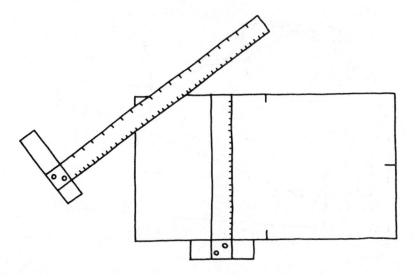

Fig. 6-3. Use a square to draw perfectly straight lines.

withstand some rather serious abuse. Rolls of brown craft and wrapping paper are commonly available up to 36 inches wide. The heavy paper used by dry cleaners can be secured in smaller quantities by the hobbyist.

Pencils for cartoon work differ from those used for scale drawing and rendering. Soft, black sketching pencils with rather thick leads are best for the first layout work. Soft lead pencils are also available in colors. It is best to establish some sort of convention with the colors. Because black is least visible, it should be used for the first lines drawn. Refinements resketched and accented in red are more visible, and they will do for the second stage. If many red and black lines are drawn, blue—which is the most visible—should be used to accent the final lines.

Drawing perfectly straight lines is necessary. A square such as the type shown in Fig. 6-3 is an economical aluminum version used by plaster workers. It is available from masonry suppliers. It is most conveniently used from the top of the board. If the centers of the table are permanently marked, finding centers and creating perfectly symmetrical cartoons is made easier.

Horizontal lines are best measured from the top of the table with the square. Use a chalk line to snap the line across the cartoon. The common carpenter's chalk line reels are useless in drawing cartoons. They deposit too much chalk and make lines which are too thick.

Braided nylon fishing line of about 20-pound test works best. A fish hook will do to hold the line on the marks. A less dangerous substitute is the spring clamp (Fig. 6-4). Blackboard chalk is harder than the cakes of chalk sold for chalk lines, and it makes finer lines.

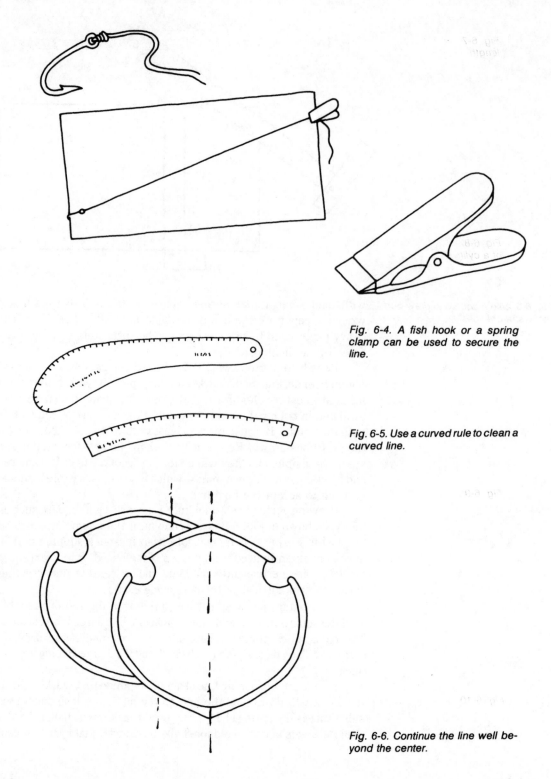

Fig. 6-4. A fish hook or a spring clamp can be used to secure the line.

Fig. 6-5. Use a curved rule to clean a curved line.

Fig. 6-6. Continue the line well beyond the center.

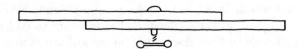

Fig. 6-7. Finding an unknown length.

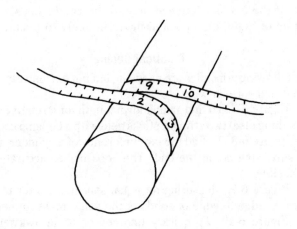

Fig. 6-8. Finding the circumference of a cylinder.

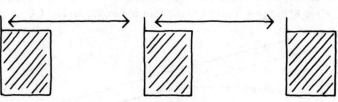

Fig. 6-9. Equal spacing.

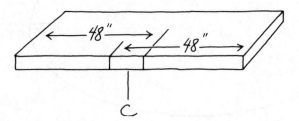

Fig. 6-10. Finding the center.

It is available in colors for ease in differentiating between lines.

Curved lines are difficult. They are hard to do freehand and even harder to do mechanically. The easiest way is to draw the line freehand and to clean it up by using a curved rule (Fig. 6-5).

When developing curves for bilateral symmetry, it is best to continue the line well beyond the center (as shown at the top of Fig. 6-6). If the line is continued only to the center (as shown at the bottom of Fig. 6-6), a pointed figure is likely to result.

Practical Geometry

The following principles are useful in, but not exclusively related to, layout and cartoon work.

Figure 6-7. To find an unknown length, or a relative length (to something else) two straight sticks held with a C clamp can be used.

Figure 6-8. To find the circumference of a cylinder, use a tape measure—but not at the end. The hook makes accurate readings impossible.

Figure 6-9. Measuring for equal spacing. Center to center of holes or edge to edge of solids is the same measurement.

Figure 6-10. To quickly find center of an awkward length, measure a known length from either end. Then divide the smaller length remaining.

Figure 6-11. To find the dimension of a curve, a yardstick or wooden batten can be marked and "walked" around the curve. If the curve is drawn on a flat surface, masking tape can be laid along the curve and the ends can be marked. The tape is then taken up and stuck down along the edge of the yardstick.

Figure 6-12 shows several useful ways of computing rough measurements without a ruler. Bricks laid in the common bond style average 4 courses to the foot in height, and 8″ CC on the run.

Fig. 6-11. Finding the dimensions of a curve.

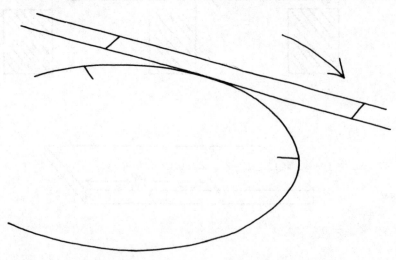

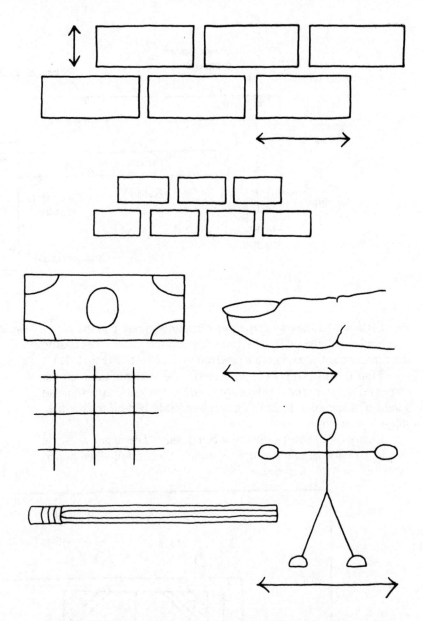

Fig. 6-12. Computing measurements without a ruler.

Cinder blocks generally measure 8 × 16 inches CC on joints. Counting the number of blocks or the number of courses gives an approximate measurement.

A dollar bill measures 6 inches. An unsharpened office pencil measures 7 inches. The first joint of the index finger of the average adult is usually very close to 1 inch. The arm span of the average adult male is very close to 6 feet.

Asphalt floor tiles usually measure either 9 inches or 12 inches.

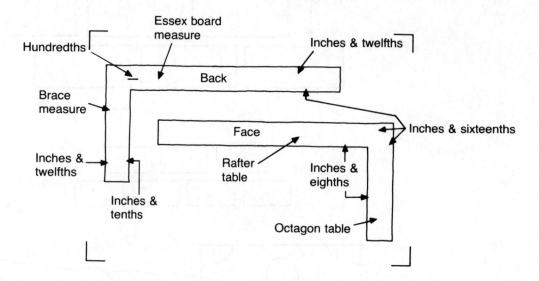

Figure 6-13 shows a carpenter's framing square and the reference tables printed on it. The frame square has many uses beside the Essex board measure table referred to in Chapter 2 (Fig. 2-12).

Fig. 6-13. A carpenter's framing square.

Figure 6-14. To lay out an octagon, the octagon table on the carpenter's square and dividers are needed. The dots represent the height of a square in inches. The dimension is laid off from either side of centerlines.

Figure 6-15 shows a variety of compasses. The upper versions (A and B) have an office pencil. Version B has a full-sized pencil (which is easy to sharpen).

Fig. 6-14. Laying out an octagon.

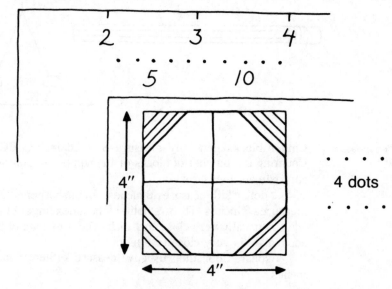

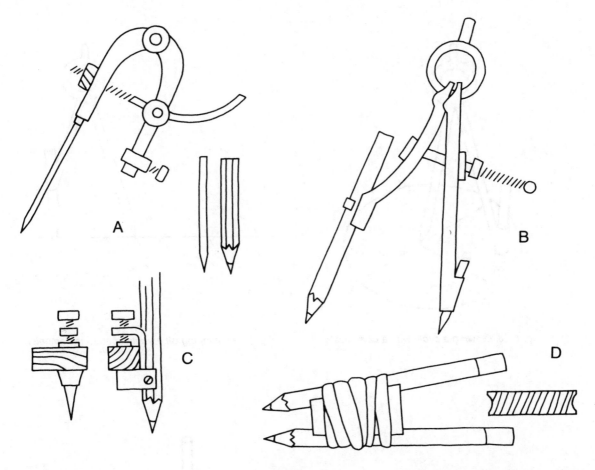

Fig. 6-15. Compasses.

The two lower versions (C and D) are somewhat different. The Trammel Points (C) are used with a wooden batten to make a compass of infinite size. Version D uses a tapered and grooved wooden block and rubber bands. By reversing the pencils, larger circles can be made. This version is very handy for scribing parallel lines.

Figure 6-16 shows drawing a circle with the compass. Be sure that the point and the pencil are in the same plane before drawing. The radius (R) equals half the diameter (D) of the circle.

Figure 6-17 shows how a compass can be used to step off any number of equally spaced increments along a straight or curved line.

Figure 6-18 shows how to draw parallel lines along a curve as for guidelines for lettering. The curve is drawn in the center of the space the lettering is to occupy. A radius is established equal to half the height of the letter. The point is set on the line and many circles are drawn. Lines tangent to all circles are parallel to the center line and the correct height for the lettering.

Figure 6-19 shows how to draw a line parallel to a raised piece

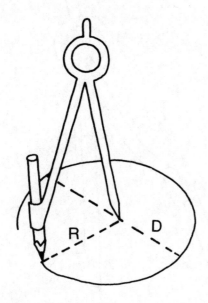

Fig. 6-16. Drawing a circle with a compass.

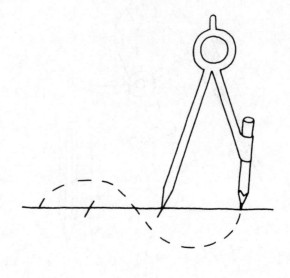

Fig. 6-17. Stepping off equally spaced increments.

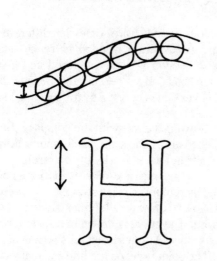

Fig. 6-18. Drawing parallel lines along a curve.

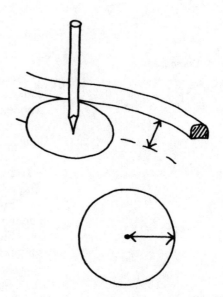

Fig. 6-19. Drawing a parallel line to a raised piece.

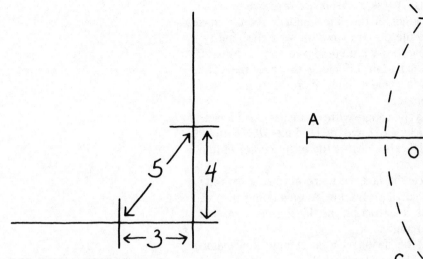

Fig. 6-20. Making a 90-degree angle.

Fig. 6-21. Drawing a right angle with a compass.

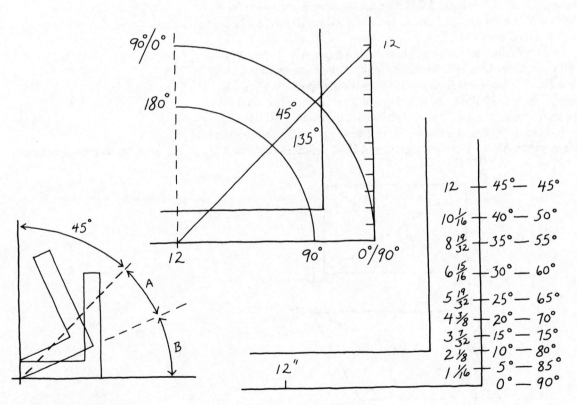

Fig. 6-22. Laying out angles.

12	45°	45°
10 1/16	40°	50°
8 19/32	35°	55°
6 15/16	30°	60°
5 19/32	25°	65°
4 3/8	20°	70°
3 7/32	15°	75°
2 1/8	10°	80°
1 1/16	5°	85°
	0°	90°

123

such as a border or molding. A disk of cardboard is drawn with the radius equal to the full height of the line needed. As the disk revolves along the border, the pencil marks off a parallel line.

Figure 6-20 shows how to make a 90-degree angle without a square. Three increments are laid off along the baseline. The intersection of two lines (4 increments and 5 increments measured as shown) create a right angle.

Figure 6-21. Drawing a right angle with a compass. Arcs longer than distance A0 are struck; ACD and BCD. Line DC is at 90 degrees to line AB. Line DC also locates the exact center of line AB.

Figure 6-22. Angles can be laid out more precisely with the framing square than with a small protractor. Angles larger than 45 degrees are drawn by first constructing the 45-degree angle and adding to it to get the final angle.

Figure 6-23 shows that the diagonals in a rectangle offer a good check to the squareness of the rectangle.

Figure 6-24 shows two methods for dividing a line into any number of equal parts. At 24A, line AB must be divided into five equal parts. Because the 28-inch line is not divisible by five, line AC is laid out 30 inches long. AC is then divided into 6-inch increments (30″ ÷ 5). Lines at angle B are drawn from AC to AB (divide the line into 5 equal parts).

At 24B the same principle is used, but angle ABC is first drawn with a square. Line AC, 30 inches long, is then drawn to intersect line BC. The square is then used to transfer the spacing to line AB.

Figure 6-25 shows how to lay out an arc when the arc is too large to use a compass. Nails are driven on drawn line AB. Height H is located at 90 degrees above the center (Fig. 6-21). Two battens longer than AB are fastened together at H. A pencil is placed at the

Fig. 6-23. Diagonals in a rectangle.

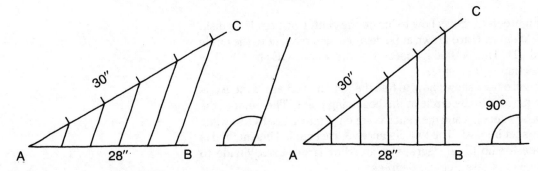

Fig. 6-24. Two methods for dividing a line into equal parts.

Fig. 6-25. Laying out an arc.

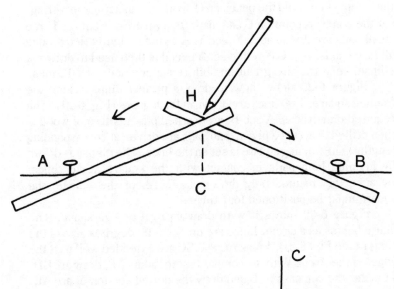

Fig. 6-26. Locating the center of a
circle or disk.

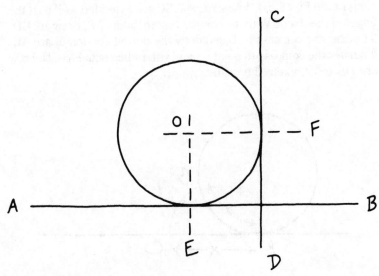

125

joint, and the battens are swung left and right while contacting the nails.

Figure 6-26 shows how to locate the center of a circle or disk. Lines AB and CD are drawn at 90 degrees, and tangent to the circle (Fig. 6-21). The method is repeated to draw lines OE and OF. The intersection is the center.

Figure 6-27 shows how to find the length of an arc. Line AC is drawn tangent to the circle at the beginning point. The point of the compass is set on A and the pencil is set on point B. Arc BC is swung to intersect line AC. The two distances X are equal. This method is accurate for up to 60 degrees of arc. For larger arcs, divide to increments of less than 60 degrees.

Figure 6-28 shows how to draw a perfect ellipse. The two center lines AB and CD are drawn as in Fig. 6-21. Set the point of the compass on A and the pencil on O. Without changing the setting, set the compass point on C and mark the two arcs, X and Y. Three small nails are driven at C, X, and Y. A string is tightly tied around all three nails. Nail C is removed. A pencil is then used to draw the ellipse; keep the string taut on both remaining nails at all times.

Figure 6-29 shows how to draw a perfect ellipse using the framing square. Two lines are drawn at 90 degrees (Fig. 6-21). The required dimensions, A and B, are marked off. A batten of wood is then drilled to accept a pencil, and nails are driven at corresponding lengths. The framing square is set on the lines. The ellipse is drawn by keeping both nails in contact with the square at all times. Because this method only draws one-fourth of the ellipse, the square must be positioned four times.

Figure 6-30 shows how to draw an oval or egg shape. The figure begins as a circle. Lines are drawn at 90 degrees across the center (see Fig. 6-21). Lines AC and BC are extended well past the edges of the circle. With the compass set to radius AB, draw arc BD. Transfer the compass to B and draw the dotted section of arc AE. Transfer the compass to point C and, with radius equal to CD, draw arc DE to complete the oval.

Fig. 6-27. Finding the length of an arc.

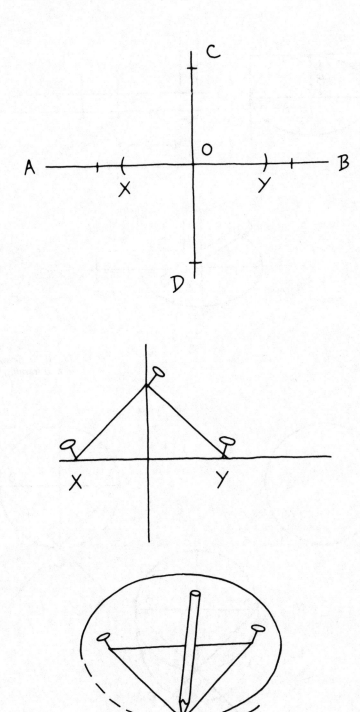

Fig. 6-28. *How to draw a perfect ellipse.*

127

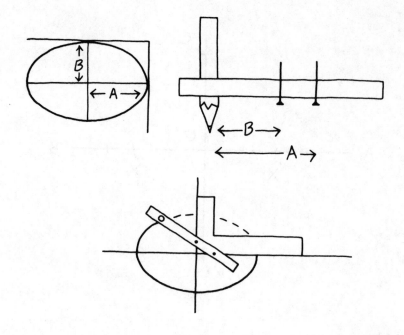

Fig. 6-29. Drawing a perfect ellipse with a framing square.

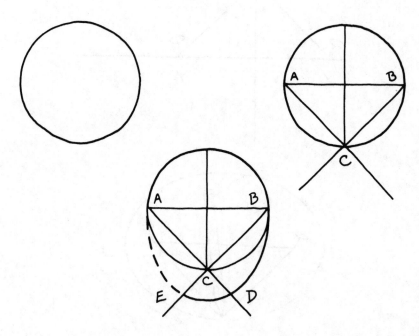

Fig. 6-30. Drawing an oval or an egg shape.

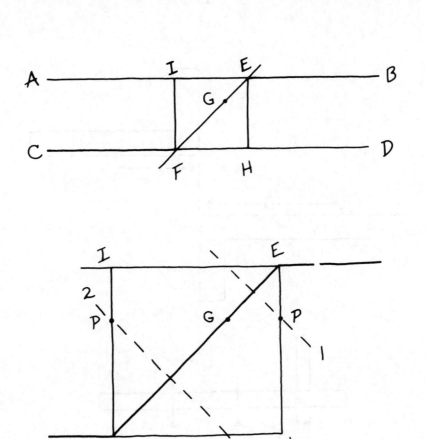

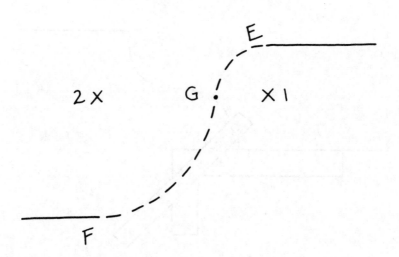

Fig. 6-31. Drawing a smooth reverse curve.

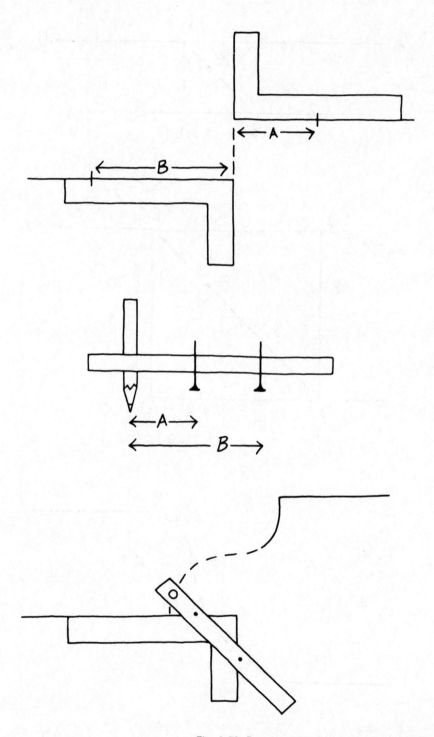

Fig. 6-32. Drawing the reverse circle using the framing square.

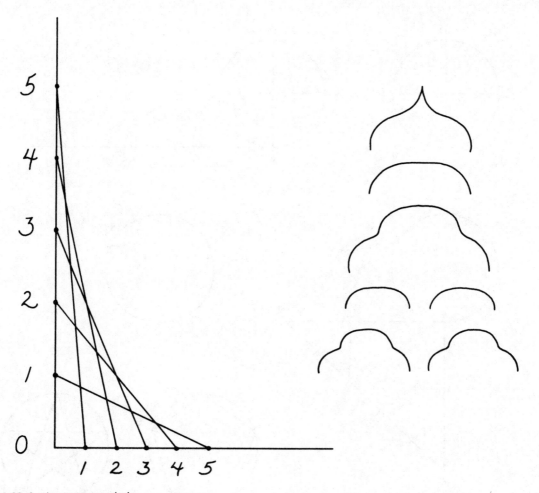

Fig. 6-33. Laying out a parabola.

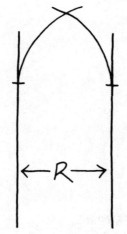

Fig. 6-34. Developing a gothic arch.

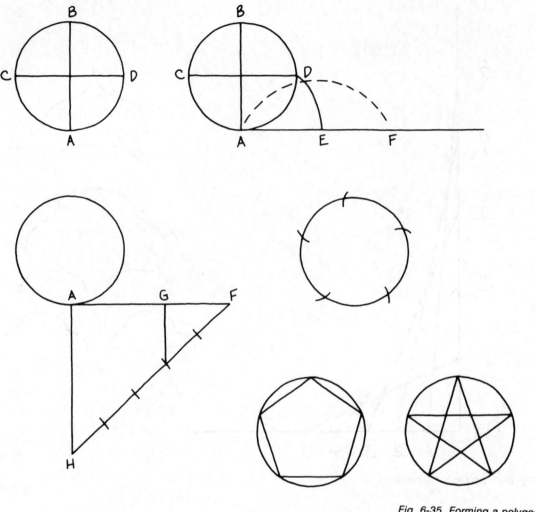

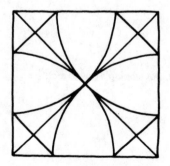

Fig. 6-35. Forming a polygon.

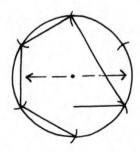

Fig. 6-36. Laying out a triangle or a hexagon.

Fig. 6-37. Drawing an octagon.

Figure 6-31 shows one method of drawing a smooth reverse curve. Lines AB and CD are parallel; they represent the start and stop of the curve. Axis of the curve is drawn (EF). Point G is the point where the curve reverses. Lines 1 and 2 are found by dividing FG and GE (as in Fig. 6-21).

The intersections of line EH with line 1 and line IF with line 2 become the centers of the arcs P. With the point of the compass on P and the pencil set on G, draw the two arcs to complete the curve.

Figure 6-32 shows how to draw the reverse curve using the framing square. Distances A and B are laid off to suit. The wood batten is laid out as in Fig. 6-29. The square is then shifted along the line the appropriate distance. Then the two separate arcs are drawn.

Figure 6-33 shows how to lay out a parabola. The two lines set at 90 degrees are marked off in equal increments (*not* equal spacing). See Fig. 6-24. Lines are drawn connecting the increments, as shown, and the resulting curve is faired (Fig. 6-5). Some shapes developed from parabola and reverse curves are shown.

Figure 6-34 shows how to develop a Gothic arch. Two arcs are struck, the radius being equal to the distance between the lines.

Figure 6-35 is real fun, it shows how to combine several processes to form an equal polygon of any number of sides. For this purpose, make a five-pointed star. In addition six-pointed snowflakes and 12-pointed diamonds are all formed the same way.

Begin with a circle that will contain the design (Fig. 6-16). With the compass, lay out the length of one-quarter the arc of the circle (Fig. 6-27) on line AF. Double the length of the line (Fig. 6-17). On the same drawing—or another sheet of paper if there is not enough room—lay out lines AF and AH at 90 degrees (Fig. 6-21).

Between lines AF and AH, draw a line divisable evenly by the number of points in the figure; in this case, it is five. If for some reason you can't, draw any line AH and divide it as in Fig. 6-24.

Now comes the tricky part. You have divided line AF into five parts, but AF only represents half of the circumference of the circle. Therefore you *really* found one-tenth. Take *two* increments along FH and transfer it back to line AF to establish point G. See Fig. 6-24B.

With the compass set to FG, the circle can now be divided into five equal parts. By connecting adjacent points, you can draw a pentagon. By connecting opposite points, you can draw a five-pointed star. This procedure works for any even or odd number of points on a circle. This elaborate procedure is not necessary for every figure.

Figure 6-36 shows how to lay out a triangle or hexagon. The radius of the circle equals one-sixth of the circumference. By joining

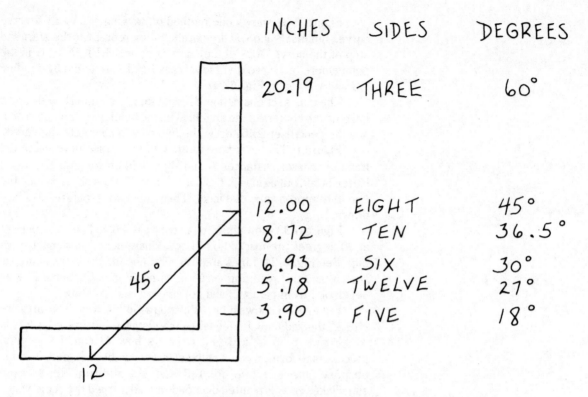

INCHES	SIDES	DEGREES
20.79	THREE	60°
12.00	EIGHT	45°
8.72	TEN	36.5°
6.93	SIX	30°
5.78	TWELVE	27°
3.90	FIVE	18°

Fig. 6-38. Drawing regular polygons.

all points, you get the hexagon. By joining every other point, you get the triangle.

Figure 6-37 shows how to draw an octagon. A square is drawn and the center is found by drawing diagonals (Fig. 6-23). The point of the compass is set on a corner and the pencil is set on the center just found. Arcs are swung from each corner. The arcs intersect the sides of the square and the ends of the arcs are connected.

Figure 6-38 shows how to draw the more common regular polygons, using the framing square to draw the angles. The question of course is how do you find .78 of an inch? See Fig. 6-13.

Figure 6-39 shows a simple spiral. Two concentric circles are drawn. The inner circle is divided into three parts (a triangle, see Fig. 6-36.) With the compass set on point 2 and the pencil on point 1, draw the arc from line A to line B. Set the point of the compass on point 3, and the pencil at the intersection of the first arc on line B. Draw this arc to intersect line C. The arcs must be faired with the curved ruler (Fig. 6-5).

A much more interesting spiral can be drawn by beginning with a square (Fig. 6-40). Centers and diagonals are drawn (Figs. 6-21 and 6-24). This gives eight points on the square. One radius of the circle is now divided into eight parts (Fig. 6-24). Eight concentric circles are drawn within the square. Beginning at circle 1 on line 1,

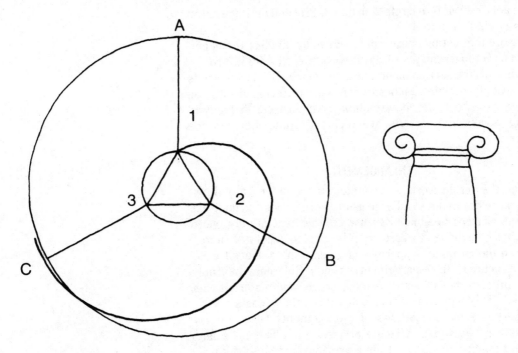

Fig. 6-39. A simple spiral.

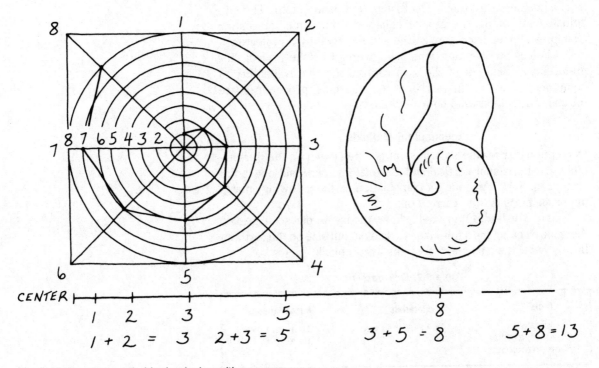

Fig. 6-40. Drawing a spiral by beginning with a square.

135

draw an arc (freehand) to circle 2 on line 2. Proceed until the spiral reaches circle 8 on line 8.

A more interesting spiral can be drawn by dividing the beginning radius into increments of the Fibonacci series (Fig. 3-5).

This ends the section on practical geometry. Because there is no way that all possible sign blank shapes and lettering layouts can be shown in one book, the above method has been used. Virtually all possible blanks and layouts are included somewhere in the geometry.

ENLARGEMENT

Now that the design work is completed, the geometrically drawn layout can be drawn out to full size using the methods and materials under the Cartoon heading. Because enlargement is only one of many ways of arriving at a cartoon, it is handled separately here.

Once the customer's approval is given—and a deposit check has been secured—the enlargement is begun. Enlargement is not a difficult process, but it demands time, space, and materials. See Table 6-2. This section is directed at cutting those costs.

There are many methods of enlargement. Often several methods can be used in a single project. For example, a large signboard might be enlarged from a previously made blank if the cartoon was kept in the files. The lettering can be taken directly from a business card (using Photostats or a pantograph). The embellishments or figures can be enlarged from some interesting examples clipped from a magazine and enlarged by a projector.

Choices and combinations are governed by the project, the preferences, facilities of the sign carver, and the availability of equipment. Two useful divisions of enlarging procedures are mechanical methods and optical methods.

Mechanical Methods

Once the paper for the enlargement is taped down on the drawing table, the horizontal vertical and diagonal lines are laid out to full scale (Fig. 6-41). Any one (or combination) of the following enlarging procedures is then carried out.

Grid Method. Figure 6-42 shows the layout of a scale grid on the scale drawing and a full-size grid laid out full size on the cartoon. In this case, the triangle represents a sign blank.

Table 6-2. Enlargement.

Tools	Materials	Miscellaneous
Photostats	Art to be enlarged	Camera tripod
Opaque projector		Level
Slide projector		

Fig. 6-41. Full-scale layout lines.

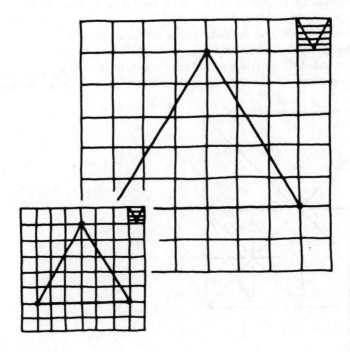

Fig. 6-42. Grid scale layout.

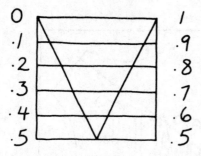

Great care must be taken to ensure that the grid lines are made carefully to scale, and that all lines are made perfectly parallel and at perfect right angles on *both* drawings. Letter or number each square to ensure that the same number of squares are used in each drawing, and that the transferred dots are located in the proper square. This absolute accuracy is necessary; errors imperceptible in scale can be devastating when enlarged.

Dots are made on the enlargement at every point that a drawing line crosses a grid line. When all such points are located, the enlargement is finished by the "connect the dots" method.

Approximating distances within a square grid can be very difficult. If this proves the case, a grid square on both the scale drawing and the enlargement can be divided as shown at Fig. 6-43. By using a compass or dividers, increments as small as one-tenth of a grid square can be picked up and transferred.

This is very precise work, and it tends to be emotionally exhausting. A much easier method is shown in Fig. 6-44. With this method, the grid is constructed "as you go" and save much time. Measuring is eliminated. Once the dimensions of the enlargement

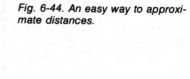

Fig. 6-43. Approximating distances.

Fig. 6-44. An easy way to approximate distances.

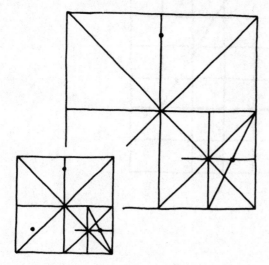

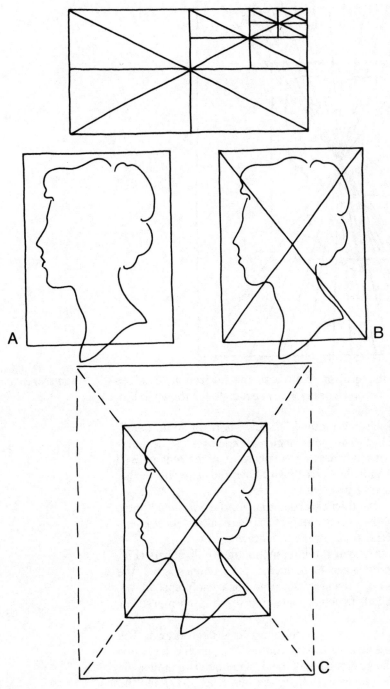

Fig. 6-45. Approximating a distance
for a rectangle.

Fig. 6-46. The radial enlarging
method.

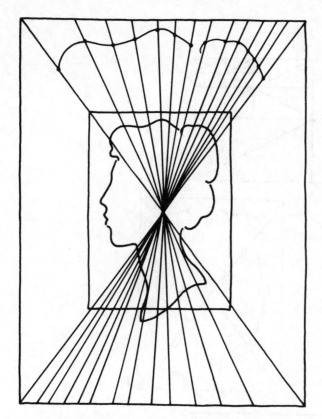

are established, the grid is relative to the horizontal divisions established. This method works for any rectangle (as shown in Fig. 6-45).

The radial enlarging method is shown here in some detail. Beginning at A of Fig. 6-46, a rectangle that encloses the design is drawn. Diagonals are then drawn to the corners of the rectangle (B of Fig. 6-46). Horizontal lines are drawn above and below the design to the established enlarged size.

The diagonals are then extended to meet the horizontal lines, and verticals are drawn (C of Fig. 6-46). The resulting rectangle is then in perfect proportion to the scale drawing.

A pushpin is driven at the intersection of the diagonals (Fig. 6-47) and a straightedge is used to draw a series of lines across the center. The lines can be widely separated or closely spaced, depending on the detail involved. Note that there is no measuring involved.

The pushpin is pulled after the lines have been drawn. The point of the compass is placed on the center. The pencil is extended along the line to the intersection of the design line. The dimension thus established is stepped off along the line (Fig. 6-17) and the enlarged point is established. The dots are then connected.

Fig. 6-47. A pushpin is driven at the intersection of the diagonals.

140

This method has one drawback; the scale drawing can only be enlarged by whole numbers. This can be a real problem unless the scale drawing is made with this drawback in mind.

The pantograph (Fig. 6-48) is a mechanical tool that can be used to produce enlargements to almost any degree. Four wood or metal legs are held in position by some sort of clamp. One end is fastened to the drawing table, and a stylus traces the scale drawing. This in turn causes a pencil to exactly copy the stylus drawing at the selected larger size. It is simple and foolproof. I don't like it. Anything that does the work "automatically" is automatically suspect, at least as far as I'm concerned.

Pantographs are stocked by several of the suppliers listed in the appendix; these tools are best purchased. Homemade varieties never seem to work quite right.

Once you have read the catalogs, try to get further information from the suppliers. Better still, ask for a photocopy of the instructions that come with the machine. Compare features. Remember that it is a machine. A good one will be costly and a cheap one will probably be useless.

Of the enlarging methods, the two shown in Figs. 6-44 and 6-47 have always worked best for me. I have used them continuously for many years, and I prefer them to either pantographs or optical methods of enlargement.

Optical Methods. Optical enlargement methods use machines that automatically make enlargements. The cautions given above under pantographs should be considered. Most sign crafters

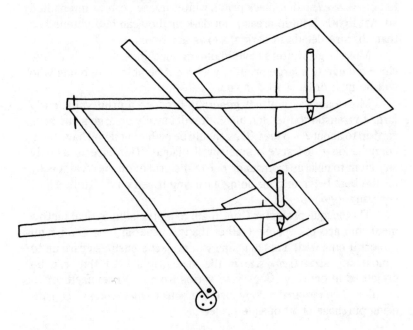

Fig. 6-48. A pantograph.

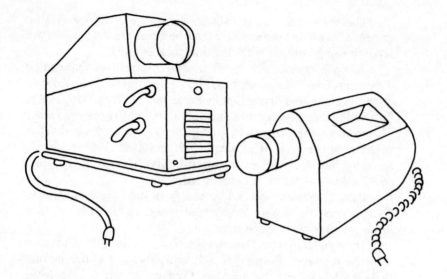

find that an optical enlarging system is necessary at some time in their career.

Fig. 6-49. An opaque projector.

A Photostat is a trade name for photographically produced enlargements (or reductions) of an original piece, called the "art." A Photostat is a high fidelity reproduction of the art made on a very high-priced camera. If the art quality is good, you get an excellent "stat." If the art is poor (blurred, lightly printed, etc.) you get a high fidelity reproduction of poor art.

In addition to enlargement, art can be *flopped* so that right faces left or *reversed* so that black prints white. Images can be intensified so that lightly printed areas print dark or they can be lightened so that obscure details in dark shadows are revealed.

Most large printers have Photostat machines. If you don't live close enough to a large printer, you might be able to find one who will do mail-order work for you.

Most cameras will not generally produce a print sufficiently large to transfer to the sign blank. It will usually enlarge a business card up to about 2 × 3 feet. This should be sufficient if you have been commissioned to carve a small wall plaque. This size is usually sufficient to enlarge from using one of the grid methods. A stat is by far the best beginning for doing a carving based on a letterhead or company logo.

The opaque projector (Fig. 6-49) is a precision optical instrument that accepts opaque (rather than transparent) art and it will project it on a wall. This machine will project a business card up to almost any size. *Copy size* is the size original art that can be projected in entirety. Copy size varies from one manufacturer to another. The larger the copy size the better when you are considering purchase of an opaque projector.

A good-quality opaque projector with 10- × -10-inch copy size retails from $400 to $700. There are others on the market that sell for about $15. They are useless.

Before considering the purchase of an opaque projector, it would be best to check with art suppliers, art schools, tool rentals, camera shops, and other sign painters with regard to short-term rentals. I have never owned one of these wonderful machines, but there have been many times when I wish I did.

Slide projectors (Fig. 6-50) are very useful for sales presentations and for use around the shop. This is my preferred method of optical enlargement.

Many homes today have some sort of 35 mm slide projector. These machines will generally project a 35mm slide to a sufficiently large size in a fully darkened room. If there are problems, the nearest camera shop will probably have a larger bulb to fit your machine. Large bulbs and long projection times can badly distort the slide. This can be overcome, to a degree, by using glass slide mounts and heat absorbing filters in the projector.

It is not necessary to use the standard color slide film in a slide projector. Actually it is better not to because fast 35mm black and white films can be used to real advantage.

By saving art and embellishments clipped from newspapers and magazines and scale drawings of blanks, a very useful slide file can be built up over time.

Fig. 6-50. A slide projector.

Because most photofinishers have a hard time with special

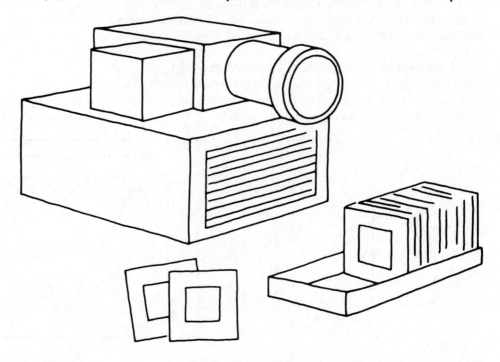

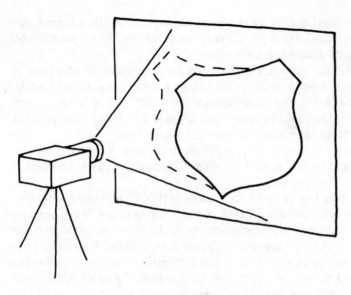

instructions, I prefer to leave my film for development and a contact sheet only. This gives you a picture for your files and it is easier than trying to find a slide. Of course, this means that you are projecting a negative image, but this is easy to get used to after a while.

Cardboard and glass slide frames are available for purchase separately. Mounting the slides is quite easy.

The only serious problem I have had in using the slide projector is the time factor. The slide I want to use *now* is either at the finisher or still in the camera. Once a file is established, there are generally few problems.

Problems in Enlargement. Two problems—distortion and awkward designs—can occur when enlargements are made. One problem is peculiar to optical methods and the second problem is shared by both optical and mechanical methods.

Fig. 6-51. An example of fore-shortening.

Fig. 6-52. Safeguards against forced perspective.

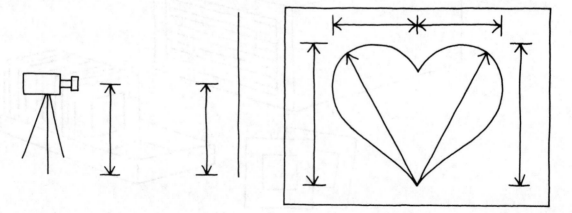

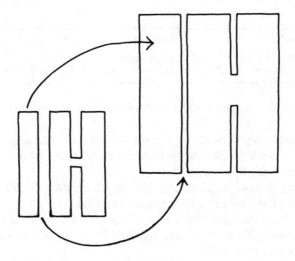

Fig. 6-53. Not everything is enlarged during the enlarging process.

Distortion can occur accidentally during optical enlargement of a design. The most likely cause is a forced perspective resulting from a careless approach to enlarging. Foreshortening of the design results (as in Fig. 6-51). Figure 6-52 shows some safeguards that can be taken to guard against forced perspective.

The reverse situation might also apply. A sign placed high above eye level, and viewed from a very short angle, might appear awkward even if it is correctly proportioned. A bit of jiggling with the projector can be used to distort the image so that in position it appears normal.

It often occurs that a design that looks very good on a business card or letterhead looks like the wrath of God when greatly enlarged. The cause is an apparent paradox that, even though explained, makes little sense. Not everything is enlarged during the enlarging process. Some parts of the design become smaller (Fig. 6-53).

A similar problem occurs when a thin line, printed as a border, for example, becomes far too heavy when enlarged to 3 inches wide on a sign. Both of these problems can be corrected by shaving off the thickness of the offending parts by using the parallel following tool such as the one shown in D of Fig. 6-15.

It can also occur that a good, small design is just a bad, large design. After you've done every step carefully and observed all the rules, the result might look like an assault on the artistic sensibilities. Such occurrences are thankfully rare, but they do occur and they *never* advertise themselves ahead of time. When one of these disasters happens to you, there are several thoughts that can ease the pain:

☐ Know that, while the responsibility for the problem is your fault, the cause isn't.

Tools	Materials
Stylus	Carbon paper
Pounce wheel	Powdered charcoal and charcoal bag

Table 6-3. Transfer.

☐ This is a situation tailor-made for the creative use of profanity.

☐ Shelve the project for at least overnight. Solutions may suggest themselves during the night or you might arrive with a fresh look at the problem in the morning.

☐ Cut the design apart and juggle the elements around a bit. Even small changes can make big improvements.

☐ Realize that your client *wants* to be thrilled when he sees the sign in place. His rose-colored glasses will often obscure things that you know are horrible.

TRANSFER

In all likelihood, the design will have to be transferred to the sign blank several times: Once when the outline of the blank is cut; again when the outlines of the lettering, etc., must be laid down for carving; and again when the outlines for painting and shading must be applied.

It is therefore necessary that the final design be drawn on a heavy, durable, and dimensionally stable paper. A pasteup of several pieces of tracing paper will have to be transferred to craft paper before transferring the design to the blank. Tracing paper is too flimsy. What is worse, it changes size and shape with changes in temperature and humidity.

Whether transferring a pasteup of tracings to craft paper or transferring the design to the blank, the process is the same. See Table 6-3.

The method of rubbing the back of the drawing with graphite is explained in the Rendering Methods section in Chapter 4.

Carbon Paper

Carbon paper is excellent for use in transferring the pasteup to the craft paper, and for transferring to the sign blank. A stylus such as Fig. 6-54 is used. This is an office supply item used for making mimeograph stencils.

There are several types of carbon paper, and all are useful. Typing carbon is the most common. Both the old fashion kind with

Fig. 6-54. A stylus.

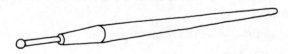

146

the greasy black or blue carbon, and the newer honeycomb plastic sheets are useful. The old style in blue is very visible on raw wood, and it is economical.

Pencil carbon is less waxy and it transfers a lighter weight line that is useful for transferring pasteups to craft paper. Pencil carbon is fairly common and economical.

Dressmakers carbon is a harder, chalkier carbon that is available in a wide range of colors. It transfers a very fine line that is easily removed from painted surfaces. It is fairly common and rather expensive.

Saral paper is an artist's carbon paper that is available in several colors. It erases easily. Sold by the 12-foot roll in single colors or by the package with one sheet of each color, it is only in large art supply stores and it is quite expensive.

Pounce

A second method transfers the design by pouncing a bag of powdered charcoal over the craft paper cartoon. Holes are made in the paper by using a pounce wheel (Fig. 6-55).

This method is preferred by many sign painters as well as artists in many other fields. I have never used it successfully in sign work, but I have used it elsewhere. The pounce wheel is hard to control in the small radius turns of letter serifs, and it often tears the paper. The pounce wheel requires a special table top of velour fabric stretched over plywood to allow the wheel adequate penetration through the paper. This method is quite successful for transferring many repeats of a design such as the same star in several locations

Fig. 6-55. Holes are made with a pounce wheel.

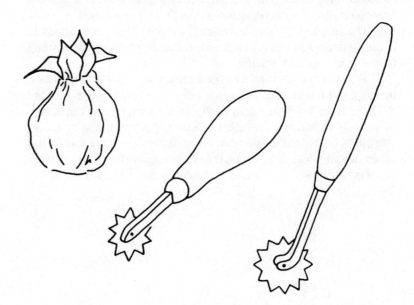

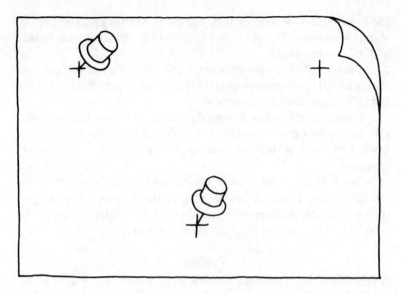

on the same sign. The method is faster than tracing the same design over and over.

Fig. 6-56. Use pushpins to transfer marks.

Lost Lines

It often happens that a transferred line is lost. It could be that the line simply wasn't traced or pounced. Working slowly, carefully, and checking often eliminates this problem.

More often a line is obliterated during the carving process or is painted over during the finishing processes. The lost line must be re-established on the blank and in precise registration. The easiest way to do this is with registration marks on the cartoon.

The simplest registration mark is a cross. Three crosses made in the negative space of the cartoon are transferred from the pasteup to the craft paper by tracing.

Transferring the marks to the sign blank is best accomplished by using pushpins as shown in Fig. 6-56. The hole in the paper and the hole in the wood are easily realigned for transferring the design in successive stages. The use of three registration marks allows one pin to be pulled to insert carbon or to check progress while the other two pins keep the cartoon in perfect registration. For complex signs involving several transfers, reinforce the marks with layers of tape.

7

Sign Blank Assembly

Having obtained the commission from the customer, the wood for the sign blank can be ordered or purchased. Upon reaching the studio, work on the layout and lettering can be carried out at the same time that the sign blank is prepared. If the sign blank and the cartoon are developed simultaneously, defects in the wood can be minimized by positioning them where they will do little harm. Alternatively, the layout and lettering can be developed with the wood grain and defects in mind. Anyway, jumping from one part of the job to the other tends to keep the work from becoming tedious.

MEASURING AND MARKING OUT

Returning to the example sign designed in Chapter 4, a 3- ×-4-foot sign blank of 1-inch-thick select Northern pine will be used. The carving is of such a simple nature that the additional expense for sugar pine is not justified.

At the yard, pick through the appropriate pile and select about 15 square feet of 1¼- ×-6-inch lumber. This comes to about 30 lineal feet.

The reason for buying 30 feet of 1¼- ×-6-inch lumber as opposed to 15 feet of 1¼- ×-12-inch lumber is that in the wider size you are almost certain to end up with flat grain if you choose the wide boards. See A of Fig. 2-3. Flat grain stock will be more prone to cup warping so choose the narrower stock. You also stand a better chance of getting vertical grain (B of Fig. 2-3) in the narrower stock. The extra stock purchased is to allow for waste and mistakes. See Table 7-1.

Back at the studio, the edge joints are planned so that as few joints as possible fall in an area to be carved. Joints falling in the area that contains letter serifs are particularly bad. If this planning requires the purchase of an extra board and cutting most of it away, then so be it. The cost of the lumber is really negligible when compared to the completed sign.

The first board is measured and cut to length by hooking the end of a tape measure over the end of the board (Fig. 7-1). Be sure to measure along the edge of the board for accuracy.

A square is used to extend the cut line across the face of the stock (Fig. 7-2) and the cut is made along the *outside* of the line. A second board is laid along the first, and the grain is matched as nearly as possible in the areas to be carved. The end(s) are trimmed to fit. The process is continued until all the boards are cut to length and matched (Fig. 7-3).

If the sign blank is to have perfectly matched ends and perfectly square corners when finished, the ends are left slightly long until the boards are permanently fastened and glued when the final cuts (dotted lines) are made.

When the boards are laid out correctly and cut for length, registration marks are made as shown in Fig. 7-4. With this shape registration mark, there is no way to accidentally assemble the boards in the wrong sequence.

If the sign is to be a *slab* (without backing framework) as this

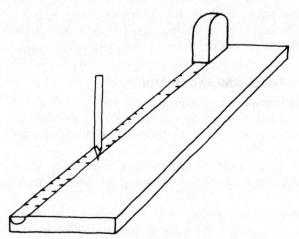

Fig. 7-1. Measure and cut the first board.

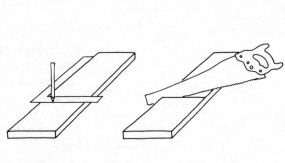

Fig. 7-2. Use a square to extend the cut line.

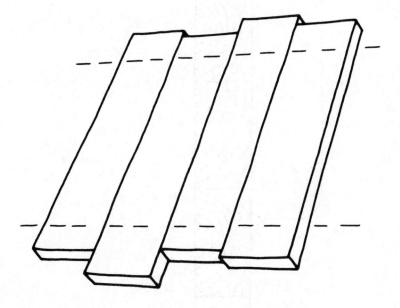

Fig. 7-3. Trim the ends to fit.

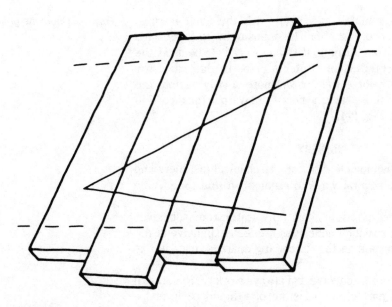

Fig. 7-4. Making registration mark.

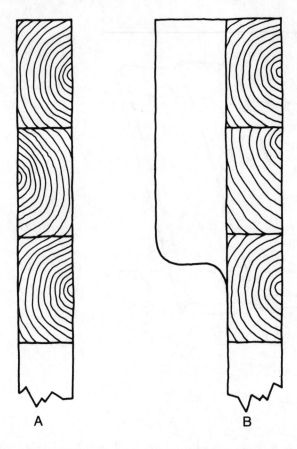

A   B

Fig. 7-5. Orient the grain.

one is, the boards should be arranged with the annular rings oriented as shown in A of Fig. 7-5. The opposing warp tendencies should keep the slab from warping. If a framework is to be used, the grain should be oriented as in B of Fig. 7-5. In this case, the tendency to warp will force the boards more tightly against the framework. Common sense says the board will warp in the direction of the rings, but see Fig. 2-4.

JOINERY

Two pieces are always joined with both mechanical fasteners and adhesive. There are several ways to accomplish this. See Table 7-2.

Adhesives. For exterior signs, only waterproof adhesives may be used. Water resistant adhesives are less expensive at the outset, but rebuilding a sign that is coming apart a year later is expensive.

One truly waterproof adhesive that always works is Resorcinol glue. This is a two-part glue consisting of a liquid resin and a powdered catalyst. It is available nearly everywhere. This is the dark purple glue used by plywood manufacturers to make exterior and marine grades of plywood. When mixed and used according to instructions, it is fail-safe.

Other sources for waterproof adhesives can be found by reading the advertisements in *Wooden Boat* and *Small Boat Journal*. These magazines cater to boat builders who must also have reliable waterproof glues.

Mechanical Fasteners. Mechanical fasteners include nails, screws, bolts and dowels. Nails, screws and bolts are used to make face-to-face, face-to-edge, and end-to-edge joints as shown in Fig. 7-6. These fasteners must be rustproof. Here again mail-order sources for boat building materials can be helpful. Nails are the least effective device in holding power and bolts are most effective. Screws are somewhere in between, it depends on their use and the grain of the wood.

Wherever possible, mechanical fasteners should be used from the back of the sign where they are not seen. When they are used from the face of the sign, there are several ways to solve the problem. Screw or bolt heads can be carefully measured and placed, and used as a design feature on the sign. Screw and bolt heads can be counterbored and plugs can be cut from the same stock glued into the holes. They can be cut off flush and sanded or they can be left "proud" as a design feature (Fig. 7-7).

Dowels are used for edge-to-edge fastening of planks (as in the case in this example). The rule of thumb for doweling is that the diameter of the dowel should be half the actual thickness of the stock (⅜ of an inch for 1-inch stock, ½ of an inch for 1¼-inch stock, Fig. 7-8). Dowels should penetrate to a minimum depth of three times

Table 7-2. Joinery.

Tools	Materials	Miscellaneous
Glue brush	Waterproof glue	Water pot
Hammer	Nails	Glue pots
Screwdrivers	Screws	Mixing sticks
Wrenches	Bolts	Rags & Newspaper
Portalign tool	Dowels	Wood plugs
Electric drill & bits	Lumber	Rasp
Dowel centers		Screwmates or
Clamps		countersink
Plane		Soda straws*
Belt sander		Scrapers, broken
Saw		glass, etc.
Square		Scraps to pad
Pencils		clamps
		Chalk

* Soda straw is inserted into the dowel holes. Blowing through the straw clears the hole of chips. Keep your eyes closed!

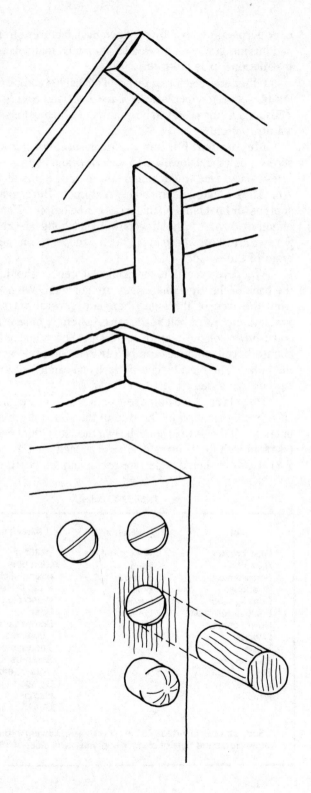

Fig. 7-6. Examples of joints.

Fig. 7-7. Plugging screw heads.

Fig. 7-8. The diameter of the dowel
should be half the thickness of the
stock.

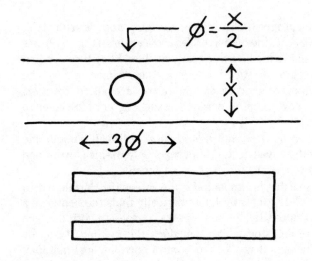

$$\emptyset = \frac{X}{2}$$

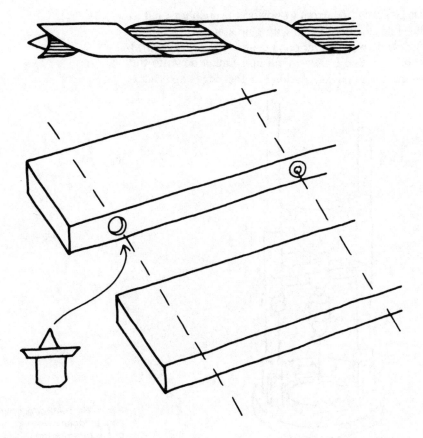

Fig. 7-9. Dowel centers.

the diameter in *each* piece of stock: 1⅛ inch for ⅜ of an inch, 1½ inch for ½ inch, etc.

Without the proper tools, doweling is hard work. Fortunately, the proper tools are inexpensive. Dowel centers (Fig. 7-9) are indispensable and so inexpensive that you should buy three or four sets just to have around. The first holes are bored in one plank. The registration marks are lined up, and the boards are pulled together. The point of the dowel center marks the exact center of the holes to be drilled.

Any drill can be used, but a *brad point* will drill smooth and clean holes without wandering. Because only ⅜-inch drills and ½-inch drills are needed, the cost is not much.

A second tool that is almost indispensable is the Portalign drill accessory (Fig. 7-10). This tool automatically finds the center of a board edge and automatically bores at 90 degrees to both the face and the edge of the stock. The tool does this without setup or adjustment. This puts it way out in front of doweling jigs that may cost much more. The tool also features a depth stop to control hole depth.

Dowels can be purchased, from woodworking suppliers, cut to length, with the ends chamfered, and with glue slots cut (A of Fig. 7-11). This is handy if you think far enough ahead to order them. I never seem to do this, and I always end up running down to the hardware store for dowel sticks. As long as the edges are cham-

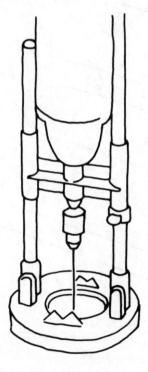

Fig. 7-10. The Portalign drill accessory automatically finds the center of the board edge.

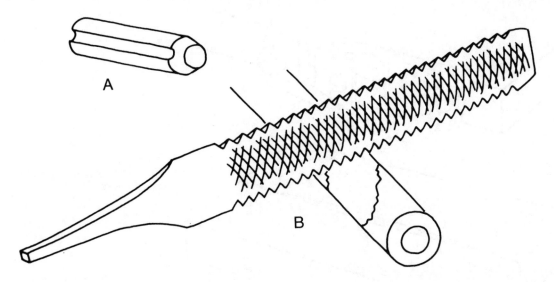

Fig. 7-11. Roll the dowel under the corner of the rasp.

fered, they seem to work as well. The glue channel can be made by rolling the dowel under the corner of a rasp (B of Fig. 7-11).

When a single slab is to be glued up from two or more separate boards, take a pass or two with a plane in the center of each board. This results in a joint that is very slightly concave (as shown greatly exaggerated in Fig. 7-12). I read of this procedure in a cabinetmaking book printed in the last century. It really does seem to make such joints stronger.

The strength of a glue joint is in direct proportion to the area of the joint. The trick is to create a large area out of a small one. In Fig. 7-13, ¾-inch stock is shown being used. Joint A has a ¾-inch area. Joint B has a 1¼-inch area, but is hard to make and impossible to dowel. Joint C is made by running a rasp or dull saw edgewise along the edge after the dowel holes are drilled. This joint provides at least as much gluing surface as joint B (and possibly more).

Gluing. The proper gluing sequence is as follows:

☐ Align the boards according to established registration marks.

☐ Coat one half of the dowels and insert them in the holes of one plank.

☐ Coat both edges to be joined and the projecting dowels with glue.

☐ Align dowels and holes and bring the joint slowly closed with clamps and blocks of scrap to protect plank edges.

Clamps. Bar clamps (A of Fig. 7-14) work very well for gluing slabs within their range. The upper limit of their clamping range is fixed and the clamps are expensive.

Pipe clamps (B of Fig. 7-14) work just as well as the bar clamps. Their clamping range is almost limitless. Extra lengths of

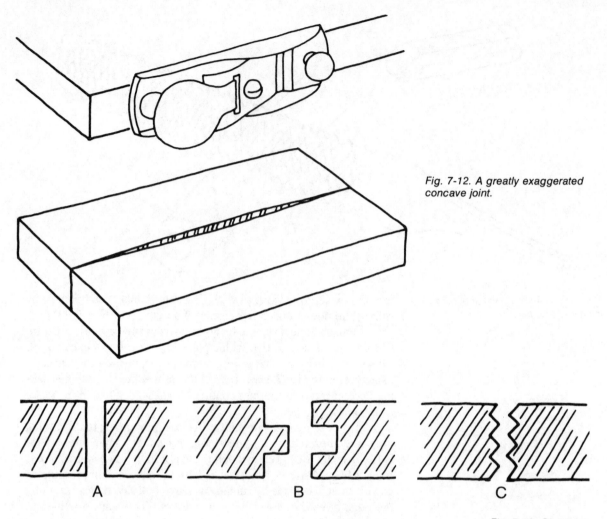

Fig. 7-12. A greatly exaggerated
concave joint.

A   B   C

Fig. 7-13. Glue joints.

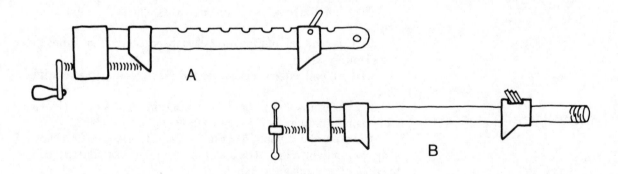

Fig. 7-14. A bar clamp (A) and a pipe clamp (B).

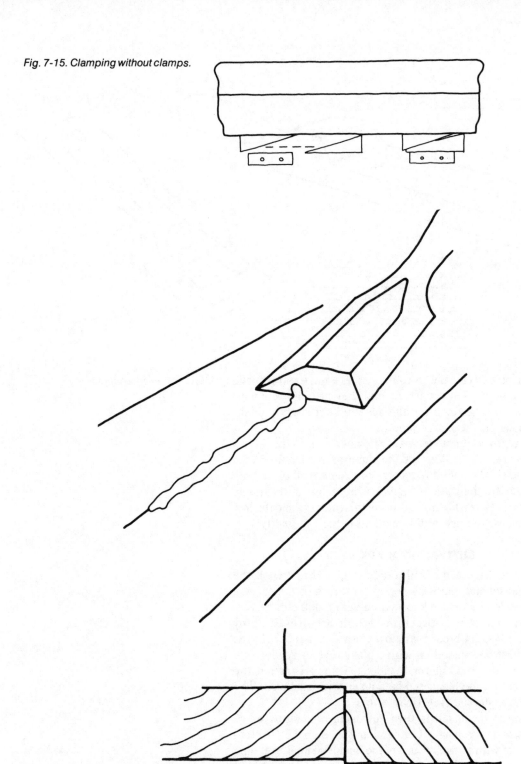

Fig. 7-15. Clamping without clamps.

Fig. 7-16. Use a chisel to remove irregularities.

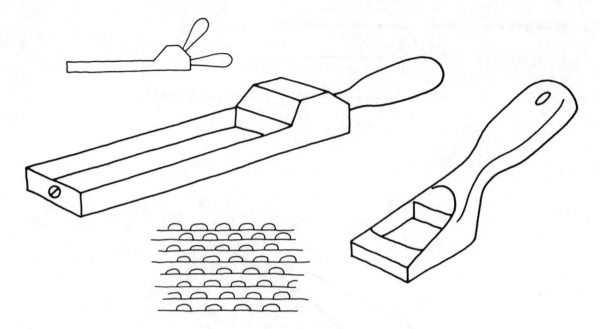

Fig. 7-17. Fast-cutting tools.

pipe and pipe nipples are easy to come by and easy to store. The clamp heads are purchased separately and they are inexpensive.

All clamps work better if the threads are kept slightly oiled. Always clean glue off the bar or pipe.

A way to get by without clamps is shown in Fig. 7-15. Blocks are fastened securely to the floor and the gluing area is covered with newspaper. The slab is pulled together, somehow, and placed between the blocks and the wall. Wedges are driven up hard to apply clamping pressure. Given the difficulties of this method, and the low cost of pipe clamps, the use of this method is hard to justify.

CUTTING THE BLANK

After the glue has dried and cured (read the glue directions), the clamps are removed and the blank set up on horses or the carving bench. Small beads of glue are knocked off with a dull chisel (Fig. 7-16). Small irregularities between the boards are evened up by using a chisel or piece of broken window glass as a scraper. Large irregularities must be evened up with a plane or belt sander.

Once the blank is smoothed and sanded to your satisfaction, the cartoon is laid out on the blank and held down with pushpins. The outline is then transferred (see Chapter 6).

The outline of the blank is then cut using a handsaw or an electric sabre saw or scroll saw. Conventional wisdom dictates that all cuts be made to within ⅛ of an inch of the line. The final trimming be done with hand tools. Because time is money, it is best to cut right down to the line with the electric saw. This does require some

Table 7-3. Cutting the Blank.

Tools	Miscellaneous
Coping saw, or Sabre saw Surform tools	Sandpaper Files, Rasps

Fig. 7-18. A rasp blade for a sabre saw.

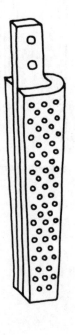

confidence and a steady hand, but it does save quite a lot of time. Cut slowly.

If you cut to within ⅛ of an inch of the line, irregularities will have to be removed and the cuts made with hand tools. The fastest cutting and safest tools I have found so far are the Stanley Surform tools shown in Fig. 7-17. The file plane #285 and the shaver #115 are the most handy.

A rasp blade is available for the sabre saw (Fig. 7-18). These have only limited usefulness. Because they cut across the grain, (the Surform tool cuts with the grain), great care must be used to avoid tearing up the edge of the blank. See also Table 7-3.

OTHER METHODS

Some designs call for the use of boards in small or random lengths or other configurations that make the use of edge fastenings or framework impossible. See Fig. 3-38. In this case, a backing or core is called for. Exterior plywood of an appropriate thickness should be used for the backing. See Table 7-4.

There are several problems to be considered in signs of this type. One is moisture that will seep between the layers and cause rot. Lots of glue will help prevent this.

Alternatively, liberal use of a good sealer such as Cuprinol or Firzite will slow down rot, but this in turn may cause problems. For example, water-based paints will not adhere over these sealers. Also, the sealer might prevent the adhesive from penetrating and curing properly. *Note*: Paint is not a sealer.

When many small pieces must be used in a mosaic fashion, it is

Table 7-4. Other Assembly Methods.

Tools	Materials	Miscellaneous
Hot glue gun Saw Square Pencils	Hot glue sticks Lumber Plywood	Chalk A helper if it doesn't work

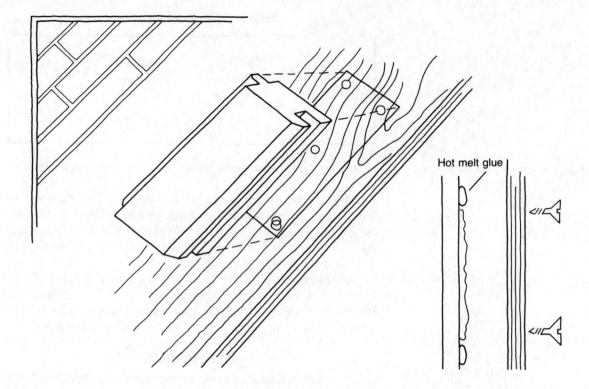

Hot melt glue

difficult to clamp the pieces adequately until the glue dries and cures. One solution is to use a combination of rustproof screws, waterproof glue and hot-melt glue (Fig. 7-19).

Fig. 7-19. Clamping with screws and glue.

An outline of the piece is drawn on the backing and the piece is removed. Holes are drilled from the front. Allow plenty of room around the screw for purchase without cracking the piece. Waterproof glue is liberally applied on all but the extreme corners of the piece. Hot-melt glue is run onto these ''bald'' spots, and the piece is held in place for about 60 seconds. If you are lucky, the hot-melt glue will hold well enough for you to get behind the backing and drive the screws through the drilled holes.

8

Hand Carving

Ideally the woodworking studio and the art studio should be separate. Paint on the carving tools and sawdust in the gold size tend to make life exasperating. Even the hobbyist should have sufficient storage and workspace to allow cleaning up completely after one operation before beginning on the next. In a professional shop—where several signs will be in different stages of completion at once—separate studios are almost a must.

THE STUDIO

A big, heavy carving bench is a must. It is practically impossible to control your carving tools (Table 8-1) when your carving blank is moving about independently. The kitchen table is definitely out for all but the smallest projects.

The big, beautiful beech carving benches with two vises and bench dogs sold by woodworking suppliers are probably marvelous (Fig. 8-1). Because they cost about as much as a used car, however, it is difficult to recommend that kind of expenditure.

The best compromise is probably a vertical-grain, Fir bench top of 2- ×-12-inch lumber mounted on the type of adjustable steel legs sold by home centers and mail-order houses (Fig. 8-2). The length of the top can vary from 4 to 6 or even 8 feet. The height of the bench top should be an inch or two above your belly button when you are standing.

Table 8-1. The studio.

Tools	Materials	Miscellaneous
Carving tools	Tool trays	First-aid kit
Clamps	Movable light	Special gloves
	Carving bench	

If the table cannot be bolted to the floor, it should be bolted to a sheet of ¾-inch or 1-inch plywood. When standing on the plywood your body weight is added to the weight of the bench for a very stable setup. It is best not to have any lips, tool trays, etc., on or built into the bench top. One or two drawers underneath are nice.

Carving tools should be stored in separate trays (Fig. 8-3). If the trays are made uniform in size, they can be stored in a rack and made to look like a chest of drawers. The rack should have a top similar to the bench, and be of the same height. If possible, it should have heavy casters. An awkward-shaped sign can then be partially supported by both the bench and the rack.

Lighting the carving on the bench is best accomplished by a mobile fixture. An old-fashioned, heavy gooseneck desk lamp (Fig. 8-4) has worked very well for me. I can always position it so that the area I am carving is never in a shadow.

Safety

Because *every* carver cuts himself sometimes, an adequate first-aid

Fig. 8-1. A carving bench.

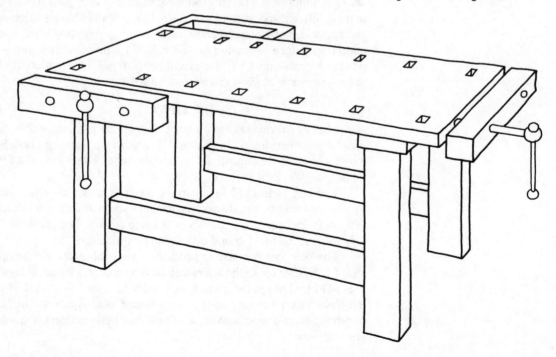

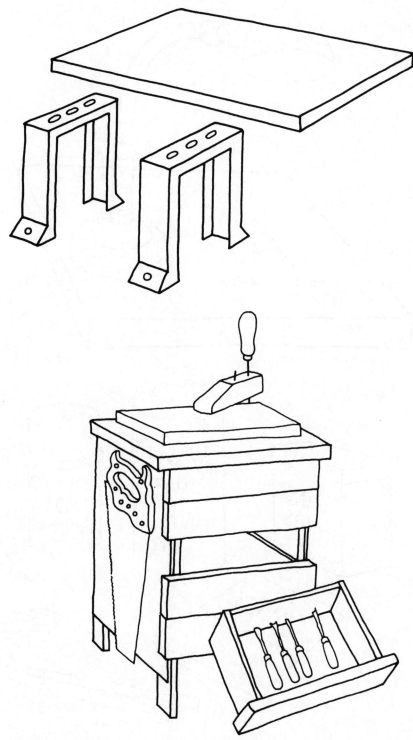

Fig. 8-2. A bench top with adjustable steel legs.

Fig. 8-3. Storing carving tools.

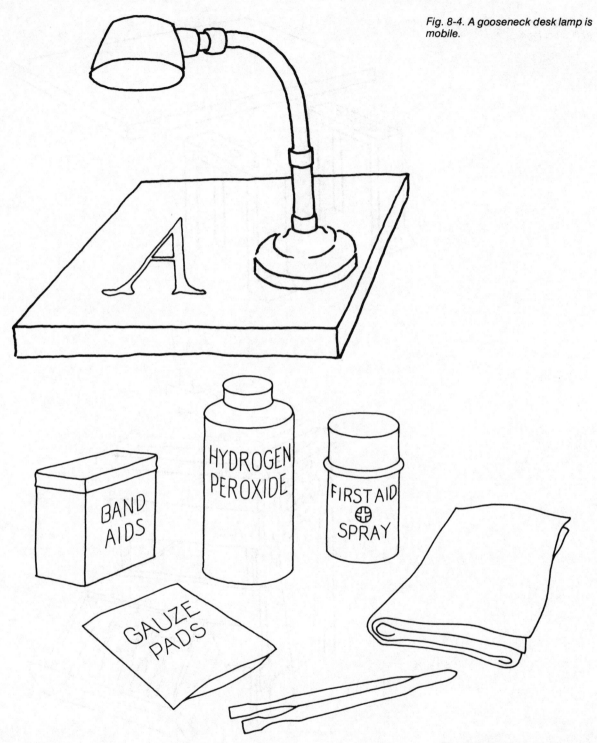

Fig. 8-4. A gooseneck desk lamp is mobile.

Fig. 8-5. First-aid components.

kit (Fig. 8-5) should be kept at the bench. Not nearby—*at*! The kit should contain a minimum of adhesive bandages, tweezers, large gauze pads, antiseptic, hydrogen peroxide, and clean, white rags. Small cuts and splinters can be handled by Band-Aids and antiseptic. Bad cuts require direct pressure with lots of gauze pads as you go for help. Blood on the carving is handled by hydrogen peroxide and rags to bleach out the stains.

Holding the Work

In order for you to carve well, the blank must be held securely to the carving bench. A surprising amount of force is used to move a chisel through the wood. If any of the force is absorbed by movement of the blank on the bench—or the carving bench in space—that force is lost. In economic terms, it is a nonproductive expenditure. If you ever hope to make a decent hourly wage, you must get the maximum out of every chisel stroke. You can easily loose about 10 percent of your efficiency by using a wobbly bench and poor clamps.

There are all sorts of commercially available clamping fixtures and jigs (Fig. 8-6) and it is probably a good idea to own one or two

Fig. 8-6. Clamping fixtures.

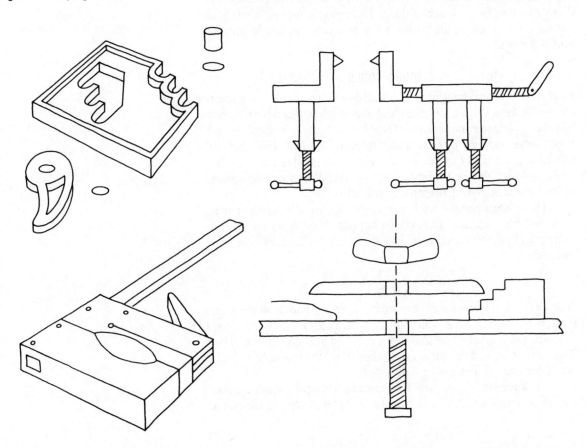

167

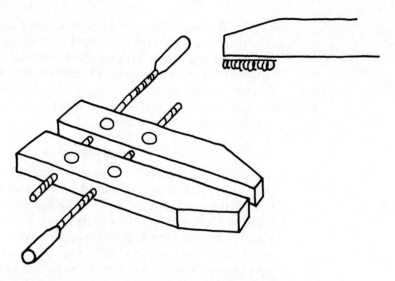

that appeal to you. The best clamp by far is the common parallel clamp (Fig. 8-7). These clamps are quick acting and positive holding. The #1 and #2 sizes are most handy and you will quickly find that you never own enough of them. It can be useful to glue pads of indoor/outdoor carpeting to the jaws of a few clamps to protect finished work.

Fig. 8-7. A parallel clamp.

CARVING TOOLS

Everyone balks at the price of carving tools. The price does seem excessive for a shaped piece of steel in a rough wooden handle. But when you consider that each tool will last at least one lifetime, and probably several, the price is reasonable. Again, given international inflation and rates of exchange, the prices of good-quality carving tools will probably never be less expensive. When you do invest, invest as much as you reasonably can afford.

There are a certain number of tools that are absolutely necessary, but they are few. Everything beyond those few may be considered refinements and luxuries that are nice to have, but not truly necessary.

Knives

A lot of truly excellent sign carving can be done with a single knife (Fig. 8-8). A long, fat handle and a short, stubby blade are used. Patterns vary widely; one that looks right for you probably will be. The veneer knife differs from the other in that it has only a single bevel for cutting along a straight edge.

For knife cut letters, use the Trajan lettering shown in Chapter 5. Use a sharp, pointed serif because the round serif is for gouge work.

168

Incised or couched letters (Fig. 8-9) can be carved with the knife, and so can all manner of "strap work" (Fig. 8-10). If you find this style intriguing, you can specialize in knife cut signs with hardly any tool investment at all.

After the cartoon is transferred to the blank, deeply V-cut letters can be made in the following manner (Fig. 8-11). Begin by making a deep cut straight down into the wood along the center of the design. A considerable amount of force is necessary to make this cut, and you might want to experiment with one- and two-handed grips on the tool. Long, sinuous cuts are made by holding the wrists rigid and drawing the forearms along the work. Short, controlled cuts are made by resting the forearms solidly on the work and moving the knife only with the fingers.

After the center cut has been made, additional cuts are made at an angle toward the center cut. This will remove a fine triangular-shaped ribbon of waste. The cut is progressively widened and deepened as needed. Where a letter or design is of varying thick-

Fig. 8-8. Excellent sign carving can be done with a knife.

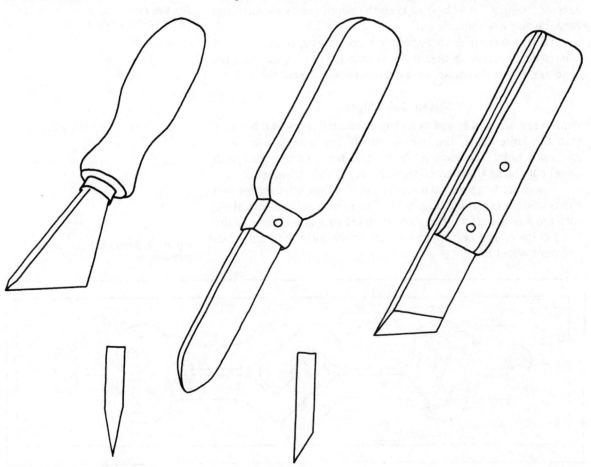

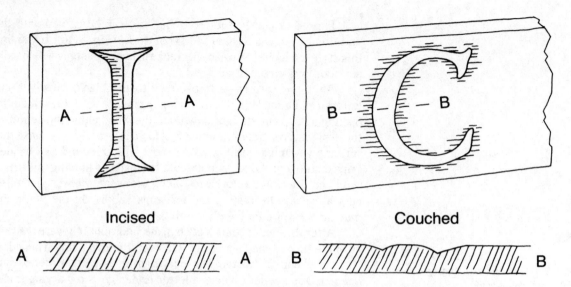

Incised   Couched

ness or "weight," it is best to keep the depth nearly uniform and vary the angle of the side cut.

Fig. 8-9. Incised or couched letters can be carved with a knife.

When you are in doubt as to how deep to carve, remember that it is easier to carve deeper later on than it is to fill in. To save needless work and to make wages, the shallower the cut the better.

Chisels and Gouges

While very acceptable and even quite beautiful work can be done with the knife alone, the use of chisels and gouges can be of enormous help. The various shapes and textures obtained with chisel cuts make this part of sign crafting a high art indeed.

There are two types of hand chisels, and they are used for two different kinds of carving (Fig. 8-12). The *bent* chisel cuts on a plane with the wood surface. The *straight* chisel cuts at an angle to the wood surface. The two operations are really quite different when you think about it.

Fig. 8-10. Strap work can be cut with a knife.

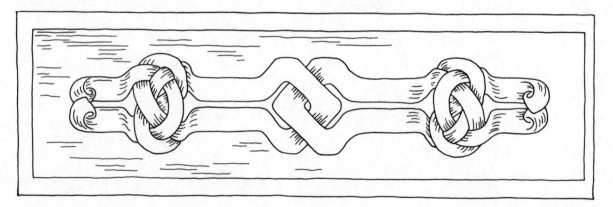

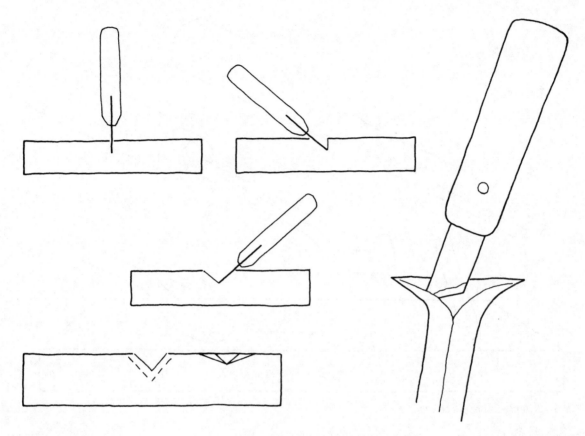

Fig. 8-11. Making V cuts.

Incised work—using the bent chisel—removes waste wood so that the design is *below* the surface of the wood. The background surface is always called the *ground*. Another name for this sort of work is *intaglio*.

Relief work—using the straight chisel—removes waste wood so that the design is *above* the ground of the work.

It should appear quite obvious that relief work is by far the harder and more time consuming of the two. As such, relief work should be avoided wherever possible. When work in relief is required, your price for the job should be adjusted up from incised work by a factor of three to five. For example, a simple incised leaf pattern (Fig. 8-13) might take about 5 minutes to execute, and it might cost your customer about $5. A raised leaf of the same design might well take you 20 minutes to execute. It then should cost your customer $20.

With incised work, when a sign is to be gilded or polychromed (painted), make shallow cuts. All that is necessary in this case is to give a slight variation in the surface of the blank (Fig. 8-14).

When a sign is to be left natural (or given a uniform, clear finish) it is necessary to carve quite deeply. Differences in texture

171

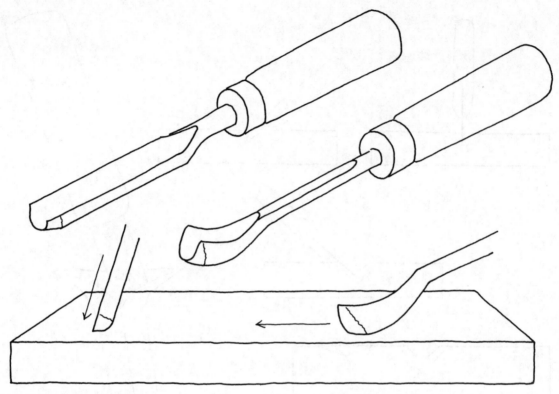

Fig. 8-12. Bent and straight chisels.

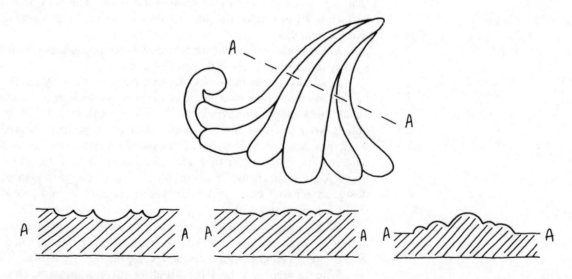

Fig. 8-13. A simple incised leaf pattern.

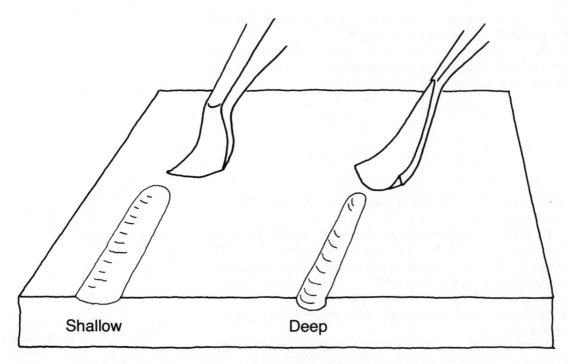

Fig. 8-14. Shallow and deep cuts.

are not enhanced by differences in color (as is the case with gilding and polychroming). What counts here are the shadows created by the carving. The deeper the carving, the more pronounced the shadow.

Relief Work

The differences between painted and natural finish also apply to relief work, but with the following difference. Gilded and light polychrome colors require much less depth in relief than natural finish or dark polychrome colors. Larger and deeper shadows are required for good visibility and effect against a dark background.

For incised work, bent gouges should be used (A and B of Fig. 8-15). Bent spoon gouges or *short bent* gouges are much more delicate than bent or *long bent* gouges, and they are preferable because they allow greater visibility around the tool. They also seem to lend themselves to greater finesse in execution than bent gouges.

The sweep of a gouge is what differentiates a chisel from a gouge. When viewing the cutting edge head-on, a chisel is perfectly flat—with no sweep. A gouge is curved in varying degrees of sweep. What makes a set of gouges expensive is that there is no universal sweep. There are different sweeps for different jobs. The only possible way around a high investment in gouges is to pick one or two lettering styles and stick with them. If you decide to use a wide variety of lettering styles, you must be prepared to invest quite heavily in a wide variety of gouges.

The following gouges are used for carving all the Trajan and Bookman Bold Italic letters recommended in this book. All are spoon or short bent gouges. See Fig. 8-16.

Sweep	Width in mm
4	14 & 21
5	7
9	12
10	7
11	2 & 5

Unfortunately, this collection of gouges from any reputable firm currently represents an investment of nearly $100.

If you do not intend to carve professionally, you might make do with a beginners set. The Speedball set #15 (Hunt #4140) is available at large craft suppliers, and it has proved itself quite good. If you do intend to carve professionally, you must make the investment in gouges. Proper tools make the carving go much more quickly, and it is skill coupled with speed that results in a decent hourly wage.

A variation on the gouge theme is the *fingernail* chisel shown in

Fig. 8-15. Examples of gouges.

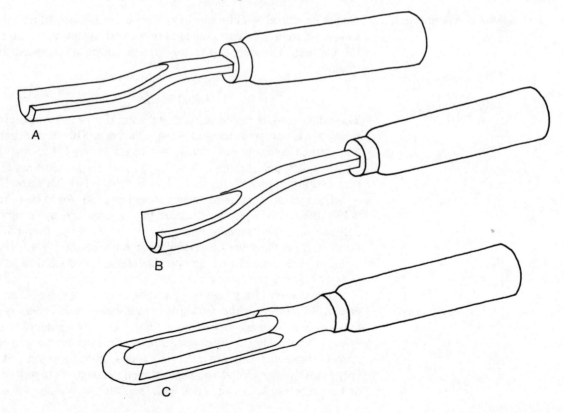

A

B

C

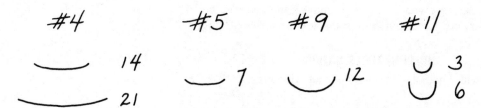

#4 _____ 14
       _____ 21

#5 ___7   #9 ___12   #11 ◡ 3
                          ◡ 6

Fig. 8-16. Gouge sizes.

Fig. 8-17. Wear specially cut leather work gloves.

C of Fig. 8-15. Though not commercially available, and somewhat tricky to use, chisels ground to this pattern can replace a whole range of gouges.

The illustration shows quite clearly how the tool is ground and honed from commercially available bevel edge or carpenter's chisel. For smaller work, a set would include ¼-inch, ½-inch, and ¾-inch sizes. Larger work might require a set of ⅜-inch, ⅝-inch, and 1-inch sizes.

When used flat side down, the chisels can be used just the same as flat chisels (paring and relief work). By turning the chisel over and placing the cutting-edge bevel side down, the chisel works as a gouge. The sweeps of a great many gouges can be simulated by varying the angle of the tool to the work. The letter carving instruc-

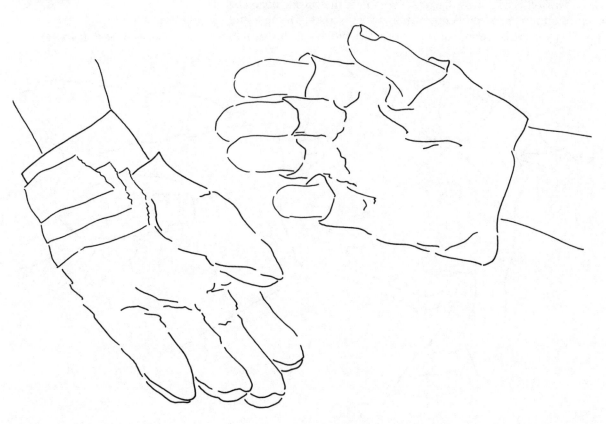

tions that follow are given in terms of gouges and sweeps, but it should take very little imagination to translate into terms of "fingernails."

HOLDING TOOLS SAFELY

Making a cut with a gouge is a two-handed job. See Figs. 8-17, 8-18, and 8-19.

Assuming that you are right-handed, the handle of the gouge is held in the right hand with the pommel in the hollow of the palm. The motive force used to supply cutting pressure should come from the toes up, with most of the forcing coming from the legs and upper back.

The pommel of the tool will very quickly raise a blister in the palm of the hand. If this is not prevented, a sign carver will be out of business in the first few hours of work. A leather work glove with the thumb and first two joints of each finger cut out should be used. A stiff pad of some sort, covered with leather, should be used to distribute the pressure over a wide area.

Steering the tool is best accomplished by changing the position of the body to follow the line of the cut. Fine control is obtained by rotating the elbow in and out from the body.

The left hand grasps the gouge very near the cutting edge and controls the length and depth of the cutting stroke. Because the point of your wrist bone rests on the surface of the sign blank, this

Fig. 8-18. Holding techniques.

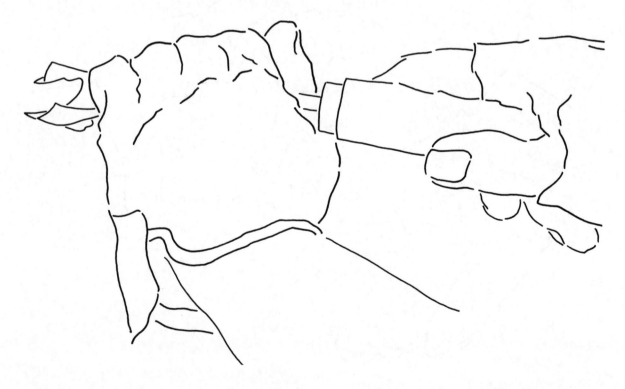

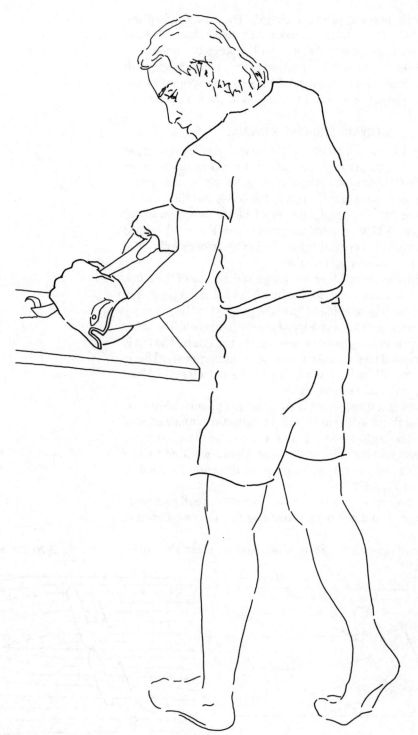

Fig. 8-19. Pressure comes from the toes up.

area will rapidly become painfully chafed. The first joint of the fingers, especially the cuticles, are extremely vulnerable. A leather work glove, with the fingers left on, will protect the fingers. A section of kitchen sponge can be inserted in the cuff of the glove to pad the wrist bone. Several layers of tape can be applied to the outside of the glove. These can be replaced as they wear out.

CARVING AND CHIP REMOVAL

The following is a detailed account of the incised carving of a single letter A in the Trajan style (to be gilded). Extrapolation to other letters and other finishes, and deeper carving, should be quite easy.

Once the cartoon is transferred to the blank and the blank is clamped to the carving bench, the grain of the wood must be analyzed. Figure 2-11 shows that the grain leaves the wood surface in two directions. It is imperative that the gouge strokes follow the grain direction as closely as possible.

Begin with the 2mm, 11-sweep gouge and a scrap of the stock you will be using. Make a cut diagonally across the grain (as in A of Fig. 8-20). Notice that one side or lip of the gouge is cutting more or less with the grain, and that the edge of the cut is smooth. The other lip of the gouge is cutting more or less against the grain. The cut is more or less ragged (depending on the degree of sharpness). This is *the* basic cut for all incised work. Study the cut closely. Make several more cuts and observe them.

When cutting letters, figures, etc., the gouge must *always* be oriented so that the smooth side of the cut forms the outside edge of the letter and the ragged side is in the waste to be removed later. This will mean walking around the sign blank, working in one direction for part of a letter, and a different direction for another part (as in B of Fig. 8-20).

A *very* important note is that cross-grain cuts are *always* made first. The letter should now look something like the one shown in Fig. 8-21.

The 7mm 5-sweep gouge is now used to clear the waste

Fig. 8-20. Cut across the grain.

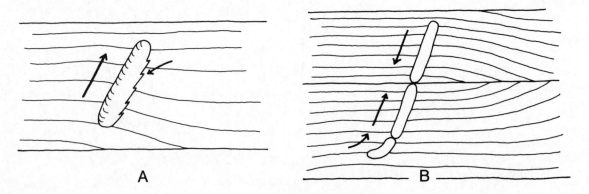

A   B

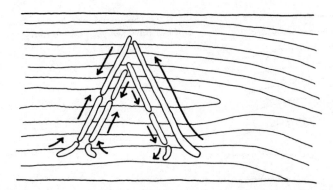

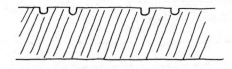

Fig. 8-21. *Always make cross-grain cuts first.*

material. Work from whatever side of the sign leaves the smoothest cut. The object is to fair the bottoming cuts gently into the side cuts. The letter should now look like the one shown in Fig. 8-22. With these cuts fresh in the mind, there are some important digressions to be made right here.

Note 1. Gold leaf stretches, but not much. The shallower the carving and the gentler the curves, the easier the final gilding will be. Try lining the inside of an egg carton with aluminum foil to see what happens.

Note 2. *Always* even up your carving with the gouge. *Never* use sandpaper on letters to be gilded. Sanding will make expensive gold leaf look like cheap gilt paint.

Once *all* the cross-grain cutting has been completed, the with-grain cutting of the cross bar and serifs is completed with the 2mm 11-sweep gouge. The letter should now look like the one shown in Fig. 8-23. Note that the junctions of the serifs and bar with the limbs have not yet been faired in. The letter looks as though it has been done with a ruler, it has no personality. Slowly and carefully fair the serifs and bar into the limbs. Again begin with the cross-grain cuts and finish with the with-grain cuts (Fig. 8-24).

The reason for making the cross-grain cuts first is that where a cross-grain cut and a with-grain cut meet, there is the likelihood of chipping out a splinter along the with-grain cut. This can be cor-

Fig. 8-22. *Fair the bottoming cuts.*

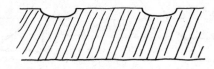

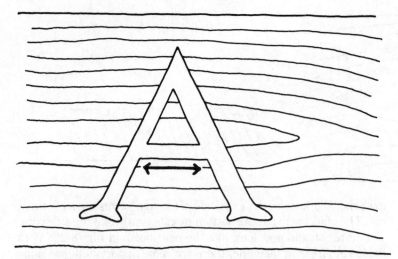

rected by making the final fairing cuts with the grain. If the with-grain cut is made first, subsequent splintering will result in an awkward-looking letter (Fig. 8-25).

The preceding detailed carving procedure is for lettering etc., that will be gilded. The cuts are very shallow, (between 1/16 of an inch and ⅛ of an inch deep). For polychrome lettering, a slightly deeper cut is made (about ⅛ of an inch throughout).

The very deep carving, ¼ of an inch to ⅜ of an inch deep, for use on natural finished signs, can be done with the 9-sweep gouge in place of the 5-sweep gouge. These cuts are shown in Fig. 8-26.

An interesting variation on the deep carving technique for natural finishes is shown in Fig. 8-27. The first step is to quickly clear out the waste from the center of the letter, without cutting the outlines first. Do not work right up to the line; leave a fairly constant space all around.

Fig. 8-24. Fair the serifs and the bar.

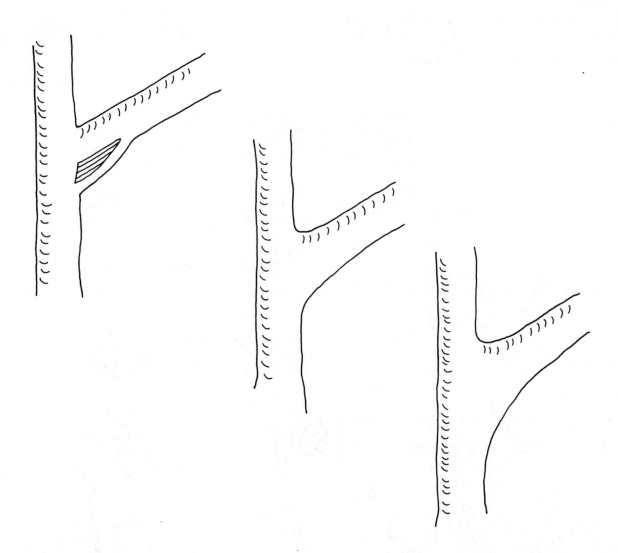

Fig. 8-25. With-grain cuts make
awkward-looking letters.

After the waste has been cleared, the letter is finished with short cuts of a flat sweep gouge started at the line and working across the letter. This technique gives quite a bit of variation between the letter and the ground. The textures are markedly different, and there is the further advantage of opening up a lot of end grain that will finish darker than the ground of the sign.

The techniques for ornamental cuts follow the same general rules as lettering cuts, but with these differences. The carving used for lettering leaves a random or nonobjective pattern of gouge cuts in the wood. These random patterns inside the incision can be likened to the facets of a rough gemstone. When leaf gilded, these

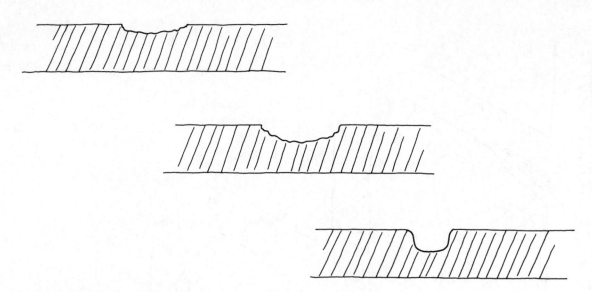

Fig. 8-26. Deep carving cuts.

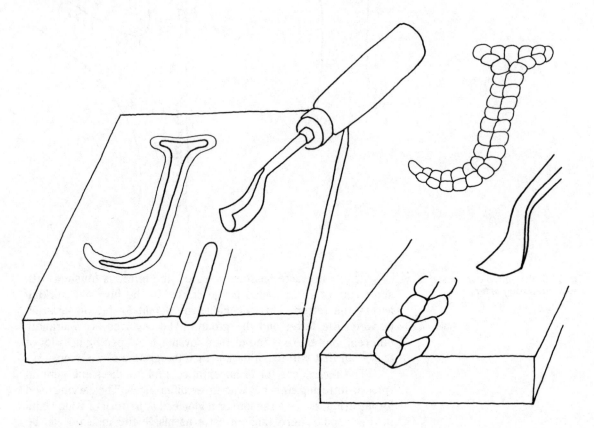

Fig. 8-27. A deep carving variation.

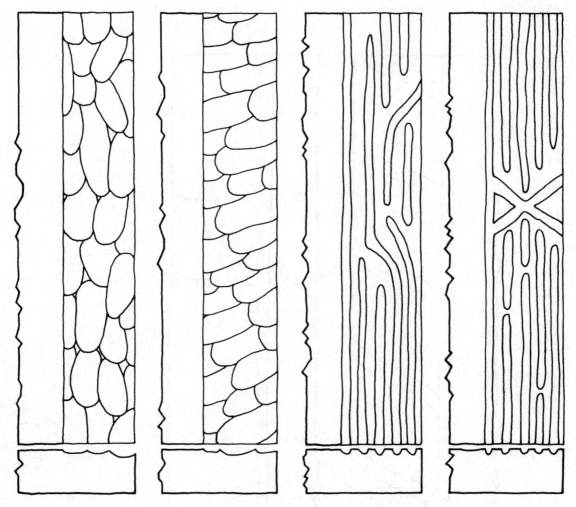

Fig. 8-28A. Borders.

facets cause the letter to glow and sparkle. This is what gives the lettering its special charm. For borders and ornaments, the cuts must be made objectively. The facets of the chisel strokes must be made the same way a painter uses brush strokes. Each final cut must be executed with care and for a reason.

Borders

The borders shown in Figs. 8-28A and 8-28B are a case in point. The clearing away of the waste is done with the final appearance in mind, and no further work needs to be done. Each border gives a pleasant contrast to the lettering.

For the two scalloped borders, each stroke leaves a cut about the same size, shape, and direction of flow as its neighbor. These borders look extremely good when gilded. They give the impression of a great deal of hand work.

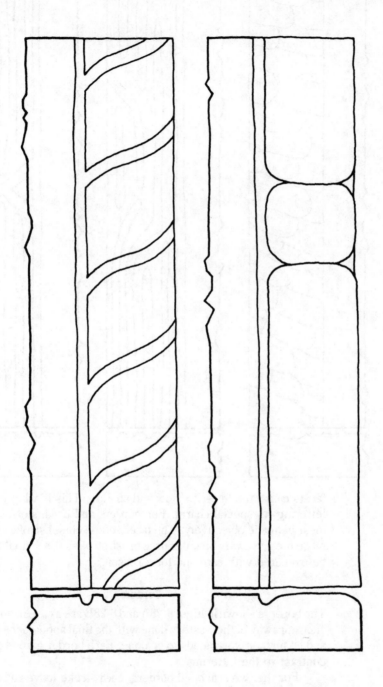

Fig. 8-28B. Borders.

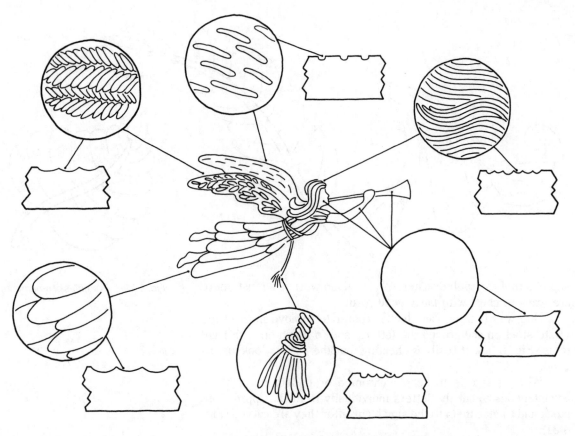

Fig. 8-29A. Examples of ornaments.

Other border strokes include reeding, bound reeds, and roping. The possibilities are nearly endless. The only thing to remember is to keep the strokes *very* shallow for leaf gilding.

Ornaments, Figures, and Embellishments

Some ornaments are shown in Fig. 8-29A and 8-29B. The final tool strokes must leave a pattern compatible with the nature of the ornament. Examples are feathers, fabrics, leaves, and hair. The object here is economy; very few tool strokes are used to simulate the feeling of—or give the appearance of—the ornament. Too many tool strokes make the result look overworked and busy. The fewer directed strokes in each ornament the better.

Relief or Raised Carving

Raised carving—where the letters, etc., are left standing and the background is cut away—is more difficult to do. This kind of work should demand a higher price than incised carving because of the time involved. But above that is the problem of mistakes. They are fairly easily corrected in incised carving, but with raised carving the

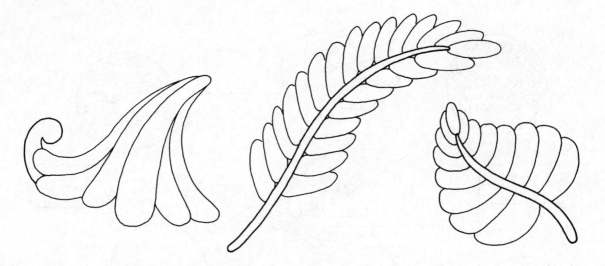

slip of a tool can spell disaster. When raised work is a must, there are ways to cheat with fairly good results.

One way is to use an electric router to remove most of the waste stock in and around the letters, and to finish up with hand tools (Fig. 8-30). It really *is* cheating, but the results look just as good.

When a sign is to be polychromed or gilded, it might be advantageous to cut the letters individually from the appropriate stock and to glue them to the sign blank after they are carved (Fig. 8-31).

Fig. 8-29B. Examples of ornaments.

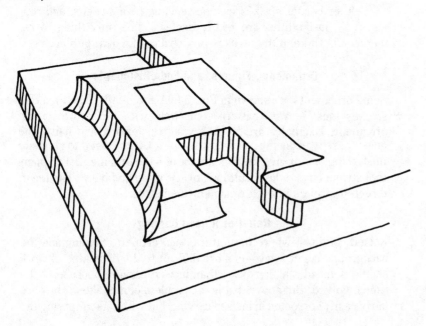

Fig. 8-30. Remove waste stock.

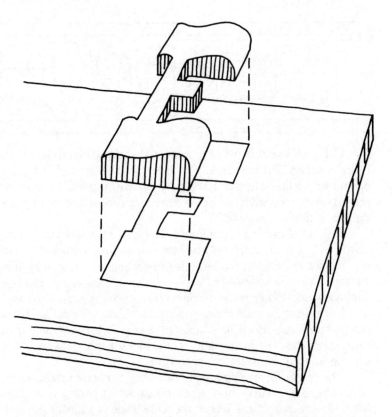

Fig. 8-31. Individual letters can be cut from stock.

A quick way to do this is to cut the letters in profile to the exact shape. The letter thus obtained is glued to a temporary backing of plywood or other sheet material. The letter blank is glued to the backing using a water-soluable glue such as Sobo or Elmer's. A sheet of paper is glued between the blank and the backing. This paper is necessary to make the technique workable.

When dry, the plywood is clamped to the bench, and the carving is executed according to design. Because there are no clamps anywhere on the letter, carving continues unimpeded.

After carving, a wide chisel is forced between the letter and the backing. This causes the paper to "split" or tear lengthwise, and it makes the removal of the letter from the backing not *too* dangerous. Experiment with scraps and thinned-out glue before you commit a great many nicely cut letter blanks to the process.

There are situations when none of the above methods of cheating will do, and the job must be done the right way. An example might be a memorial carving for a church. A beautifully figured piece of quarter-sawn white oak might be used with the grain running through both the ground and the lettering on the clear finished piece. There is no way that router cuts or stick-on lettering will do in this case (Fig. 8-32).

187

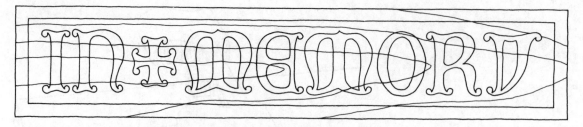

For a job like this, use the knife and shallow sweep gouge to make couched lettering as in Fig. 8-9. Cut the ground just a bit deeper within the letters than around them. Be prepared to spend an eternity with sandpaper and be sure to charge about five times what the job at first seems worth.

The relief carving of appliques (larger versions of the letters shown in Fig. 8-31) is the only instance so far that requires the use of a chisel in addition to the knives and gouges previously discussed. The chisel is used to carve the outside curves or radii on applique work (all inside curves being considered as incised work).

Fortunately, a good chisel is a hardware store item. You need not pay the price of imported carving tools. A 1½-inch or 2-inch carpenter's chisel of good quality works as well as an imported tool costing up to three times as much (Fig. 8-33).

The reason for specifying the wide blade is not for making large cuts. The chisel works best when taking small paring cuts (Fig. 8-34). The few instances where the wide blade is a hinderance can be dealt with by using one of the knives.

When applique relief carvings are to be polychromed or left natural, it is best to simplify the carving to a series of well-differentiated planes (Fig. 8-35). This allows the shadows to show that the piece really is carved. The careful modeling of planes—as in a sculpture—will generally appear to be simply painted on the surface. Try polychroming the "heads" side of a half-dollar to see what I mean. All the carefully executed relief work disappears, leaving something that looks cheap. Of course, the darker the colors used, the greater the differentiation between the planes should be.

When relief carving is to be leaf gilded, the modeling of the planes should be much more sophisticated and lifelike. Think of the silver "finish" on the half-dollar. The finish cuts should be objec-

Fig. 8-32. The grain runs through the ground and the lettering.

Fig. 8-33. A carpenter's chisel.

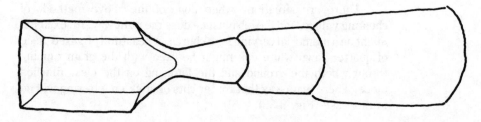

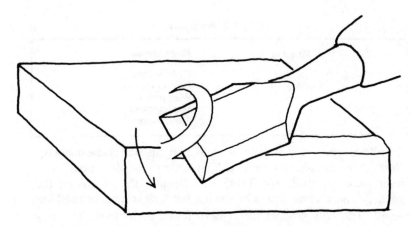

Fig. 8-34. A small paring cut.

tively made, as discussed previously, and never sandpapered. The scintillating effect of many reflective facets is exquisite.

Defects

Occasionally, defects in the wood (or mistakes in carving) are so glaring that they cannot be ''fudged'' away in the carving process. This can happen when a tool cut suddenly reveals a hidden pitch pocket or worm hole in the blank, or when a particularly nasty piece of grain splits out, taking half a letter with it.

A patch called a *graving piece* must be let in where the problem is. The piece must be carefully cut to the correct size and glued in place. The graving piece must be cut from the same stock as the blank, and the grain must be at least similar in appearance. Small graving pieces can be whittled from scrap and glued into drilled holes. Large, hidden defects are, fortunately, rare. If encountered, starting over from scratch should be considered. A large graving piece must fit perfectly or it will simply create new and even larger defects.

The use of wood fillers to correct defects should be avoided.

Fig. 8-35. Differentiated planes.

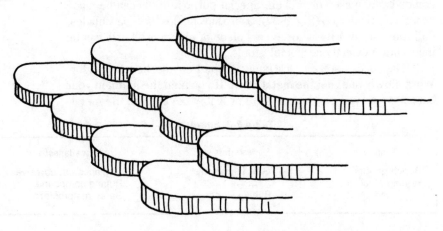

189

Table 8-2. Problems.

Materials	Miscellaneous
Scraps	Putty knives
Glue	Palette knives
Fillers	Wax paper
	Mixing sticks
	Sand paper

All filters tend to pop out after a while, and this will cause unnecessary strife with your customers. If no other recourse is possible, a filler must be used. See Table 8-2. Despite the claims on the package, none of the fillers on the market look, carve, or sand like wood. The only product that I have found to be even remotely acceptable is an auto body filler called Black Diamond. One particularly horrible mistake I made was filled with this product over five years ago and it has not yet shown signs of failure. I still hold my breath each time I drive past the sign.

Sharpening and Tool Maintenance

Most carving masters still require their students to learn hand sharpening of carving tools the old-fashioned way. This is silly. Customers pay you for carving not for sharpening tools. Power sharpening equipment is much faster; time *is* money. In addition, power sharpening equipment actually results in better quality work. There is no temptation to keep on working with a dulling tool when a sharp tool is available in seconds. See Table 8-3.

Bench Grinder

A bench grider is a useful tool to have if you can afford one. A small unit is relatively inexpensive, and it should serve a sign crafter quite well (Fig. 8-36).

Carving tools occasionally need regrinding if the blade becomes badly nicked or broken. Special-purpose tools can be made up for a particular job (Fig. 8-37). Sabre saw blades, hacksaw blades, dull files, screwdrivers, or even a piece of old umbrella rib can be made into perfectly acceptable tools.

The blades are first carefully shaped on the bench grinder. Work slowly and cool the metal often. If you hold the metal in your bare hand as you grind it, you will probably never burn the metal.

Table 8-3. Sharpening.

Tools	Materials	Miscellaneous
Bench grinder	Grinding wheels	Replacement abrasives
Honing machine	Abrasive	Buffing compound
	Buffing wheel	Spray rustproofer

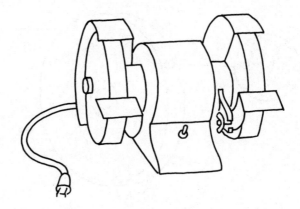

Fig. 8-36. An example of a bench grinder.

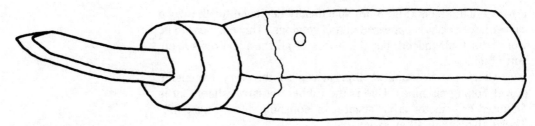

Fig. 8-37. A homemade grounding tool.

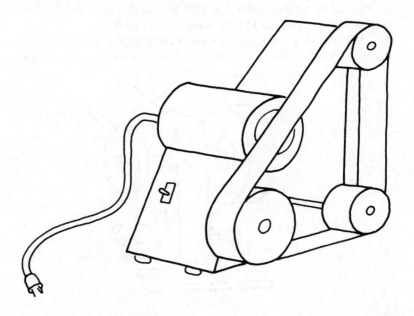

Fig. 8-38. A power honing tool.

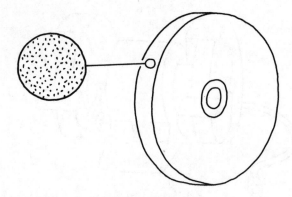

Your hand will burn first. A quick handle can be made up from scrap. Then the tool is ready for honing.

Honing Tools

Power honing tools (Fig. 8-38) specifically designed for the wood carver have recently appeared in tool catalogs. These appear to be wonderful tools indeed, but the prices of all the good ones seem quite high.

There are economical alternatives to the very expensive power honing machines. One is the rubber abrasive wheel that is mounted on a motor arbor adapter or polishing head (Fig. 8-39). These also seem rather expensive.

Another alternative is the lapidary wheel with replaceable abrasive belt (Fig. 8-40). This is quite inexpensive. Whichever alternative you select, be certain to select a #400 grit or finer abrasive. For removing the fine burr left by the abrasive, a wide cotton buffing wheel and black emery stick are used.

Because only the bottom section of the gouge's sweep is dulled during carving, there is a tendency for often-used gouges to change

Fig. 8-40. A lapidary wheel.

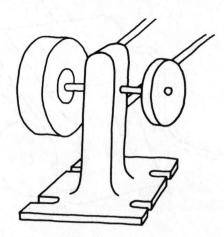

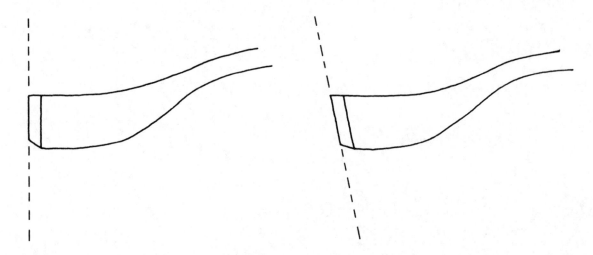

Fig. 8-41. Honed gouges sometimes change shape.

shape as shown in Fig. 8-41, after repeated honing. This is perfectly acceptable; some carvers even prefer this shape. A gouge so shaped cuts through the stock at the side first, and then through the bottom of the cut. This tends to make the cutting of quick radius turns, such as letter serifs, rather easier.

The tool is too dull to cut with long before the original bevel is lost. To sharpen the tool, merely hone along the original bevel until the tool is sharp. Polish on the buffing wheel to remove the sharpening burr, and to get the final degree of sharpness that makes cutting wood like cutting silk.

There are all sorts of cockamamy tests used to tell when a tool is "properly" sharpened. Slicing paper and shaving hair from the body are examples. This is nonsense. A tool is sharp when it cuts wood. Keep a piece of scrap near the honing machine and test for sharpness by cutting across the end grain. When the tool cuts cleanly, the tool is sharp.

There are rust-preventive sprays available that keep treated tools from rusting. All the sprays I have tried work. This includes a spray can of vegetable oil used to keep food from sticking to a frying pan. A can of this is very inexpensive insurance for your tools.

9
Power
Carving Methods

There are those craftsmen who insist that all things should be done using the old ways, and that the use of power tools should be despised. We should be thankful for these purists; it is they who keep alive the traditions of the past. But the use of power tools makes sense today because time is money and power tools buy time. If a sign crafter is to have any hope of making a living and supporting a family, power tools are essential.

The chief advantage of power tools does not lie in the speed with which they remove waste from a carving—no matter how dramatic that speed might be. The chief advantage lies in the precision and control built into the tools. Power carving tools place in the hands of the advanced amateur the final degrees of accuracy and control that are the hallmarks of a master craftsman.

POWER CHISELS

Power chisels have been around for a long time. They are primarily used in stone carving or monumental wooden sculpture. These large, heavy, and very expensive tools, (Fig. 9-1) have only limited usefulness, and they have found only limited acceptance among sign carvers.

The recent development of a small, lightweight, and inexpensive electric chisel offers promise for sign carvers (Fig. 9-2). This

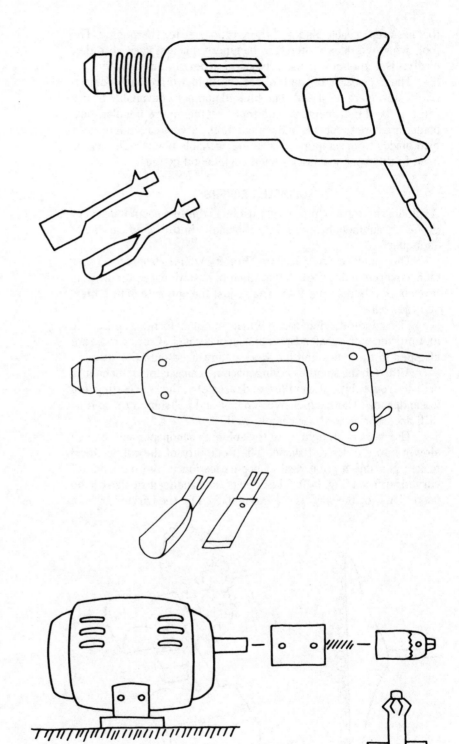

Fig. 9-1. A power chisel.

Fig. 9-2. An electric chisel.

Fig. 9-3. A spindle carving machine.

195

tool uses replaceable blades so there is no need for sharpening. The tool, which vibrates rather than hammers, makes work go rather easily. This tool makes using physical strength unnecessary.

The drawbacks of the tool are the light weight and comparitively slow working speed. The limited number of available blades can also be a detriment. As the tool becomes more popular, new blades are sure to appear. In the meantime, carvers can fashion their own blades from scrap or by adapting available blades. The tool is used in the same manner as hand chisels and gouges.

SPINDLE CARVERS

A spindle carving machine is very useful in the sign shop. It can very profitably augment hand carving, especially in the relief carving of appliques.

The spindle carving machine (Fig. 9-3) differs from most other tools covered in this book in that the tool is stationary; the work is brought to the tool (Fig. 9-4). That is just the opposite of the chisel and the router.

The spindle carving machine, in its simplest form, is an electric motor fitted with a shaft adapter and Jacob's chuck. Cutting tools are clamped in the chuck and the work is advanced onto the cutter.

Although the spindle carving machine can accept all manner of drill and router bits, power files, and rasps etc., the best cutting tool is sandpaper. The inexpensive sanding and polishing kits sold as drill accessories work extremely well.

The work is brought up to the spinning sandpaper and worked slowly into the desired shape. The flexibility of the rubber head makes possible a great deal of sophistication in the modeling of curved surfaces (Fig. 9-5). The edge of the sanding disk also can be used. This, by the way, is the method used by the carvers of fine,

Fig. 9-4. The work is brought to the tool.

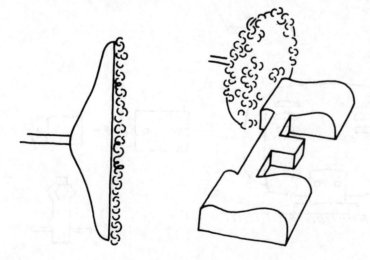

196

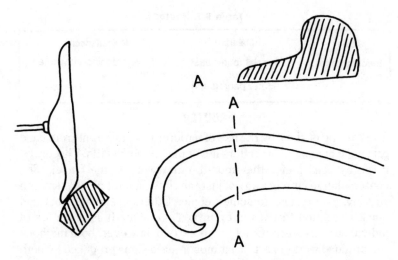

Fig. 9-5. Sanding curved surfaces.

Fig. 9-6. Cutter storage rack.

lead crystal glassware. That should indicate how well the tool can be made to work.

Expanding rubber drums and ready-made sandpaper sleeves are available in a great many sizes (from about ½ inch to 3 inches in diameter.) Sleeves are available in several grits. Using this tool requires much changing of cutters. If the cutters are stored on an orderly rack of some sort (Fig. 9-6), the problem of finding the right cutter in the midst of 30 or 50 cutters is eliminated.

One or two small gouge cuts are necessary to begin the tool tracking properly. The piece is then shaped using the sandpaper. If the work is to be painted, it is finished by using finer and finer grits of sandpaper. If the piece is to be stained, left natural, or leaf gilded, it can be worked all over with the shallow-sweep gouge using objective tool strokes (as described in Chapter 8).

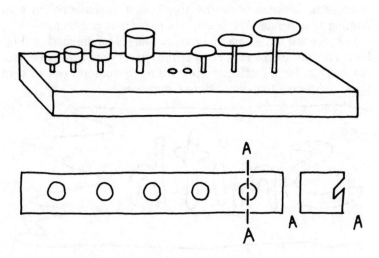

Table 9-1. Router.

Tools	Materials	Miscellaneous
Electric router	Special router base	Bit sharpening attachment
Router bits	Sign router	Letter fonts
	Router pantograph	

ROUTER

The carving of signs by the use of a router is so different from hand carving that many sign crafters never master both skills. Those who carve by hand prefer the smooth, quiet work of the chisel. The contemplative cutting away of just the right amount of silky smooth shavings is a delight to some people. Others prefer the roar and quick execution that a router makes possible. It is a matter of individual preference. One thing is certain, however, both methods can produce works of art. That most routed signs produced by both professionals and amateurs are of such poor quality and so sloppily done is not the fault of the tool. See Table 9-1.

There are very few genuine artists using routers. Because the most popular routed sign is the name board, it stands to reason that a good business could be developed just about anywhere in the country by someone willing to take the time to master the tool.

The routed nameboard most often encountered (and responsible for the bad reputation of routing) is a simple dark stained board (Fig. 9-7). Some people go so far as to cut jagged ends on the board. After the name is routed freehand down the middle of the board, it is handed to the waiting customer who is told to go home and varnish it. If the person doing the routing has studied caligraphy, there is hope for the result. But the predominance of quick-and-dirty nameboard suggests that this has not been the case.

What follows is a general discussion of routers and bits, and their uses. Understanding the tool is just as essential to sign crafting as understanding brushes is to portrait painting.

There are three general types of routers on the market (Fig. 9-8). The choice depends largely on the type of work to be done. It is not unusual for a craftsman specializing in router work to own several different tools for different purposes.

Fig. 9-7. A poorly routed nameboard.

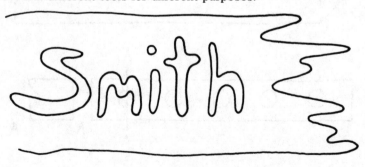

Fig. 9-8. General types of routers.

The smallest tool is sold primarily to the home hobbyist. It is useful for small jobs, and for sharpening the large router bits. The intermediate size is sold for home workshop use. It is probably the most versatile tool. The large size is usually sold for large, commercial use.

In choosing a router, it is best to compare features. The overall size and weight of the tool are important considerations. This is especially true if you intend to use the tool for eight hours a day. Light weight is not a real advantage. Mass tends to absorb quite a bit of the tool's vibrations, and it takes quite a bit of the fatigue out of the work. Balance is vital. If the tool is hard to control *when lifted off the work* decent work will not result. The gyroscopic action of the running tool has a great deal to do with the balance of the tool. Ask to plug in several models and hold them in the air. Move them about with only wrist action. The most comfortable tool will be the one for you.

Other considerations are the weight/size ratio. Large mass is helpful and large bulk is not. Visibility is important. Just because a tool has a built-in lightbulb doesn't mean you will be able to actually see where you are cutting. Make sure the tool housing does not confine your vision to a very narrow area of the workpiece. Do not worry if the base plate obscures your vision; the base plate will be replaced. If the tool has some provision for keeping chips out of your eyes—such as a vacuum attachment—make sure that this does not adversely effect control or visibility.

Look carefully at the tool *collet* (collar). The collet and associated hardware should have a heavy-duty look to them. The adjustments should be easy to get at and work smoothly. In addition, the handles should feel good and provide positive control and comfort.

199

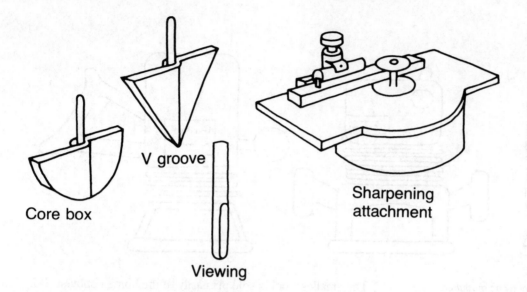

V groove

Core box

Viewing

Sharpening
attachment

Router Bits

Fig. 9-9. Examples of bits.

Router bits are marvelous things (especially for the compulsive gadgeteer). There are so many of them for so many different purposes. There are special up-cutting bits for normal work, down-cutting bits which eject chips through the bottom of a through-cut, carbide bits, and more.

For the beginner, the bits shown in Fig. 9-9 will do very well. Normal high-speed bits (not carbide) should be chosen at the beginning. They are inexpensive and easy to sharpen. The power honing tool (Figs. 8-39 and 8-40) can be used to sharpen router bits. Nevertheless, the bit sharpening attachment for the rubber router recommended.

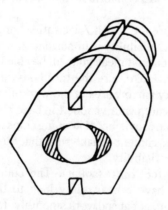

Fig. 9-10. Note the elliptical collet.

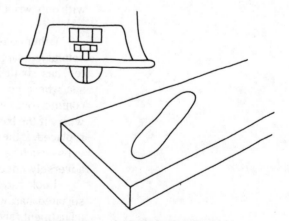

Fig. 9-11. Extend the bit below the sole plate and make a diagonal cut.

A router bit is a precision tool even if the low cost of even the best bits tend to create the opposite impression. The fact that bits are inexpensive should not be cause for the craftsman to take them lightly or to treat them as disposable items.

Because even a dull bit will remove a great deal of waste very quickly, it is often incorrectly assumed that a bit can be pushed until dull, burned, and misshapen. A router bit must be sharpened as carefully and completely—and as often—as the finest gouges. When a bit looses its razor sharpness, two things begin to happen. First, the wood fibers are torn off rather than cleanly sheared. This results in a ragged cut. Second, the stresses placed on the router collet are greatly increased. This eventually results in an elliptical collet (Fig. 9-10). No amount of clean cuts are possible with a bit running off center in an oval collet.

The main cause of router bit failure is a dull bit. Feed pressure must be greatly increased to keep a dull bit cutting. This extra stress *always* seeks a way out (usually at the weakest part of the bit). Sharp bits are a must. When sharpening bits, make extra sure to sharpen both flutes equally. That is, take the same number of passes along the sharpening wheel on both flutes. The bit must remain perfectly symmetrical.

The choice of carbide or high-speed steel bits is a matter of preference. Difficulties in manufacture make carbide tipped bits considerably more expensive. Carbide bits require less frequent sharpening; but the sharpening is more difficult, and it requires a special set of abrasive wheels. The extra cost of carbide bits is therefore significant.

Making a Router Cut

Begin by chucking a ½-inch core box bit in the collet. Be certain to make the chuck up tight. Extend the bit below the sole plate about as shown in Fig. 9-11. Make a cut diagonally across a piece of stock as

Fig. 9-12. Natural resistance of the grain could cause the bit to wander.

shown (Fig. 9-11). A study of the resulting cut reveals many things about a router. First, one side of the bit is cutting with the grain; the other side is cutting against the grain (see Fig. 8-20). Second, one side of the bit is cutting like a gouge; the other side is cutting like a chisel (see Fig. 8-12). Therefore, the router should be thought of as removing waste in the same manner as the hand gouge. The with-grain cuts should be used to form the outside of letters etc., whenever possible. Also, all cross-grain cuts should be made first, and the with-grain cuts faired into them. See Figs. 8-20 through 8-25.

You will also notice that the router has a much greater capacity for wandering off the line than the gouge. The speed with which an irreparable mistake can be made is intimidating at first. Smoothly shaped letters are possible, but much practice with an eye to the grain of the wood is required.

Figure 9-12 shows what might occur with the cutting of a letter C. At just the point when the natural resistance of the grain might cause the bit to wander, the bit has crossed into an area of softer density. The normal tendency of the blade to "dig in" on one side and "kick out" on the other side is further complicated by the changing density. What happens is exactly what causes a pole sticking up out of the water to appear to change direction. Lines of force tend to change direction when encountering media of different density. Density varies within the plank for a variety of reasons. Hartwood, sapwood, pith, and defects (Figs. 2-2 through 2-11) all play a part.

One way to keep such problems from ruining a sign is to refrain from using the single-stroke lettering generally used in sign routing (Fig. 9-7, and A of 9-13). Use of a weighted letter style such as the Trajan makes correcting mistakes much easier (See B of Fig. 9-13).

Because single-stroke lettering is particularly desirable in "while-you-wait" situations such as craft shows, it might be best to develop skill in a lettering style incorporating several single strokes per letter (Fig. 9-14). In such lettering styles as these,

Fig. 9-13. Single-stroke lettering (A) and Trajan lettering (B).

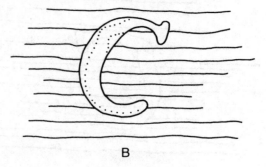

ABCD ABCD
abcd abcd

A   B

202

ABCD ABCD abcde ABC THE Style

Fig. 9-14. Several single strokes are incorporated in each letter.

minor deviations become charming irregularities rather than glaring errors.

There is a style of router lettering using the single-stroke technique that raises router work to a high art (see the beginning of this section). To do this, modifications must be made to the sole plate of the router.

First, the existing sole plate is removed and used as a template for making the new plate (Fig. 9-15). The new plate is made of soft or hard wood—depending upon availability. If a spindle carving machine (Figs. 9-4 and 9-5) is available, the work will go quite quickly.

When the new plate is completed, it should be sanded to a fine, smooth finish and given several coats of hard floor wax.

Fig. 9-15. Use the sole plate as a template.

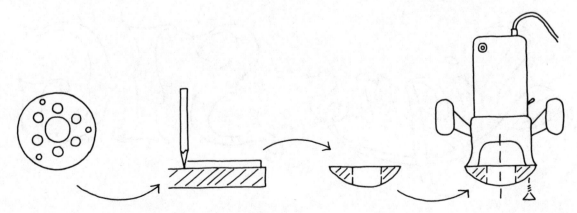

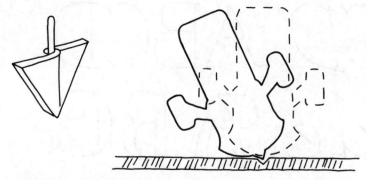

Fig. 9-16. Use a chamfering bit.

The new sole plate is attached to the router base using the original mounting screws. The result is somewhat unorthodox in appearance, but it is correct.

A chamfering bit is solidly chucked in collet and fully extended below the new sole plate (Fig. 9-16). The rig is used by rocking the router on the base plate while cutting. This results in a weighted V cut in the blank. Lettering styles developed from this weighted V can be either simple or elaborate (Fig. 9-17). Signs carved in a caligraphic script using this technique look particularly good. Perhaps even better are signs carved in the art deco manner. A carver specializing in art-deco-routed signs should suffer from an embarrasingly large backlog of orders.

For routing of all borders, ornaments, figures, and embellishments, follow the same recommendations given in Chapter 8 for incised carving.

Template Routing

Template routing involves the use of special router accessories and templates to produce incised lettering and ornament. Some examples of machines and templates are shown in Fig. 9-18.

Special problems are encountered with these machines. First

Fig. 9-17. Lettering styles.

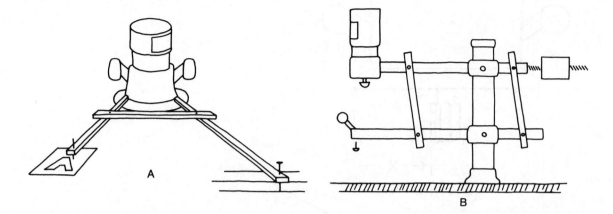

 at positions A and B

A

B

Fig. 9-18. Router accessories.

is the cost. While some pantograph machines are quite inexpensive (you get what you pay for), others require a huge outlay of capital. The machine is expensive enough, but the fonts of letters are the real killers.

The second problem is that once you have purchased one of these machines, you are locked into it. Only the type faces on hand can be used and the composition is severely limited. There is just no freedom to create an individual work of art; you get only what the templates will allow. Individual tastes vary, but I wouldn't own one of these machines if given to me. Perhaps I flatter myself, but I believe I can do a better-looking job, and do it in less time than it takes to set up the templates. Perhaps if I had sufficient call for template-routed signs I'd feel differently.

Straightedge

The simplest template is a straightedge that keeps the router along a perfectly straight line—without any irregularities. This is especially useful for work in the modern hard-edged graphic style.

The first requirement is a spacer strip (Fig. 9-19). The width *exactly* equals the distance from the edge of the router bit to the edge of the standard router base. This, of course, means separate strips for each bit.

The spacer is laid along the edge of the letter, and a straightedge is clamped to the sign blank along the edge of the spacer (Fig. 9-20). The spacer is removed, and the cut is made by pressing the router base against the straightedge as the cut is made.

A straightedge template can be made to accommodate any letter slope by screwing a piece of hardboard to a cleat (Fig. 9-21). When used with the spacer strip, this template ensures an identical slope on all letters. Of course, this works for only the straight edges of the letters; all the curves must be done freehand. By using letters

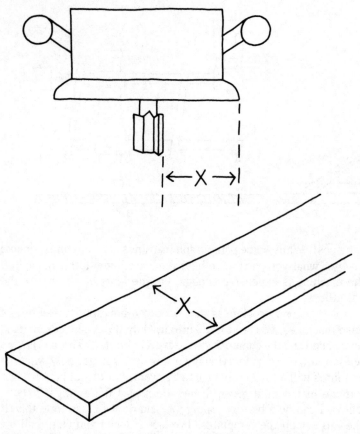

like those shown in Fig. 3-38, the amount of freehand work can be reduced.

Fig. 9-19. A spacer strip.

Template-following guides are sold as accessories for most routers (Fig. 9-22). These bushings exactly follow a plywood or hardboard template laid on the surface of the blank. Because the measuring and drawing of a perfect template are hard work, this accessory is used only for production runs of identical pieces. This sort of order seldom—if ever—falls to a small shop.

Pantograph

The pantograph is a tool that holds the router in a fixed position relative to a stylus (Fig. 9-23). The same cautions apply to router pantographs as apply to pencil pantographs (Fig. 6-48). Advertising literature might lead some to suppose that the problems of bit wandering are corrected by the use of these machines. This is *not* the case. Because the pantograph operator is one more step removed from the router, bit wandering is *increased*. It is probably better to stick with grid enlarging and freehand routing.

Some pantograph machines reproduce a three dimensional

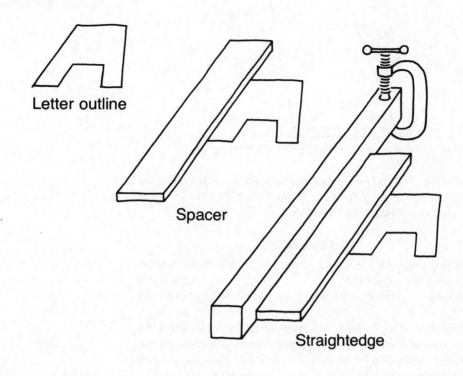

Letter outline

Spacer

Straightedge

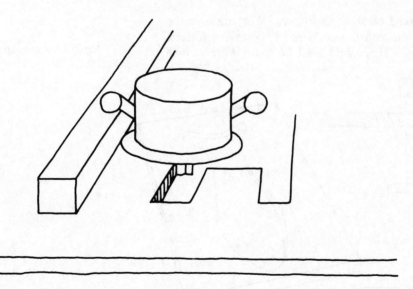

Fig. 9-20. A straightedge is clamped in place, and the spacer is removed.

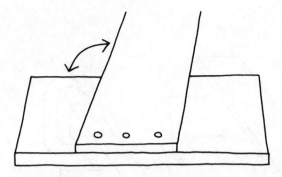

Fig. 9-21. A straightedge template.

object (B of Fig. 9-18). These work well, but they are again limited to mass-production runs of the same item. These are nice orders to get, but seldom encountered in practice.

Relief Carving

Relief carving, especially on larger signs, is the forte of the router. Depending on the nature of the job, a day's work with hand tools could translate to an hour's work with the router. See Figs. 3-35 and 3-39.

Accurate relief work depends largely on the order in which the waste is removed from the blank. Adequate material to support the router base is necessary for an even depth of cut. Because you are removing this material as you go, you are removing the support as well. *Never* leave an "island" in the middle of an open area (Fig. 9-24).

The sequence should be about as follows. Working over the whole of the sign, begin with the outlines of the raised letters, ornaments and borders. This might well be done with a small

Fig. 9-22. A template guide.

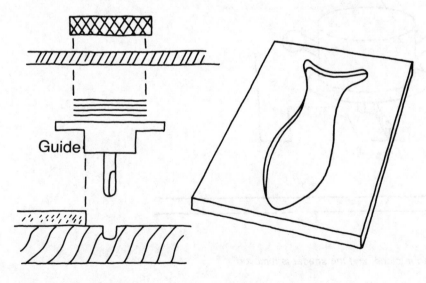

Guide

208

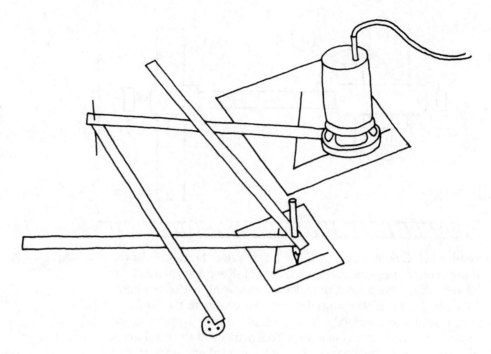

Fig. 9-23. A pantograph.

Fig. 9-24. Never leave an island in an open area (arrow).

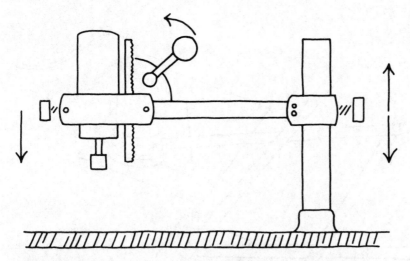

Fig. 9-25. An over-arm router.

veining bit. Changing to a core-box bit, remove the centers of the letters and the negative space around them. Keep a sharp watch for islands; they have a habit of suddenly appearing out of nowhere. Clean out waste ground working from the center to the border.

Working to a perfectly flat ground of uniform depth is all but impossible with a hand-held router. Tool marks will always show as imperfections in the ground. Trying to sand them away always makes them look worse, (not to mention the time consumed). To get a perfectly flat ground requires a tool called an over-arm router. This is an amazingly expensive machine (Fig. 9-25). Designs that require a flat ground should be constructed as relief appliques (Figs. 8-31 through 8-33).

A randomly textured ground will look just as good, in most cases, as a perfectly flat ground. If the core-box bit or the veining bit are used to clear the ground, with thought given to objective strokes, the final result will be quite pleasing.

Combinations

There is almost no end to the ways in which both incised and relief work can be used in combination on a single sign (Fig. 9-26). The only real problem is determining the order in which the waste is removed so that there remains some support for the router base.

There is a way to use the router completely without the router base. If rotary rasps are used in place of router bits (Fig. 9-27), a great deal of relief and even full-round carving can be done quite quickly.

SANDBLASTING

A fairly recent development in sign carving is the semicontrolled erosion on a blank surface using a sand blaster (Fig. 9-28). The

210

Fig. 9-26. A combination of incised and relief work.

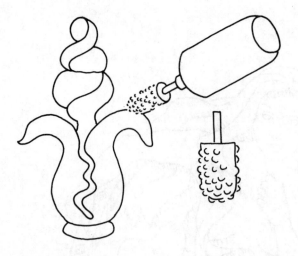

Fig. 9-27. Using a rotary rasp.

design is generally worked out as a relief. The negative space is worn away by blasts of air-carried abrasives. The design usually results in a very unusual piece that is simultaneously slick and funky. It fits the mood of the times. The slickness comes from the precise control of the design elements, while the funk comes from the individual and unpredictable erosion of the background.

The design is first laid out in a cartoon. Then it is transferred to a self adhesive frisket or stencil material. This material is a high-density plastic sheet material that protects the design from the erosion of the abrasive. See Table 9-2. The friskit is then cut away from the waste areas of the design, and the background is blasted away (Fig. 9-29). There is an occasional problem encountered with the adhesive of the friskit material. When this occurs, a supplemental adhesive spray should be tried.

Many sign crafters are reluctant to try their hand at sandblasting because of the high cost of frisket materials and the capital investment in sandblasting equipment. These problems can be overcome by asking suppliers to lower their minimum order requirements on a "one-time-experiment" basis, and by striking up an arrangement with someone who already has a sandblaster. Sand-

Fig. 9-28. A sandblasted sign.

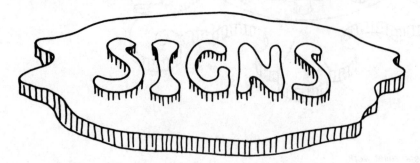

Table 9-2. Sandblasting.

Tools	Materials	Miscellaneous
Sandblaster Air compressor Abrasives	Friskit material Stencil knife	Gloves Hood/mask Dust mask Spray adhesive

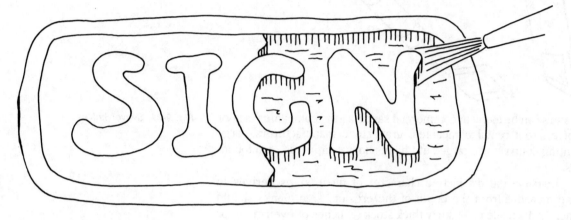

Fig. 9-29. The background is blasted away.

Fig. 9-30. Cut the frisket along the design lines.

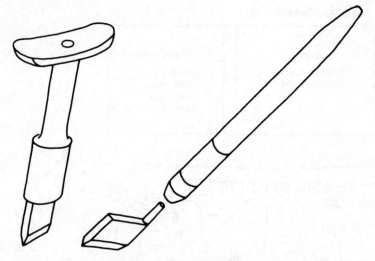

Fig. 9-31. Swivel knives.

blasters can be found at commercial sandblasting companies (a poor choice), tool rental companies, gravestone manufacturers, large painting contractors, large auto body shops, shipyards, and foundries.

Because the distinctive character of these signs derives in large measure from the depth of the erosion, sign blanks should generally be made up of fairly thick stock (2 inches or even more for larger signs). Softwoods such as redwood, cedar and sugar pine are preferable. Experiments with hardboards, flakeboards, and hardwoods can produce some interesting results.

The surface of the blank should be prepared as carefully and smoothly as possible. A smooth surface is essential for proper adhesion of the friskit material, and for crisp outlines.

Once the friskit material is adhered to the blank, it is pressed and rolled down again and again to ensure intimate contact with the blank surface in all design areas. The friskit is then cut along the design lines, and the areas to be sandblasted are exposed (Fig. 9-30).

There are several types of knives used to cleanly cut the friskit. My preference is for the swivel knife used in leather crafting. A second choice is the graphic arts swivel knife developed for a similar purpose. The one shown in Fig. 9-31 has replaceable blades.

A degree of control over the erosion process can be obtained by removing selected portions of the friskit at various stages during the blasting. This results in different depths and—by very precise control—different textures within the sign.

Overall texture is governed by the relative coarseness of the abrasive used. Because commercial abrasives are very carefully screened to size, changing abrasives is a time-consuming and painstaking operation. You can do your reputation no end of harm by contaminating abrasives when using borrowed equipment.

In your first experiments with sandblasting, try to find as many ways as possible to peel the friskit off the blank. Try also to see how hard it is to "blow through" the friskit. When you blast your first sign, you will have a catalog of moves to avoid. Have extra friskit material and a knife with your when you are blasting.

A protective hood and heavy gloves are essential safety precautions when you are doing *any* amount of sandblasting. If the hood you borrow doesn't have an air filter arrangement, built in, a dust mask is essential.

A borrowed hood is almost certain to have scarred glass that obscures vision and prevents precise work. Buy your own glass lens and take it with you when you borrow equipment.

10

Finishing

Finishing the sign is as much a part of the total sign as the designing or the carving. Finishing should be just as painstakingly thought out and executed as any other part of the sign. It is at this stage that a great deal can be done to turn the effort into a genuine work of art. Also, a less-than-perfect effort can be considerably helped by a carefully detailed paint job. See Table 10-1.

There are several finishing methods. They include a "natural" finish, polychrome (different colors of paint), and metal leaf and powders. There are of course many variations of application and technique possible within each finishing method. A large number of variations are possible by combining several finishes within a single sign. There is so much room for experiment and expression that a sign crafter should never find career boredom a problem.

BRUSHES

The paint brush is the basic tool of the painter. But no single brush will do for every job. There is as much or more variety in paint brushes as there is in carving tools.

The first thing to know about good brushes is that you will have to look for them. Most paint and hardware stores sell brushes that are good enough for house painters, but *not* good enough for sign

Table 10-1. Painted Finish.

Tools	Materials	Miscellaneous
Flat brushes	Penetrating sealers	Brush cleaning rack
Lining brushes	Penetrating finishes	Solvent
Lettering brushes	Varnish	Solvent storage cans
Novelty brushes	Stains	Neat's-foot oil
Dagger striping brush	Sign paint	Clean rags
	Aluminum paint	Newspapers
	Artist's acrylics	Index card stock
	Acrylic media, mat & gloss	Brush storage boxes or containers
	Gold paint	Window glass
		Food colors
		Analine dyes
		Sanding block(s)
		Sandpaper

painters. You might as well try to carve a sign with a hatchet as try to paint a sign with a whisk broom. *Large* art supply stores and mail-order catalogs are the place to look for brushes.

The second thing to know about good brushes is that you pay for what you get. Good brushes are still made by hand. Quality brushes are not inexpensive, but a brush that lasts five or ten years is quite economical. Invest in the best, and treat the best with the care and respect they deserve.

Flat Brushes

Flat painting brushes (Fig. 10-1) are used to apply a uniform coat of finish over a large, flat area. The best of these brushes are made of

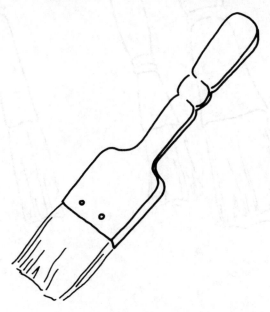

Fig. 10-1. A flat brush.

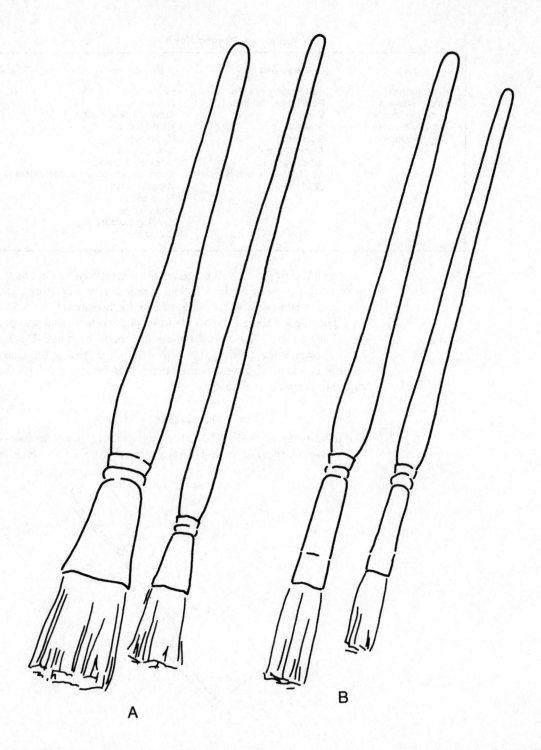

A

B

Fig. 10-2. Lining brushes.

badger hair set in a nickel/silver ferrule, and they have a rather short round wood handle. The 1½-inch and 2½-inch sizes are all that should be needed for even the largest work.

Lining and Lettering Brushes

Lining and lettering brushes have long, round tapered handles. They have ferrules that begin round at the handle and end round or slightly flattened at the bristle.

Lining brushes (A of Fig. 10-2) are used to apply finish to smaller flat surfaces and to molded or relief-carved surfaces. Squirrel-hair brushes or badger-hair brushes are worth the cost. Brushes ½ inch and 1 inch should be sufficient for most work.

Lettering brushes are confusing. The best are "hand cupped." This results in a brush that is round when dry, but develops a sharp, flat chisel edge when applied to the work. These brushes leave a long, perfectly straight line of uniform thickness. The best of these brushes is the Grumbacher #9355 (it has a copper-colored ferrule). Because line work is such an important part of sign painting, it is hard to imagine how anyone could do without several of these brushes. Although quite expensive, the professional should have at least the #1, #4, #6, and #10 sizes.

Novelty Brushes

There are so many brush variations that it would seem that there couldn't be any that are not available off the shelf. But there are useful brushes that must be made up for special purposes. For these brushes, I have found that the inexpensive "artist" brushes are a good choice. If you destroy one, you haven't lost much.

In A of Fig. 10-3, the "finger" brush is an artists brush adapted to simulating wood grain. The "fish tail" brush (B of Fig. 10-3) is useful for wood grain, knots, and many other decorative strokes.

Fig. 10-3. Artist's brushes.

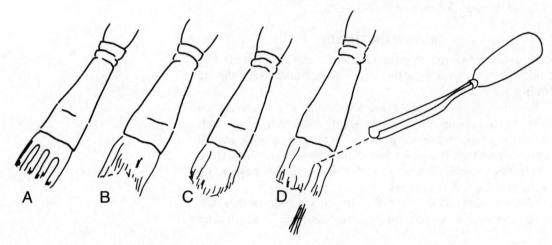

A   B   C   D

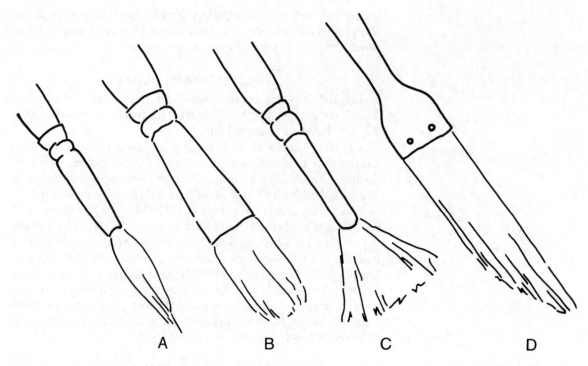

A B C D

Fig. 10-4. Novelty brushes.

The "spoon" brush (C of Fig. 10-3) is also used for decorative strokes. To make these novelty brushes, artist's brushes are shaped with carving tools or razor blades (D of Fig. 10-3).

Figure 10-4 shows some examples of off-the-shelf novelty brushes that are useful as they are. The fine-point watercolor brush (A), the oval wash brush (B), the fan fitch (C), and the dagger striper (D) are best purchased, as needed, in sizes to suit the particular job. The numbers and sizes of brushes given are the minimum you can reasonably get by with. Adding brushes to the collection seems to be a hobby in itself for many sign painters.

BRUSH MAINTENANCE

Good brushes are a large investment, and like any investment, they should be protected. Cleaning them in a slapdash fashion and storing them in a jar is a bad idea.

Because oil-based paints are used almost exclusively on wooden signs, brushes must be thoroughly cleaned in a good solvent. The least expensive acceptable solvents are gasoline and #2 oil or oil-burner fuel. If common sense prevails—no smoking, store the solvents outside, dispose of material carefully—there is no hazzard to using these solvents.

Three or four various sizes of empty tin cans placed in a rack such as shown in Fig. 10-5 makes for handy cleaning. The antlerlike arrangement makes a good handle. This is a convenient place to rest drying brushes.

To clean a brush, a small amount of solvent is placed in each can. The dirty brush is first wiped on newspaper to remove as much paint as possible. The brush is dipped in the first can, agitated, and wiped dry on the newspaper. The process is repeated with the second and third cans. The brush is clean when no traces of color are left after wiping on the newspaper.

As brush cleaning progresses throughout the day, the dirty solvent is poured into the next larger can, the smallest can receiving fresh solvent each time. At the end of the day, the contents of all cans are dumped into a screw-top can that is stored outside for later disposal. The cleaning cans should also be stored outside. Solvent-soaked rags and newspapers should also be stored outside, but in a place where the fumes will evaporate.

At the end of the day, the brushes should be treated and stored safely. The brushes are gently squeezed dry in a clean rag. The brush tips are dipped into a jar of neat's-foot oil (Fig. 10-6), and then held upside down. The oil is then worked through the bristles back toward the heel of the brush; use your fingers. The neat's-foot oil restores "life" to natural bristles, keeps any paint residue from hardening, and is easily cleaned out of the brush on the next painting day.

Small brushes can be safely stored in a covered box, (A of Fig. 10-7). This keeps them clean and free of sawdust. Necktie boxes are about the right size. Flat brushes are wrapped in an envelope of brown paper and placed in a cardboard sheath for extra bristle protection (B of Fig. 10-7).

Fig. 10-5. An organized brush-cleaning area is very important.

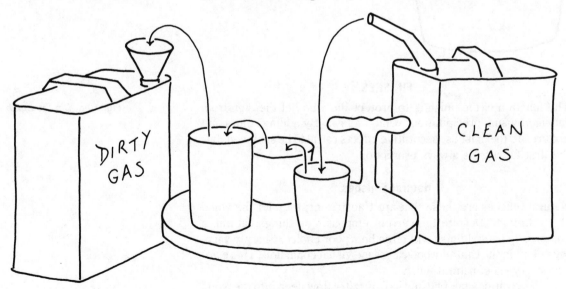

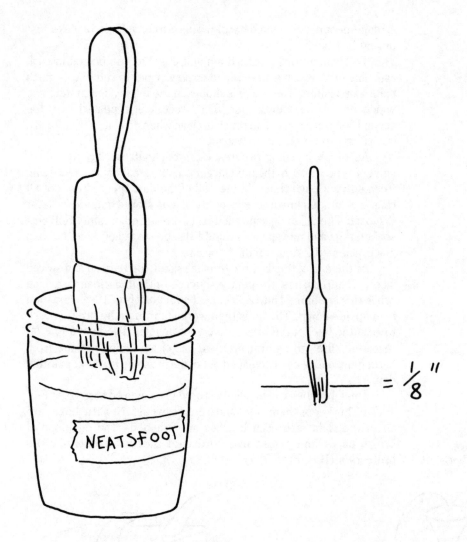

NEATSFOOT

$= \frac{1}{8}''$

FINISHES

The function of the finish is to protect the wood of the sign from damage by sun, precipitation, wind, and rot. By adding colors and textures to the finishes, decorative effects can also be achieved, but the first function is always protection.

Natural Finishes

Natural finishes are those that are transparent; they let the wood show through. Despite the current emphasis on things natural, a completely natural finish will often be a poor choice. Sharply varying colors in the natural wood can cause visual confusion. There are several types of natural finish.

Penetrating sealers (Cuprinol, Firzite) flow deep into the wood

Fig. 10-6. Dip the brush.

222

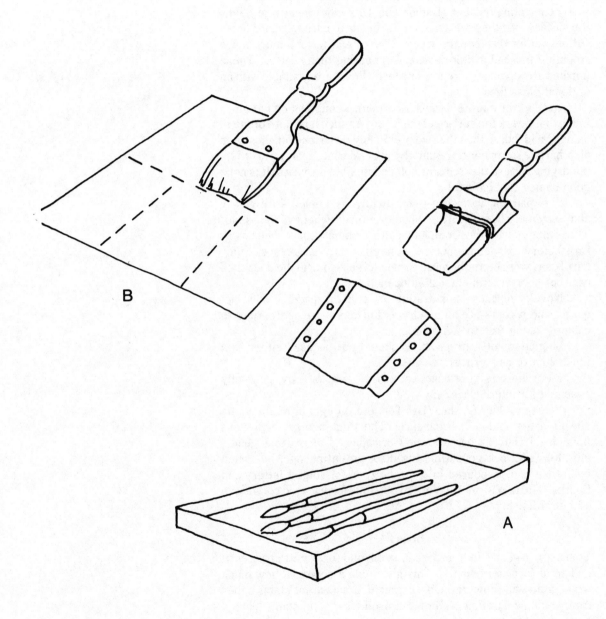

Fig. 10-7. Storing brushes.

and seal it completely against moisture penetration. This is the most natural of the natural finishes because it does nothing to alter the surface of the wood. It does tend to add warmth to the color of the wood. This type of finish is very easy to renew or repair.

Penetrating finishes (Danish Oil, Dex Olje) penetrate below the surface, and they are acted on by the air to cure to a hard finish within, rather than on, the wood. These tend to look much more smoothly finished and professional appearing than sealers. These finishes are also easy to renew or repair. Some are available with an optional gloss finish.

Outdoor or marine varnish is a matt, semigloss or full-gloss finish that lies *on* the surface of the wood. As such it is more prone to damage and failure than the two previously described finishes. It is also harder to renew or repair. Spar or Marine Spar varnish is a nondrying varnish that remains soft and flexible for years. It is not a good choice for sign work.

Sign painting varnishes—specifically so labeled—are glossy and extremely durable. They should be used whenever possible. Those put out by the Commonwealth Company have been very satisfactory for me. Do not be tempted to buy large cans. Many small cans work better because the shelf life is long in the unopened can, but shorter after the can is opened.

Novelty finishes—penetrating oil, seal oil, padding oils, lacquers, and waxes—are all nondrying finishes more appropriate to cabinetmaking than to sign painting.

Shellac is not waterproof. It should not be used either as a finish coat or as a primer.

Floor finishes (urethane varnishes, Fabulon) are generally specified for interior use only.

"Deep plastic" finishes (Bar Top, etc.,) might or might not be specified for outdoor permanence. The thick-bodied, high-gloss finish is durable, but hard to renew or repair. This material generally does not look good when used for an entire sign, but when colored it can be poured into the bottoms of routed letters and figures. The bright, shiny colors so obtained form a good contrast to a natural finish.

Stains

Stains are available in transparent, semisolid (or semitransparent), and solid (opaque) finishes. This gives you a choice of how much wood grain will show through the finish. Transparent stains penetrate as do penetrating sealers. Semisolid and solid stains leave a coating on the surface of the wood.

The best use of stains at present seems to be a nonwaxy transparent or semisolid stain to give color and even off grain figures. This is followed by a penetrating finish or by varnish.

Varnish stains and exterior solid stains marketed as options to house paint are not sufficiently durable for sign work.

There are no bright colors of nonwaxy stains on the market to my knowledge. To get bright transparent colors, analine dyes, sold by theatrical scenery supply houses, should be used. The problem with these is that there is no record regarding their permanence in sunlight. Reds are especially poor in this regard. Experiments with fabric dyes and food colors can be tried, but again there is the question of permanence.

Paints

Paint is an opaque medium available in matt, semigloss, and full-gloss finishes. The best paints for sign work are sign paints. These may, by law, use lead and other poisonous heavy metals as pigments. They are considerably more durable as a result. Before drying begins, the vehicles and dryers used in sign paints allow for considerably more brushwork than many other types of paint. Once the drying begins it is quite rapid.

The enamels sold in small cans at hardware stores are a poor choice for sign work. This is true even if it says "signs" on the label. They are too thin bodied and too lightly pigmented for outdoor durability. The drying time commences immediately. This allows very little time for brush work.

House paints are acceptable for sign work but only oil based paints should be used. The gloss varieties sold as trim paints are preferable because the colors are brighter and permanent. Again, there is little body and little working time with most house paints.

Chalking flat white house paint should *never* be used for sign work. Latex house paints do not have the penetration or durability of oil paints so they should not be used.

Novelty Paints

Aluminum paint is a light-bodied penetrating paint using powdered aluminum as a pigment. As such, it serves as both a penetrating sealer and an undercoat. Four or five coats of aluminum paint over raw wood provide a hard and shiny ground with good "tooth" for finish coats. Signs undercoated with aluminum paint are much brighter and more eye-catching than signs undercoated with flat white or tinted undercoaters. Even very dark colors and black seem to benefit. Look for brands that brag about the amount of aluminum they use, and how finely the powder is divided. For some reason, the least expensive brand I can buy always seems to be the best. As a finish coat, aluminum is a poor choice. This paint should be purchased by the gallon because so much is used, and because the shelf life is long—even for opened cans.

Artist's acrylics (Liquitex, Hyplar) are surprisingly durable when used as a finish coat. To test their durability before trying them on signs, I painted several wooden fishing plugs with, both brands, over aluminum paint undercoating, and over the recommended primers and gesso. After several years, the plugs painted over aluminum are still sound. The undercoatings and gesso failed in just a few days. The acrylic mediums—both flat and gloss—show a similar durability to the paints themselves. Signs I have subsequently painted in acrylics have not failed to date. The oldest is over six years old.

Artist's oil colors are too soft and take too long to dry for sign use. They do work well as pigments for mixing glazes, and for tinting sign paint. A drop or two of Japan dryer should be added to mixtures containing artist's oil colors.

Modeler's enamels, sold in very small bottles at hobby shops, are at least as durable as sign paint. The unusual colors make them attractive for striping and fancy work. They adhere quite well over full-gloss sign paint without any surface preparation.

Antiquing and painting mediums and glazes are available ready-made for furniture finishing. These do not work at all well for signs. It is better to make your own.

PAINTING A SIGN

The first step in painting a sign is to have both the sign blank and the painting area clean and free of dust—especially sanding dust. Tack rags and a vacuum cleaner should be used.

The sign blank is ready for undercoating when the carving is complete. If reasonable care has been taken during the carving, no further preparation should be necessary.

A soft, natural-bristle brush (Fig. 10-8, *not* one of the badger hair brushes) should be reversed for use with the aluminum paint. Traces of aluminum powder cannot be completely removed from the brush.

The front, back, and edges of the sign are all undercoated in the same way, except that the sanding and buffing steps are eliminated on the back of the blank. Paint the back of the sign first.

The brush is dipped about ½ of an inch deep, and tipped against the edge of the can to remove excess paint. The brush is held quite high up on the handle. Long strokes are used to apply the paint somewhat freely—but not to excess—in the direction of the grain. The paint is carried right up to the edge, but care is taken that drips do not run over the edge. The brush is rinsed quickly and set aside. The first coat will dry and penetrate quite quickly.

Note. The aluminum pigment settles out quite quickly. The paint should be thoroughly stirred before beginning, and at about 10-minute intervals during painting.

A second coat is applied in the same manner and allowed to dry.

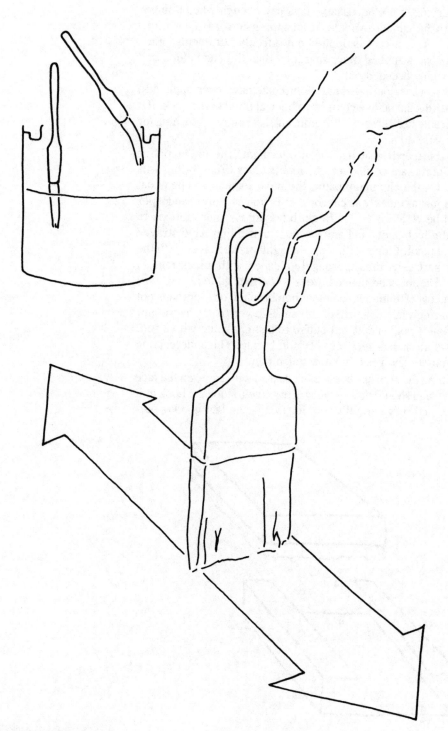

Fig. 10-8. A soft, natural-bristle brush.

Complete drying is not necessary. It is dry enough when a finger pressed onto the paint does not leave an impression of a fingerprint.

Note. The first coat is applied quite freely but evenly. Each succeeding coat is applied more sparingly than the one before, and more thoroughly brushed out.

The process is continued until four coats have been applied to the face and edges, and five coats have been applied to the back. If it seems desirable to alternate with-grain and cross-grain brushing for alternate coats, do so.

After the fourth coat has dried overnight, the undercoating should be lightly sanded all over. A sanding block (Fig. 10-9) works quite well. On the aluminum paint, the most expensive open-coat paper clogs just as quickly as cheapest stuff you can buy. Sandpaper grit should be #150 to #180. Begin by using circular motions to knock off the high spots and any sawdust that might have strayed onto the wet paint. Finish with long, straight strokes taken with the grain. The surface is then thoroughly cleaned with a tack rag.

Note. Do not sand incised areas to be leaf gilded.

A fifth coat of aluminum paint is then brushed on—perhaps not quite so sparingly as the fourth coat—and allowed to dry overnight. This last coat is not sanded, but buffed to a slight shine with a soft, but coarse cloth such as terry or very soft burlap. The undercoating is now complete and ready for the finish paint.

Assuming the sign has been undercoated with care, on the face at least, the sign should now be very attractive to look at. Look at it you should, and very carefully too, for this is the last good oppor-

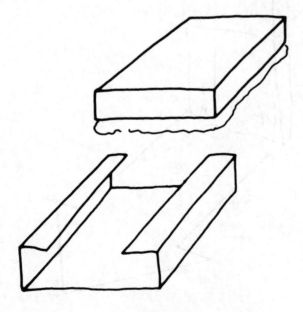

Fig. 10-9. A sanding block.

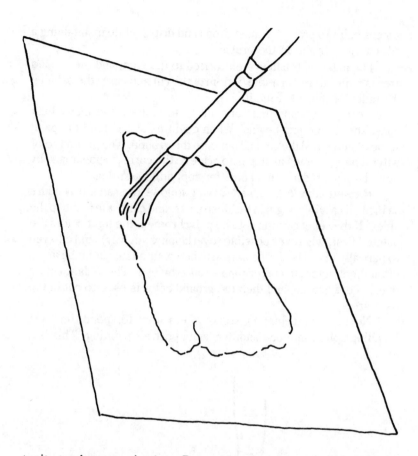

Fig. 10-10. Carry the loaded brush to a palette.

tunity to clean up mistakes. Retouching the undercoat is far easier than retouching the finish paint.

Painting Carved Areas

After the undercoat is dry and buffed, the carved areas are painted before the painting of the ground is begun. This allows some mistakes and overlaps on the ground that are corrected when the ground is painted in.

Incised carving. Lettering brushes (B of Fig. 10-2) are used to paint the incised areas. Assuming that a good-quality sign paint is used, coverage will be complete in one coat. There will be little puddling of the paint in the bottoms of the letters. This puddling should be guarded against. Get down close and look into the carved areas after they have been painted. Check often.

The brush is first gently squeezed in a clean rag to remove any excess neat's-foot oil. It is then dipped about one-third deep into the paint. Rather than tipping the brush on the can edge (as in Fig. 10-8), the loaded brush is carried to a piece of index card stock. There it is paletted several times (Fig. 10-10). This has the effect of removing excess paint to protect against drops and drips, while maintaining a full charge of paint in the brush.

The paletted brush is then carried to the sign, and the incised area is painted. Begin at the bottom of the cut and carry the paint up the sides of the cut (Fig. 10-11).

Note. It is sometimes difficult to tell where the incised cut ends, and the ground begins. When doubt exists, extend the paint somewhat beyond the cut and out onto the ground. The ground color will then be "cut in" in stages to achieve the correct appearance by eye. This procedure also holds for applying metal leaf.

Raised carving. Raised carving follows the same procedure as incised carving; begin in the deep parts, and carry the paint up the sides. If the relief carving is to be polychromed, the light colors are painted first, wherever possible (overlapping slightly), and allowed to partially dry. The dark colors are then painted in; cut in the areas of the light colors to correct appearance by eye. These dark colors overlap the ground, and then the ground color is used to cut in the dark areas.

Note. Some beginning sign crafters want to spend time wet blending colors into one another, as in portrait painting. This is a

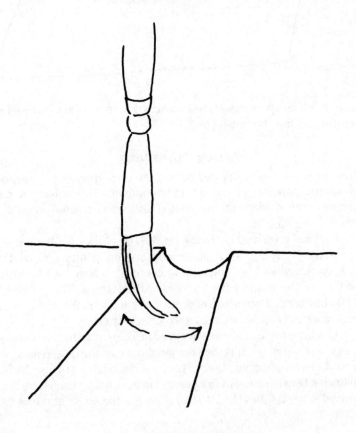

Fig. 10-11. Painting an incised area.

230

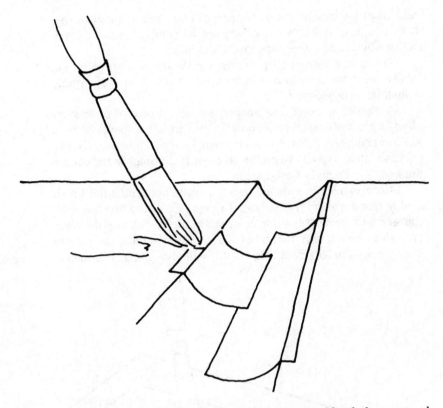

Fig. 10-12. Overlap the edges of all metal leaf.

mistake. As the sign is viewed from a distance, blended areas tend to "read" as a blurr. See also the section on glazes.

Ground Coat

The finishing ground coat of oil based sign paint is carefully painted onto the ground areas of the sign. The lining and flat brushes are used, the paint is laid on with final brush strokes following the long axis of the sign. If the sign is tall, brush up and down; if the sign is wide, brush back and forth. The slight irregularities caused by the brush strokes are used to emphasize the horizontal or vertical flow of the design.

Care must be taken to slightly overlap all raw edges of any metal leaf (Fig. 10-12). This will protect them from wind and driving rain.

Assuming a careful undercoating job and that a quality sign paint is used for the ground, one coat is sufficient. The sign is then allowed to dry for a few days, and then transported to the site for mounting.

GLAZES

A glaze is a transparent or semitransparent coating applied over the finish paint job in *some* cases. Glazing can be used to simulate the effect of age (patina), or it can be used to emphasize the carved sections by giving deeper-appearing shadows.

Glazes are prepared by tinting a quantity of sign painter's varnish with the appropriate artist's oil color. A slower-drying varnish is recommended.

A blob of oil color is squeezed out onto a palette of window glass or clear plastic. A small quantity of varnish is spooned into a shallow container. A brush is used to work varnish into the oil color (a brush full at a time). When the oil color is thoroughly and evenly thinned, the brush is rinsed clean.

More varnish is spooned into the container, and a full brush load is transferred to the palette. The very tip of the brush is then charged with some of the thin color and worked back into the clear varnish to give a very thin transparent color. Holding the palette over the area to be glazed (Fig. 10-13) will give you a clear idea of

Fig. 10-13. Hold the palette over the areas to be glazed.

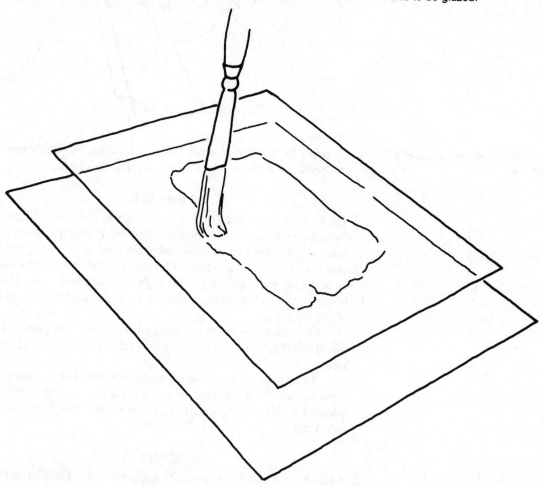

232

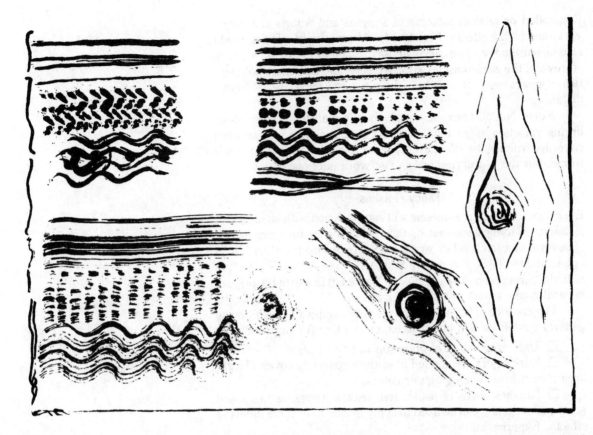

Fig. 10-14. Controlled and random patterns.

the effect of the glaze. More color or more varnish can be added until the right effect is achieved.

Glazing is begun with the lightest or most transparent mix. Apply it over the entire area to be glazed. Rather than puddle the glaze to get a darker effect, a tad more color is worked into a brushful of varnish and applied a bit at a time to local areas.

Note. The varnish in the container gets progressively darker as color is transferred from the brush.

If too much glaze is inadvertently applied to a local area, the brush should be quickly rinsed in solvent, and then squeezed out in a clean rag. The dry brush is then used to lift off the excess glaze.

To glaze a large flat area, such as an entire ground, a somewhat larger quantity of glaze can be mixed in a separate container. The color should be about the medium intensity you intend to use. Extra varnish or color can be mixed in on the spot by using the sign as the palette. Be certain to keep glaze out of areas that are not to receive glaze, and *always* keep glazes off gold leaf.

While the glaze is wet and workable, it can be gone over with a dry, flat brush (one of the novelty brushes, Fig. 10-3, used dry), a cotton ball, or a wad of crumpled plastic wrap or aluminum foil.

Controlled or random patterns of stipples and whorls can create very interesting effects (Fig. 10-14). Alternatively, glazing might also obscure a very fine carving effort. Judgment must be used. In any event, the glaze must be worked freely, and with more boldness than appears right. Remember, the glaze too must "read" from a distance.

Note. Not all varnishes work equally well for glazes. Slow-drying varieties might tend to creep back together into an even coverage, ruining the effect. Sign painter's varnish has not done this to me, but the fast drying makes fast work necessary.

Fancy Finishes

Every once in a while, someone will approach you with an ideal that is unique. Carving a wooden sign that will give the final appearance of several thousand dollars worth of exquisite Russina Malachite is one example. To do this sort of thing well takes incredible skill in both the carving and the painting, but the result is worth the price of several commissions in satisfaction alone.

The creation of fantasy finishes is very complex. The following general guidelines will help you experiment with fancy finishes.

☐ Use many colors of glaze (up to five or six).

☐ Dark colors are applied first; they generally cover a larger area than the succeeding lighter colors.

☐ Brushes, wads of paper, foil, leaves, twigs, sponges and scraps of carpeting can be used to apply glazes to achieve different effects. Experiment!

☐ Allow glazes to dry completely before applying the next color.

☐ Have pictures to work from. Check your library for articles on rocks and minerals, wood, furniture, theater scenery and general art books.

Striping

Striping can be used in several ways on carved signs. Figure 10-15 shows some of these. Decorative pinstriping looks good on some signs. Fancy Victorian signs might benefit by applying gold size and leaf over the finished ground paint to accent the carving. The most common use, however, is outlining incised and gilded lettering to establish a contrast between the lettering and a light-colored or white ground.

The dagger striping brush is used. Work at whatever hour of the day you feel most serene, and your hand is most steady. The trick of striping is to use a glaze (*not* a paint) as the striping medium. This can be done by making a glaze of varnish and oil colors or by beating in a fairly large quantity of sign painters varnish into sign

Fig. 10-15. Examples of striping.

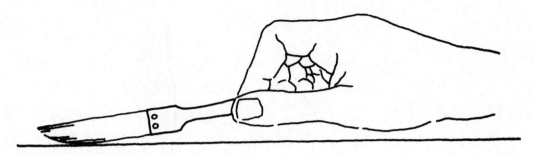

Fig. 10-16A. Hold the brush this way for straight lines.

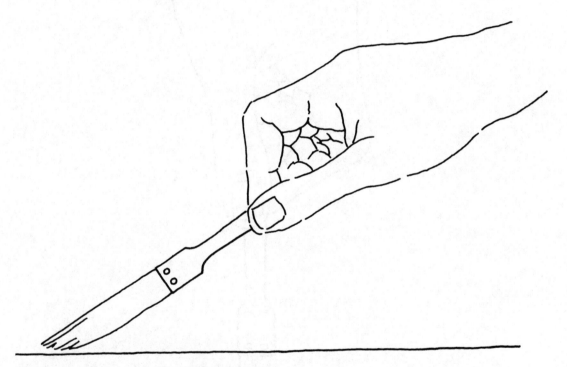

Fig. 10-16B. Hold the brush this way for moderate curves.

paint. The object is to achieve a "slippery" and very smooth flowing medium.

The funny-shaped brush is used by grasping the small handle between the thumb and the index finger (Figs. 10-16A, 10-16B, and 10-16C). For long, straight lines, the handle is held almost parallel to the surface. For curved lines, the handle is lifted, depending on the radius of the curve. For very tight radius curves, serifs etc., the brush is held almost perpendicular to the surface. Practice and confidence are more important than skill or a steady hand.

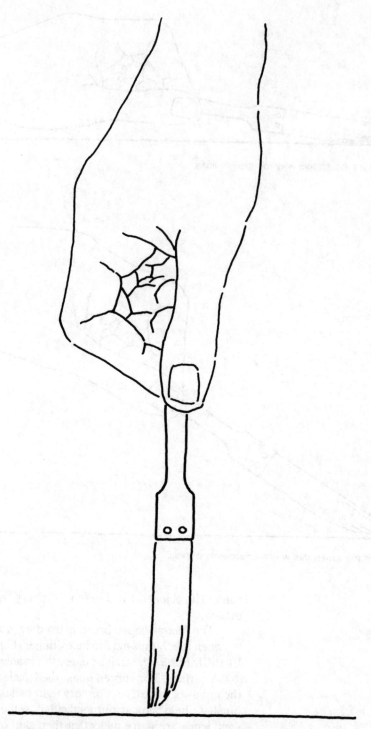

Fig. 10-16C. Grip the brush with your thumb and index finger for tight curves, serifs, etc.

Table 10-2. Metallic Finishes.

Tools	Materials	Miscellaneous
Gilder's cushion	Bronze powders	Brushes
Gilder's Knife	Bronzing liquid	Amonia
Gilder's Tips	Artist's Acrylic Media	Candle
Metal leafs:	Gilding size, fast & slow	Window glass
XX Gold	Skew box	Vaseline
Dutch Metal		Talcum powder
Colored gold		Cotton balls
Silver		
Paladium		

METAL FINISHES

There are several different metallic media available. Each is applied differently, and is used for a different purpose. See Table 10-2.

Bronze Powders

Dry bronze powders have a distinct advantage over ready-mixed paint. First, you can mix quantities suited to the job. This paint is always fresh. Second, you can mix several colors of bronze powders in the same paint job to get colors and shadings impossible with ready-mixed colors. Third, dry bronze powders are available in many unusual colors such as bright red, lilac, and emerald green.

Dry bronzes are traditionally mixed with a bronzing fluid or banana oil. While these work well, they are slow drying, and tend to darken the colors slightly. Recently I have been using artist's acrylic gloss medium with great success. This vehicle is quick drying, seems even more durable than the traditional oils, and the colors seem brighter.

The method of applying the bronze powders over a tacky varnish ground (used in chair stenciling and tole painting) leaves a surface that is too delicate for sign work.

Gold Paint

Ready-mixed paint is available in several different "golds." None, of course, is real gold; it is a finely divided brass or bronze powder. Because the powder tends to pack quite hard in the bottom of the jar, these products are difficult to use.

Artificial Gold Leaf

The type of artificial leaf applied in the same manner as genuine gold leaf is called variously dutch metal, brass leaf, or pinchbeck. The leaves of this material are larger than real gold (5½ × 5½ inches) and quite a bit thicker. This gives the beginner something easy to work with while acquiring skills.

Dutch metal gilding must be varnished over because otherwise the material will rapidly tarnish. Even varnished it will eventually tarnish.

The tendency to tarnish can be used to advantage in some cases. Tarnishing is accelerated by brush application of clear ammonia to the unvarnished leaf, after it has been applied to the sign. The tarnishing action takes 8 to 12 hours to complete. The result is a tortoise shell-like effect that is quite handsome. Two or more ammonia applications might be required to achieve a very dark tarnish. The leaf must then be rinsed with clear water, allowed to dry, and varnished for permanence.

The tarnished effect does not look good on any but the largest lettering; the effect distracts from legibility. The effect looks quite good on figures, borders, and embellishments when the intent is to simulate great age.

Aluminum leaf and silver leaf are applied like gold leaf. Both tend to tarnish (aluminum more rapidly) and they must be protected by varnish. Palladium leaf is a silver-colored leaf that does not tarnish and needs no varnish.

Silver-colored leafs are seldom used in sign work, except for an occasional embellishment. From a distance, in sunlight, silver-leafed work seems to evaporate into nothingness.

Leaf Gold

Leaf gold is wonderful. It is also phenomenonally expensive and exasperating stuff to work with. Once the skills are developed, there is a mesmerizing effect to the material and to the application of it. The beauty of gold is just as romantic today as it ever was. Working with the material involves intense concentration, trance-like relaxation, and excitement—all at once. It is GOLD, the substance of wars, fairy tales, pirates, kings, and enchanted princesses. It is also the most beautiful thing you can do to a carved letter.

In the discussion of letter carving (see Chapter 5) repeated mention was made of two things: shallow carving and NO sandpaper. I assume that these cautions have been observed.

An undercoating of aluminum paint—well brushed out in the letters, with no puddles—will fill in any irregularities in the carving and might appear to need sanding. Buffing the aluminum paint smooths the carved areas, yet it retains the look of crisp, clean cuts. The carved surfaces of each letter now look like the surface of a wind-ruffled pond in the moonlight.

Note. Reading many books on the topic of gilding—especially older books—might lead one to believe that *only* a clay substrate may be used for gilding. This is not true. The buffed aluminum paint works extremely well.

If gilded letters are to be individually outlined with the striping brush, the ground can be painted in before gilding. The striping will cut in the border of each letter and protect the raw edge of the gold. If the letters are not to be outlined, the gilding of letters is executed *before* the ground is painted. The ground paint will then cut in the outline and protect the leaf. In either case, the final paint will be used to cut the letter to a crisp outline and protect the leaf (Fig. 10-17).

Gold leaf comes in "books" of leaves. The size of each leaf is 3⅜ × 3⅜ inches and there are 25 leaves per book. The most common variety is 23K XX leaf. This leaf is about 1/250,000 of an inch thick. One book contains about 1/1,200 of 1 pound of gold. One book laid by a skilled master will cover an area 1½ square feet. A "pack" of 20 books will cover an area of about 30 square feet.

A second variety of 23K XX gold leaf is also available. Called patent gold, it differs in two respects. First, it is thicker (about 1/10,000 of an inch thick). Second, it is quite firmly adhered to the paper leaves of the book. This makes outdoor gilding and gilding of vertical and overhead surfaces much easier. Naturally, because it is thicker it is more expensive.

Fig. 10-17. Applying the final paint.

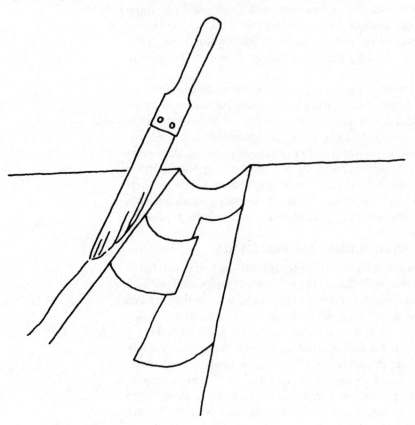

Patent gold is seldom needed by the sign carver, although the thicker leaf might prove more durable in extreme weather locations. The thicker leaf might also be easier for the beginner to use. Dutch metal would be the obvious choice for learning and experimentation.

Note. When you order patent gold, make sure you know what you are getting. The term *patent gold* is occasionally—erroneously—used as a synonym for Dutch metal by some shop clerks who should know better.

Gold Size

There are several varieties of gold size available, and there is sometimes confusion about them.

Oil Size. Oil size or "slow size" is indeed slow. It must be allowed to dry anywhere from 8 to 18 hours before developing the correct tack.

Quick Size. Quick size is also an oil size. The difference is that a small amount of dryer has been added. This reduces the viscosity somewhat, and it speeds drying.

The beginner should experiment with both varieties. Sign crafters in the rain belts of the Northwest and Southeast will likely find that slow size never is ready to work with, while those in the Southwestern deserts might find that they must work too rapidly to keep up with quick size.

Another variable is the color of the size. Some size is clear and treacherous to work with. Great pains must be taken to avoid puddles or holidays. A second variety is tinted with chrome yellow medium. This is easier to use over the aluminum paint because holidays and puddles show up quite clearly. Whether quick or slow tinted or clear, all size benefits from a drop of turpentine added before storing for a period longer than a few days. Of the several brands available, my experience is that those brands imported from Europe (especially Germany) are superior to domestic products.

GILDER'S TOOLS AND PROCEDURES

The *gilder's cushion* or *klinker* (Fig. 10-18) is a block of wood that is padded and covered with chamois or kid leather, suede side up. The padding can be anything that gives a *slight* resiliency to the surface. Too much or too little is not good, but the optimum range is quite wide. The resiliency of a well-done hamburger is about right.

The leather is treated by rubbing it with the powdery chalk from the leaves of the gold books. The cushion improves with use. Pains must be taken to ensure that the cushion is never contaminated by gold size, paint, or sanding dust. The shield along three sides can be made of any material. Its only purpose is to block stray air currents.

Fig. 10-18. A gilder's cushion.

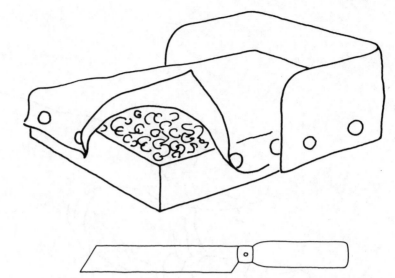

Fig. 10-19. A gilder's knife.

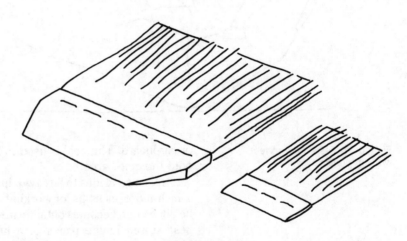

Fig. 10-20. A gilder's tip.

Gilder's Knife

The gilder's knife (Fig. 10-19) is a long, thin, perfectly flat bladed tool that is absolutely free of rust and nicks in the blade. This is the *only* cutting tool of the sign carver that is not kept razor sharp. Sharpen to razor sharpness and then draw the cutting edge across a piece of smooth steel or glass rod to dull the edge slightly. The blade must be kept free of rust, but it must not be contaminated by oil or rust-preventive spray. A loose wrapping in waxed paper seems to work well.

Gilder's Tip

The gilder's tip (Fig. 10-20) is a thin, flat badger-hair brush about 4 inches wide cemented or stitched between two layers of thin wood

241

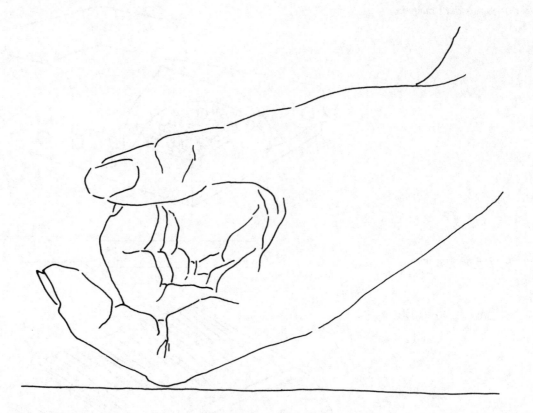

Fig. 10-21. Testing for correct
working consistency.

or cardboard. This tool is used to lift the leaf from the cushion and onto the sized area.

It is a good idea to buy two tips and cut one of them into 2-inch, 1-inch and ½-inch tips for working with cut leaf. The tips must never be allowed to become contaminated with gold size or dust. Tips are best stored in the pages of a heavy book, bristles toward the binding.

Sizing

The gold size is brushed onto the areas to be gilded in as thin and even a coating as is reasonably possible. The lettering brushes work well for this job. The sizing must be done the requisite numbers before gilding is to commence. Because I like to gild in the early morning, I do the sizing the last thing at night.

The size is tested for the correct working consistency or degree of *tack* by lightly pressing the back of a knuckle onto the size (Fig. 10-21). If the size pulls vigorously at the skin, yet the skin comes away clean, the size is ready.

Note. If the size mysteriously dries more rapidly than anticipated (it does this once in a while), there is no remedy. Allow the size to dry completely and start over again.

A newer method of sizing works somewhat differently. With this method, artists polymer medium (Hyplar, Liquitex, etc.,) is used in place of the normal gold size. The leaf is applied to the wet medium. All the following gilding instructions apply to both sizing methods. So far, both methods appear to work equally well. Polymers haven't been around as long as the slow drying size. Therefore some experimentation should be carried out by individual artisans.

Gilding

The first step is to locate the source of, and block any stray breezes that are in the work area. Stoke up your pipe and blow great clouds of smoke around the area or walk about with a lighted candle and study the flame. Lock the door and put up the out-to-lunch sign. Someone opening a door will send up enormously costly clouds of gold.

Crank up whatever music seems to help. I like to think that the precision of Brahms invades my soul and improves my work. See to it that the lighting is good.

Set out the cushion, the knife, the tips and the books of gold. In the following instructions it is assumed that the gilder is right handed. Lefties must adjust.

Examine a book of gold. The leaf adheres slightly to one side of the leaves of the book. Orient the book so that the gold is up (Fig. 10-22).

Place the cushion on an unsized area somewhat to the left of the area to be gilded first. Work across the sign from left to right.

Slide the knife under a leaf of gold and lower it gently to the cushion. The correct lowering speed will float the leaf off the knife, and the leaf will land perfectly flat on the leather. This takes practice, but is probably the easiest part.

If the leaf lands improperly, and is rumpled up, the knife is used

Fig. 10-22. Gold leaves adhere slightly to one side of the pack.

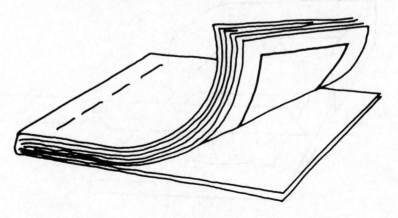

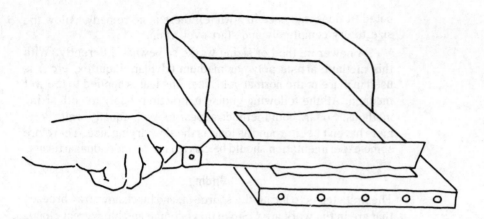

Fig. 10-23. Hold one edge of the leaf with the knife.

to hold one edge down (as in Fig. 10-23). A very short and very gentle puff of breath is aimed *above and beyond* the leaf. This puff of breath creates a very slight vacuum under the leaf. This raises it up and allows it to settle flat on the cushion. You can practice your blowing techniques by using the ash of a piece of cigarette paper on a sheet of typing paper. The pressure required to move the ash around on the surface is about the pressure needed to move the gold leaf about.

Note. Never *ever* even think of touching the gold with your fingers. The leaf will be destroyed instantly. At around $2 per leaf, the lesson is quickly learned!

The area to be gilded is judged for size by the eyeball method. A leaf is cut somewhat oversize, as in Fig. 10-24. The knife is laid on the leaf and drawn toward you. The cutting stroke is smooth, continuous and light. The knife stroke continues until *all* the knife blade has cleared *all* the leaf. Lifting the knife while the blade is still in contact with the leaf tears the leaf.

The size of the piece of leaf to be used is a matter of skill.

Fig. 10-24. Cut the leaf oversized.

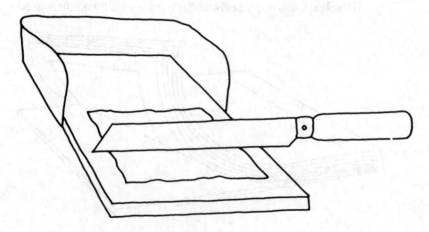

Beginners should subdivide the leaf into smaller parts until skill is gained.

The gilder's tip is used to lift the cut leaf from the cushion and to lay it on the size. A tip slightly smaller than the cut piece of leaf is used. In order to lift the leaf, the tip must be prepared in some way.

The traditional method of preparing the tip is to stroke the tip vigorously through the hair of your head or against the sleeve of a woolen sweater in order to build up a charge of static electricity that holds the gold. In warm, humid weather this doesn't work. To charge the tip under these conditions, the following method will probably work after some experimentation.

The smallest possible amount of Vaseline is smeared over the widest possible area of a piece clean of window glass. The very tip of the tip is drawn across the treated glass to apply a microscopic amount of Vaseline to each hair.

After charging the tip by whatever method seems to work, the very tip of the tip is touched to the very edge of the cut piece of leaf. The edge of the leaf will be either the upper edge or the right edge (depending on which edge will keep the tip from contacting the size). If size is picked up on the tip, the tip is ruined—for the day at least.

The piece of gold is lifted by it's edge and floated through the air on the edge of the tip (Fig. 10-25). The tip is brought down so as to contact the work about ⅛ of an inch beyond the sized area. The leaf settles on the size and is instantly and irretrevably grasped by the size. No repositioning is possible.

For deeply carved letters, a slight puff of breath at the last possible instant, directed downward at the leaf, will force the leaf into a concave shape just as it settles onto the size. It takes practice.

The thing to aim for is one single and unhurried precise motion from cushion to size: press, lift, float, blow/press, all in one perfectly timed almost balletic motion.

There is no doubt that this is a difficult skill to master. It is probably almost as hard a maneuver to accomplish as a sparrow alighting on a moving branch in a high wind. You will know you have arrived when you can gild as effortlessly and unconsciously as the sparrow outside your window can fly. At that point, you will have achieved a status reserved only for magicians and wizards. Showing off this skill to a few select persons in your studio is good for the ego. It also helps business to show off these "gee whiz" skills to architects and decorators from time to time.

Once the first piece of gold is laid, the succeeding pieces are laid in an overlapping shingle fashion (Fig. 10-26).

Many small pieces, called *skews* overlap onto adjacent pieces of gold or onto unsized areas. The largest of these are carefully torn off using the tip, and lifted onto the ends of serifs and small holidays, etc.

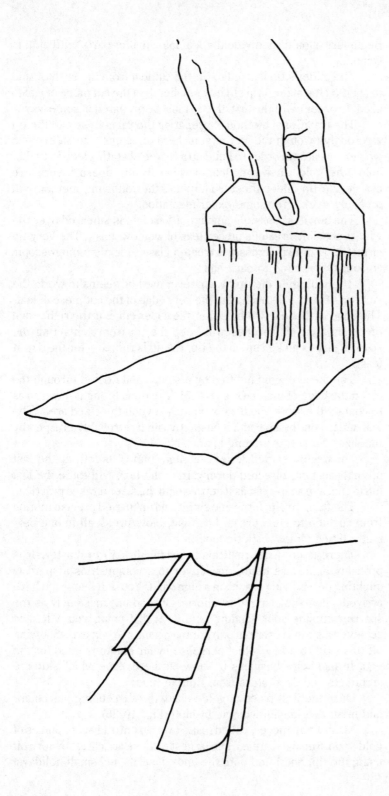

Fig. 10-25. The piece of gold is lifted by the edge.

Fig. 10-26. The gold pieces are overlapped.

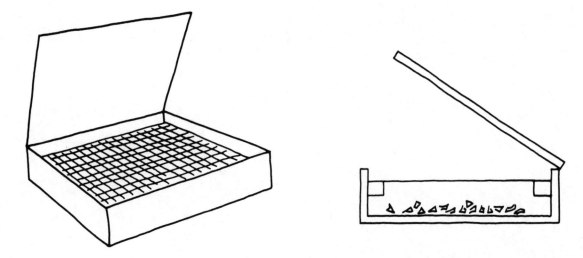

Fig. 10-27. The skew box.

When a section is completed, the leaf is lightly tamped into the size with the end of the tip to ensure intimate contact with the size. The remaining skews are placed into the skew box (Fig. 10-27).

The skew box is a cigar box with a piece of window screen fitting just below the lid. The skews are worked through the screen with the tip and into the box. This small size has less tendency to become airborne. The lid of the box keeps the skews inside. Once a year or so, when the price of gold goes way up, take the skew box to your nearby friendly gold buyer.

After the gold has been in place a few days to allow the size to fully harden, the gold can be burnished if you prefer. Cotton balls dipped in talcum powder work well for burnishing. Care must be taken not to burnish through the very thin leaf.

Pure gold is called XX or XXX or *deep karat* gold. This is never varnished. All other leaf materials must be varnished to postpone tarnishing. These include lemon gold, usual gold, green gold, and pale gold (among others). All have tarnishing alloys mixed with the pure gold to achieve the colors. The only exception is the paladium leaf noted previously.

As soon as the gold is burnished, the sign should be trotted out in the sunlight and admired. After all that intense effort, you need the gratification. The play of sunlight on the burnished facets of the carving make the whole effort immensely worthwhile.

11
Mounting the Sign

The setting of the sign is part of the design. Indeed, the side of a building or the air around a free-standing sign are the negative space that sets the sign off and makes it attractive.

The mounting of the sign must be taken into consideration in the design phase. If the mounting is to be invisible or unobtrusive (as in Fig. 11-1), the mechanics and fastenings must be thought out in such a way as to remain unseen. It is one thing to drive a bolt *through* a board. It is quite another thing to try to drive a bolt *behind* a sign that sits flat on the wall.

If the sign mounting is to be visible (as in Fig. 11-2), then the mounting must be designed as carefully and beautifully as the sign itself. One of the saddest things to see is a carefully made sign nailed up on a bracket that is clearly an afterthought (Fig. 11-3).

A sign must be hung in such a way as to ensure safety. The sign should be safe and so should people, cars, and buildings in the vicinity of the sign. A sign measuring 3 × 4 feet might weigh only 50 pounds, but a sail of the same dimensions could easily drive a 200-pound racing sailboat at frightening speeds in a good breeze. Therefore the fastenings used to support a 3-×-4-foot sign should be capable of supporting at least 250 pounds without failure. Right? Well, consider this.

It is not uncommon for winds to blow up to 100 miles per hour, and more. A 100-mph wind will exert a force of 45 pounds per square

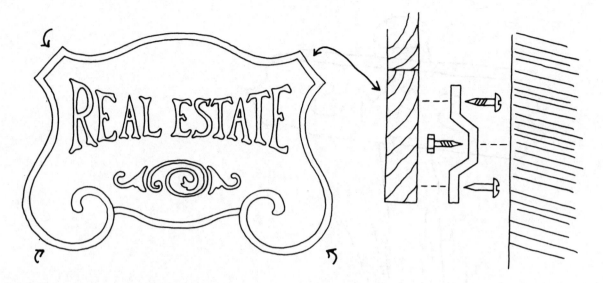

Fig. 11-1. Locations of fasteners.

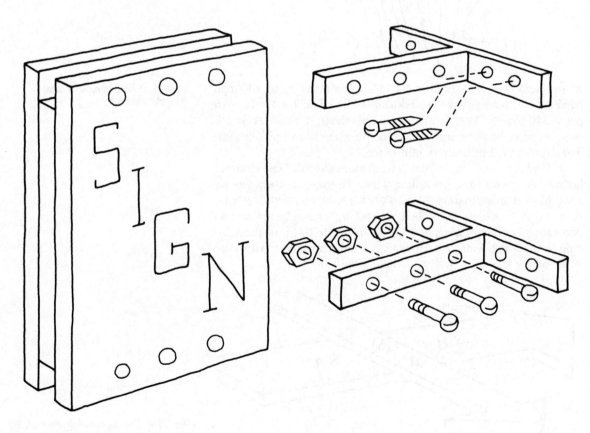

Fig. 11-2. Visible fasteners.

Fig. 11-3. An example of after-thought mounting.

foot of sign face. For the 3-×-4-foot sign to stand up to 100-mph winds, the fastenings have to be calculated like this: $3 \times 4 = 12 \times 45$ ppf = 540 pounds. That's well over double the first guess. After all, the guy with the little boat will go home when the wind kicks up. The sign can't. But there is still more.

Wind is a "live" load. That is wind moves about. Gusts blow at higher speeds than the prevailing wind. To make matters worse, gusts blow at an approximate 40-degree angle to the prevailing wind (Fig. 11-4). It is quite possible for a hanging sign to be slapped on one side by a 50-mph wind, and a second later to be hit on the *other* side by a 70-mph wind. A sign mounting must be able to withstand some heavy shocks as well as simple wind load.

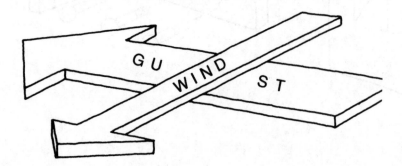

Fig. 11-4. Gusts blow at an angle to the prevailing winds.

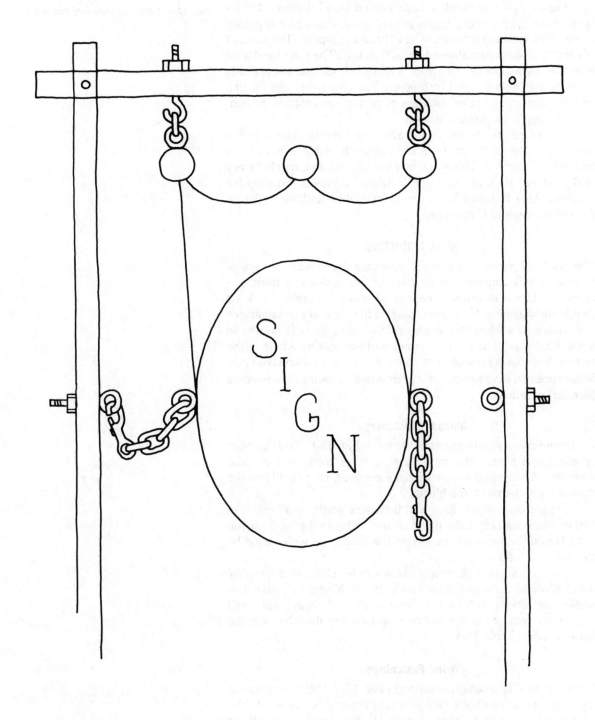

Fig. 11-5. Note the enlarged mounting details.

Figure 11-5 represents a large carved sign I did for a beauty shop ; here the mounting details are enlarged. The sign was placed close to the road and is meant to be a ''traffic stopper''. The size is 4 × 7 feet (the maximum allowed by local codes). The calculated wind load was 1,060 pounds. This wind load and shock load could easily snap the supporting 4-×-4-inch posts. The two safety chains, that restrain movement in a mild breeze, have dog leash clips at the end. The hanging eyes above are open.

The proprietor of the shop—who asked me to make the sign this way—takes the sign down and carries it inside every time a high wind threatens. This is not an easy job, but fortunately he is a husky fellow. He takes the sign in when he closes the shop for vacation. Also, he takes the sign in every night—faithfully—during the entire week of Halloween.

WALL MOUNTING

The walls of newer commercial buildings are almost always of masonry block construction because of fire codes and insurance reasons. There is often a veneer of wood, shingle, brick or aluminum sheathing. Unless you can find the plans of the building or someone who worked on the construction of it, there is no way to know what is underneath the veneer without making a hole in the veneer and looking inside. Try to do this in an unobtrusive spot. Make sure you have the owner's permission as well as the tenant's permission to do so.

Masonry Fastenings

Common masonry fastenings are shown in Fig. 11-6. Lead anchors or expansion plugs with lag or hanger bolts work well in solid masonry. Where solid masonry blocks are used, try to drill into the mortar joints between the blocks.

Toggle bolts and hollow wall fasteners work equally well in hollow block masonry units if you hit the cavity in the block. If you must fasten the sign into the web of the block, the web should be treated as a solid unit.

Very small and lightweight signs can be glued to a masonry wall. Miracle Adhesive Company's Black Magic adhesive has worked extremely well for me. Nevertheless, I always add small pegs to the back of the sign and corresponding shallow holes in the masonry. See Table 11-1.

Wood Fastenings

Common wood fastenings are shown in Fig. 11-7. Older commercial buildings and private homes are generally constructed of wood. The construction methods used almost always involve boards or plywood nailed over studs, and covered with a veneer of some sort.

Fig. 11-6. Common masonry fasteners.

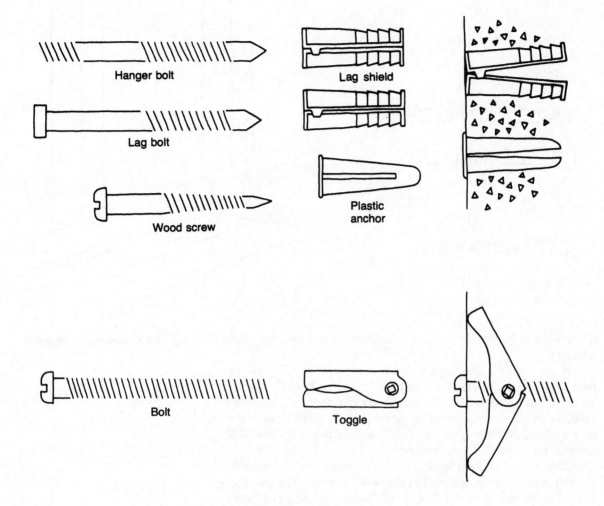

Hanger bolt

Lag bolt

Wood screw

Lag shield

Plastic anchor

Bolt

Toggle

Table 11-1. Wall Mounting.

Tools	Materials	Miscellaneous
Electric drill	Lead anchors	Ladders
Masonry bits	Expansion plugs	Extension cords
Wood bits	Lag bolts	Assorted hand tools
Wrenches	Hanger bolts	Pencils, chalk, etc.
Level	Toggle bolts	Wood blocks
Measuring tape	Flat steel stock	

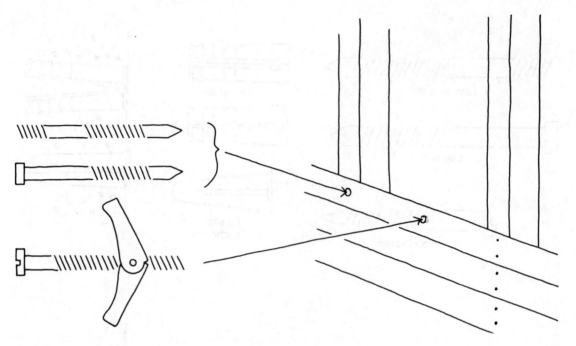

Fig. 11-7. Common wood fasteners.

If the veneer is masonry in good condition, it can be treated as masonry.

If the veneer is a siding material of some sort, it will probably be nailed to the wall studs. A row of nail heads should be visible. Where a siding material that does not expose the nails has been used, a careful examination along the foundation or the edge of the roof might show nails driven into the studs in the trim. The stud location must then be transferred to the location of the sign.

If there is still no way to find the stud, a hole must be made into the siding in a position where the patch will be covered by the sign. Poking about with a piece of wire or coat hanger will help you locate the stud.

Where it is impossible to fasten the sign onto studs for esthetic or other reasons, toggle bolts can often be used between the studs.

Once the fastening locations are known and the cartoon of the sign blank is drawn, the mounting can be designed.

Mounting Design

Figure 11-8 shows several methods for mounting a sign to a flat wall: A shows a hole through the sign with a decorative brass acorn nut and washer: and B and C show hanging brackets of steel fastened to the back of the sign. In either case, be sure to allow some space for air to circulate and water to evaporate.

In some cases, it might be best to actually place the fasteners in the wall before the sign blank is made. A template, such as the one

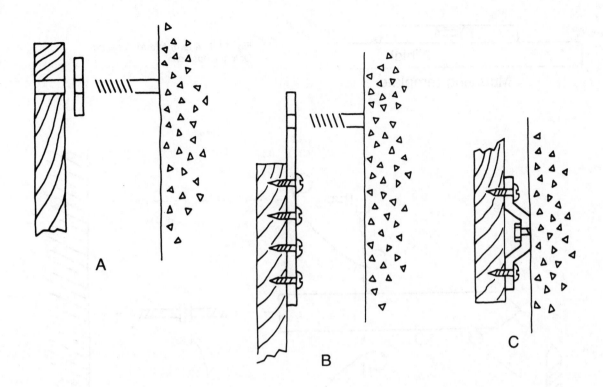

Fig. 11-8. Sign-mounting methods.

shown in Fig. 11-9, can be made up to the *exact* position of the fastenings. This template will ensure that the sign will indeed fit. Make sure that the template is clearly labeled for orientation (left, north, or up).

Another thing to make sure of in the design phase is that you don't design yourself into an impossible situation. For example, in Fig. 11-8C, be sure to leave enough room inside the bracket (C of Fig. 11-8) to swing the wrench that you will be using.

OFFSET MOUNTINGS

Offset mountings can be simple or elaborate, and the amount of work involved can be quite misleading. The simplest mountings can often be the most difficult to execute, and an elaborate mounting might give you far more room to work. The services of a local welder might be required. See Fig. 11-10.

Roof Mountings. Roof mountings must generally be designed so as to remain unseen from below. Brackets of flat steel stock are easily cold formed to the required shape and fastened with screws, bolts, or lags (Fig. 11-11). Be sure to raise the sign off the roof somewhat to allow for drainage.

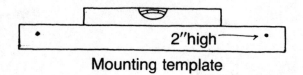

2" high

Mounting template

Fig. 11-9. A template for locating
fastener positions.

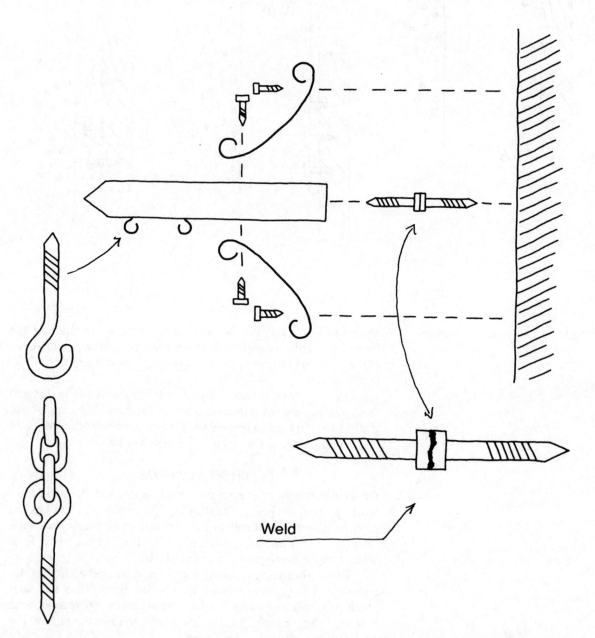

Weld

Fig. 11-10. Fasteners might need welding.

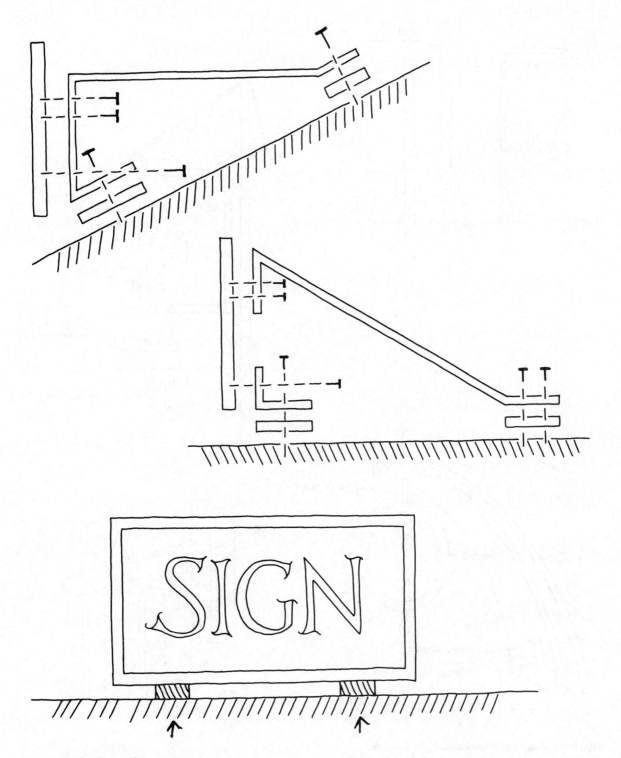

Fig. 11-11. Roof mountings.

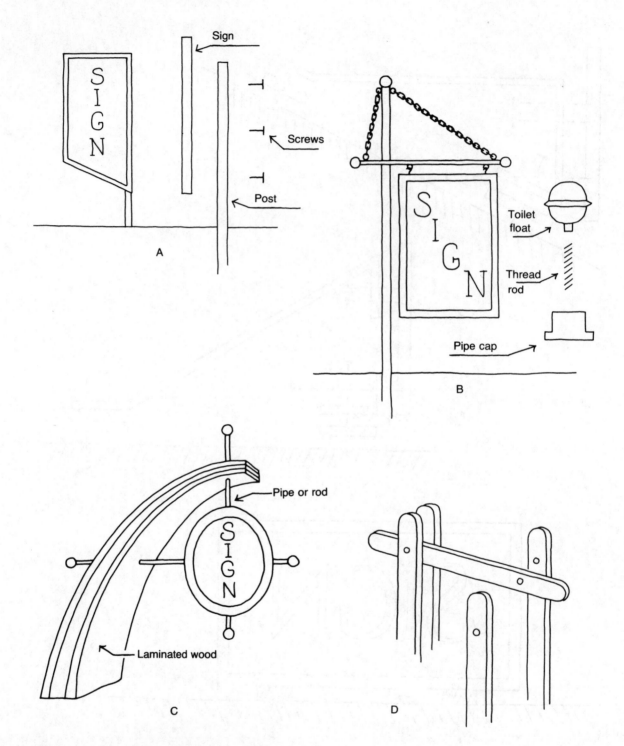

Fig. 11-12. Examples of freestanding mountings.

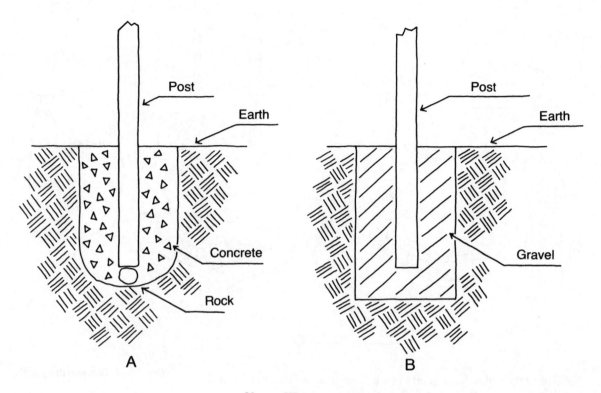

Fig. 11-13. Anchoring freestanding mountings.

Note. Whenever very large or heavy signs must be mounted—especially on a roof or high on a wall—it might be a good idea to subcontract the installation to a large sign or billboard company. They have the equipment and experienced riggers to ensure that the job is done right. The cost will be passed along to the customer in any event. Because these big companies seldom employ woodcarvers, they do not represent "competition." If they like your work, they might begin to subcontract work to you.

Freestanding Mountings

Freestanding mountings are a wonderful area for design and self expression. Some ideas are shown in Figs. 11-12 and 11-13. The primary thing to remember is to set posts quite deeply into the ground. Use only redwood, cedar, locust, or pressure-treated timbers for contact with the ground. See Table 11-2.

Table 11-2. Freestanding Mountings.

Tools	Materials	Miscellaneous
Post hole digger, or	Sand	Wheelbarrow
Gas driven earth auger	Gravel	Shovels
Level	Ready mixed concrete	
Plumb bob		

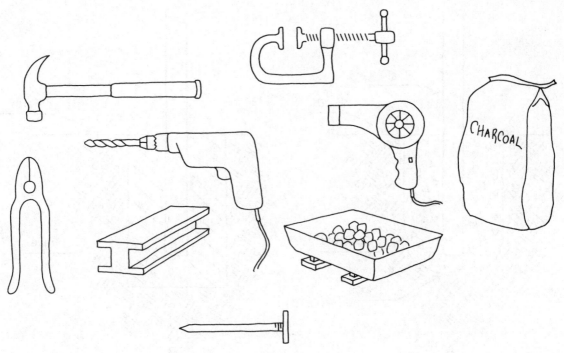

Fig. 11-14. Blacksmithing tools.

This might also be a good area in which to subcontract. For very large signs, a large company is a must. But for even a small sign, arming a teenaged neighbor with a rented post hole digger might be a very good idea.

BLACKSMITHING

I learned the art of blacksmithing simply because I needed to make the hangers for the type of sign shown in Fig. 11-15. I found it easy to come up with the tools I needed, and even easier to make the "wrought iron" brackets.

The tools shown in Fig. 11-14 are simple and direct. See also Table 11-3. The hibachi and charcoal briquettes were already on the patio. The "anvil" consisted of a hunk of heavy steel plate and a

Table 11-3. Blacksmithing.

Tools	Materials	Miscellaneous
Hibachi or barbecue	Charcoal or bricquets	Chalk or welder's soapstone marker
Assorted hammers	Flat steel stock	Hairdryer or small fan
"Anvil"	Large common nails	Heavy leather gloves
Electric drill & bits		Bucket of water or garden hose
Bolt cutter, or		
Cold chisel		
C-clamps, visegrip pliers, etc.		

Fig. 11-15. Gently hammer a head onto the rivet.

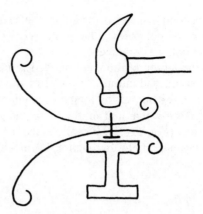

short length of 2-inch water pipe found at the town dump. These are set on old fence posts sunk deeply in the ground. The drill and bits as well as the nails and bolt cutter were in the shop. If you don't have a bolt cutter, a large cold chisel will do. The flat steel stock can be purchased in small quantities at industrial and millwright suppliers and large hardware stores.

First get a good fire going in the hibachi. An old hair dryer makes a good bellows. The steel is placed well into the fire. When glowing red, it is pulled out and worked to the required shape on the anvil by using assorted hammers. The steel is surprisingly soft, and it requires a more gentle touch than you might first expect. For extreme or complex bends, several reheatings might be necessary. Working the steel after it looses its red heat will cause the steel to fracture at the bend.

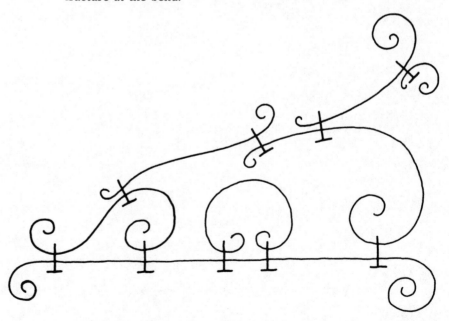

Fig. 11-16. An example of a "wrought iron" mounting.

261

After the needed shape is formed, the steel can be sprayed with the garden hose to cool down. Clamp the cooled components together and drill holes as needed.

Estimate the length of the rivet needed to fasten the several thicknesses of steel, and cut a heavy nail to the required length. the rivet until it is red hot. Using long pliers, slip the rivet into the rivet hole. Place the whole unit on the anvil and gently hammer a head onto the rivet (Fig. 11-15). It really is that easy. Figure 11-16 shows an example of a simple "wrought iron" mounting made in this fashion.

12

Selling Carved Signs

I t has been my experience, and the experience of many people I have talked to and read about, that it is difficult to start a small business and even harder to succeed with it. The reasons for this are many, but the *main* reasons are not immediately apparent.

For example, it is rather easy to develop a truly better mousetrap. But having invented it, it comes as a terrible shock to discover that the path to your door is overgrown by nettles and weeds. The world is ignoring you completely, and that's not the way it's supposed to be!

In the meantime, an entrepreneur who knows nothing about mice or traps gets a tremendous close-out deal on the same old trap. On network TV and in the national papers he advertizes it as the greatest thing since sliced bread, and the world beats his door down. You starve with the truly better mousetrap, while he becomes rich on the same old thing.

In the world of crafts, it is as easy as going broke to develop a product line that everyone admires, yet no one buys. All crafts, and this includes carved signs, are products. Products fail in the marketplace for one of two reasons.

Reason one is that no one wants it. There is a world of difference between people liking your product, and wanting it enough to pay the price.

Reason two is that the people who might want the product enough to pay the price don't know that the product even exists, let alone where to find it. These two reasons boil down to one word: marketing.

It is easy to invest money in wood and tools. It is easier still to invest time in learning to carve well. These are the fun things. Investing time and money in market research and market development are not fun. They are costly in terms of both money and time. And besides, commercialism is something that many artisans want to avoid. That's *why* they become artisans in the first place. But the only way that you can really know that your work is marketable is when others think enough of your work to buy it.

CUSTOM SIGNS

Selling custom signs is very much like being a missionary in a foreign country. It is like getting people to believe in a God that they cannot see. There is simply no valid reason for the natives to place faith in an intangible, no matter what the missionary's vision and experience. A beautifully carved and gilded sign that exists only in your mind will not sell. Therefore you must do what all missionaries do; get out and meet people and talk and talk and talk until someone else catches the vision too. One way to do this is to start small, work at home, and treat the whole thing as a hobby.

Selling from Your Home

The first step is to carve a name board for your home. Place it where everyone will see it. If a neighbor admires it, talk him into accepting one as a gift. Go to his home and do the installation yourself. Make these first signs beautiful and start a trend. Give your work away even if you do want to start a business eventually. Think of the first dozen or so signs as an apprenticeship.

As you do the work, be sure to talk it up with everybody you meet. Even if you are stuck for words it should not be too hard. I have intentionally used a great deal of "advertising copy" in writing the text of this book. Pick it out and use it freely.

Almost everyone knows one or two housewives who sell refrigerator dishes, cosmetics, or costume jewelry on the "party plan." Look up the more successful of these women and make up nameboards for them. While you're at it, offer to make them some sales aids such as shown in Fig. 1-21. They will get the message right away. Perhaps they will give you a wonderful free education in selling and commission structures on the spot.

Be sure to take *good* color photos of your work. One should be a closeup of the sign and a second should be a middle-distance shot showing the sign in it's setting. Make enlargements of the best of these and start a portfolio that you *always* have with you.

Fig. 12-1. Examples of sales aids.

As your reputation begins to grow, there are several other methods you can use. But always remember that your personality and reputation sells signs. Signs never sell themselves.

Business Signs

In almost every business community, there is an older and more densely packed part of town. The shops are generally small and the rents are generally low. Costume jewelry, boutiques, record shops and beauty parlors gravitate to these locations.

Look for the best street in this part of town. It is almost certain to be well traveled. Look for the three *worst* signs on the street. The businesses should suggest that a carved sign would be appropriate. Visit each store and engage the proprietor in conversation. Then select the business owner who seems to be the most kindred spirit and make him the same offer you made to the party plan lady.

In such locations, there are also businesses that have absolutely no use for the show windows in the stores they rent. Printers, plumbers, and insurance offices are likely candidates. You can often rent such show windows very inexpensively, or even get them free just for washing the windows. Try to find a shop where the proprietor is willing to take the time to talk about you and your work.

When you decorate a window (as in Fig. 12-2), there are some things you must be sure to include. Most important of course is your name and phone number. Second, be sure to have some interesting props as well as examples of your carving. Props can be such things

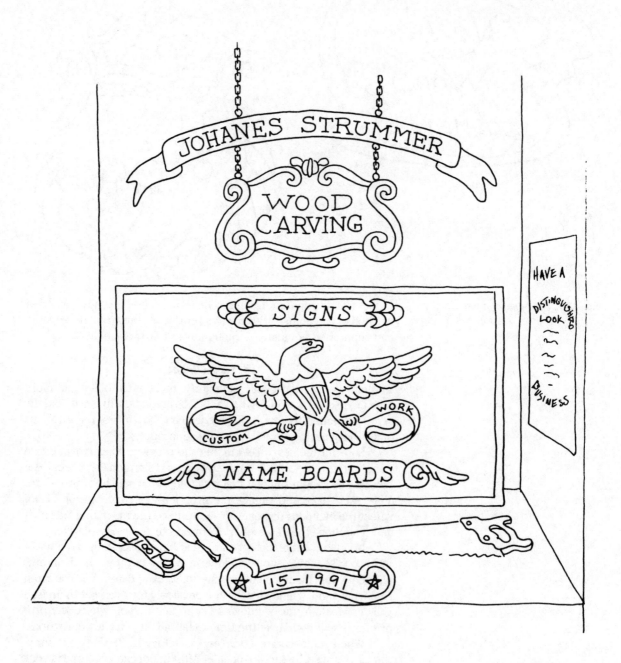

Fig. 12-2. A window display.

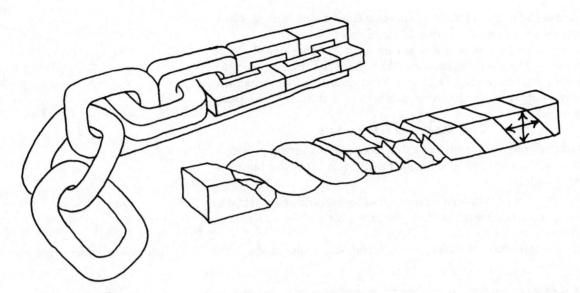

Fig. 12-3. Examples of props.

as driftwood, but the best props seem to be antique tools and wood shavings.

Include pieces that are unfinished or show the various stages of carving and finishing. Examples of two all-time winners are shown in Fig. 12-3. Hand letter some small, well-worded captions on pieces of show card. Be sure that they are legible from the street.

Include a *good* photo of yourself carving one of the items in the window. Make sure the picture is well composed, has an "artsy" look to it, and shows your face.

As you begin to secure commissions, contact your local paper about stories on your work. Ask by name for the reporter who is most likely to be interested. Make sure you have several black-and-white glossy photos of yourself and your work for the paper to use. Don't depend on the paper's photographer. Remember that newspapers won't write you up just because you and your work are interesting. The papers have to be *told* that you and your work are interesting.

Wholesale

There are many ways to wholesale carved signs through established businesses. This can be much more profitable than starting your own shop. By selecting the outlets carefully, you can continue to work in your basement or garage. At the same time, far more potential customers will see your work than if you had a single retail location.

Make up smaller versions of the store window display and take a photo of it to the stores of your choice. Businesses that could profit from associating with you might be home centers, real estate agents, ships chandlers, gift shops, and hardware stores. Most businesses will want a very compact display.

Another type of business to contact is the large sign shops in the area. Many such businesses do not have the time or space to devote to wood carving. Of course, this means that their name will be on your work, but the money helps to ease the pain somewhat.

Craft Shows and Flea Markets

Working craft shows and flea markets can be rewarding provided that you make the necessary adjustments required by the nature of these outlets.

☐ Your table or booth must be flamboyant, and you must talk, dress, and act the part. The trick is to give quality while acting like a huckster.

☐ You must specialize in while-you-wait nameboards. This

Fig. 12-4. An example of a flier.

268

means rapid freehand work with a router without benefit of a design or making a cartoon. You must have a quantity of prefinished sign blanks on hand.

☐ Don't ever expect to take orders to be finished and delivered next week. Flea marketers want their purchases *now*!

☐ Have your portfolio of color photographs and a pile of business cards available at the booth. Handouts and fliers (Fig. 12-4) can also work well.

☐ You will need a booth with several electrical outlets for lights, a vacuum cleaner, and for running the router. Also be prepared for the complaints from neighboring booths about the noise and mess.

All of this represents a substantial investment—both financial and emotional—that might or might not be rewarded. Seasons, weather, and a great many more variables come into consideration. And then some shows just bomb no matter what you do. On the other hand, thousand-dollar days are also possible.

By far the hardest part of show selling is pricing. Almost all experienced show vendors will tell you that there is *simply* no guaranteed pricing formula. Experience and experimentation will eventually pay off.

Retail Business

Opening a retail shop or studio is probably the ultimate dream of all craftspeople. The shop will look *just* the way you want it to, you will make lovely things, and people will come to you with handfuls of dollars to lay on you. Of such dreams is the cloth of fairy tales woven.

To be sure, the fairy tale is important. Successful shop owners are the ones who preserve the illusion in the midst of harsh realities. Tourists will visit such shops and the word will spread, but only because the shop is an anachronism; the public wants to believe the fairy tale too.

This should say a lot about the creation of such a shop. It almost *must* be in a tourist area, and it will take an enormous amount of hard cash up front to create the image of genteel poverty and dedication to craft and excellence.

The federal government, in conjunction with many state and local agencies, holds countless small business workshops and seminars every year. The small business failure rate in this country has reached the proportions of a major epidemic. If the dream is one that infects you badly, then you must do a lot of hard work and long hours of research into just what problems lie ahead. Taxes, licenses, permits, insurance, unemployment, workman's compensation and a host of additional problems lie in wait for you.

Begin at a local college and find a professor in the business department. Find out all you can about programs put on by colleges, the government, and organizations. Attend all the seminars and workshops. Take notes and believe what these people tell you.

Your local library will have (or can get) many books on small business, crafts, marketing research and new product development. Read and take notes.

The unfortunate facts are these. Out of every 1,000 new businesses started this year, over 500 will fail. This year! Out of every 1,000 that are left, 950 did it the hard way. Of the remainder, 45 have rich parents who want to keep the kids busy somewhere else. The remaining five are miracles that shouldn't have happened. They are delusions perpetrated by capricious gods, designed to tempt the rest of us into failure and dispair. Miracles only happen to other people.

PROBLEMS

There are always problems related to running a small business. In this section we will cover only the problems that you are certain to face in the sign carving business.

Local Ordinances

As the function of the politician is to forbid what he cannot otherwise compel, there are laws called ordinances or codes designed to ensure that all signs everywhere conform to legal definitions of beauty and propriety. That so many existing signs are attrociously offensive gives loud witness to the effacacy of the codes. Nevertheless, codes exist and you must abide by them. Copies will be available at the local government offices. Because your tax dollars are at work, you will in all likelihood have to pay for your copy.

The simplest code gives restrictions about setbacks from rights-of-ways (roads and sidewalks), maximum size allowed, and relative size as figured on a percentage of the total square footage of the building front. Naturally it gets better for a corner building.

More complex codes require a rendering to be submitted to an approving committee that is somehow endowed with impeccable taste, and meets only when certain planets are in conjunction. I know of one code that limits palettes to five specific colors of paint!

Local Permits

A permit allows you to proceed with the erection of a sign that conforms to the code. You must see to it that the permits are secured (more money). This could take several trips to city hall, and involve such things as proving that you are insured, or you might have to post a bond. When things get to be a real hassle, the business owner can be designated as the contractor. This might

QUICK & CHEEP
25 BIRD ST. HOBOKEN N.J.
201 123 1234

TERMS	33.33% of the total price F.O.B. our studio in Hoboken, NJ, is to accompany any order to enter that order into production. 33.33% of the total price will be paid upon customer's receipt of color photograph of completed work. 33.34% of total price due upon customer's receipt of work.
CONDITIONS	ALL orders must be in writing and to be effective must be accompanied by a 33.33% deposit as specified above, and must be acknowledged in writing by us and at the price shown on our acknowledgement. Our written consent must be obtained in order to cancel any order, and terms of the cancellation must indemnify us against loss, as in TERMS above. No cancellations may be made for finished work.
AGREEMENTS	We will not be liable for losses, damages or delays resulting FROM STRIKES, accidents or other causes beyond our control. All clerical errors are subject to correction.
SHIPMENTS	All work will be shipped on a ""Freight Collect'' basis unless ""Prepaid'' shipment has been specifically negotiated with us in writing.
CLAIMS	All work is inspected for proper packing before leaving our studio. Accordingly, our responsibility ceases upon acceptance by the carrier. It is the cosignee's responsibility to initiate and carry through all claims for delay, damage, or loss in transit. We will render all possible assistance in securing satisfactory adjustment of such claims.
SPECIAL FIXTURES	We will fabricate special mounting, lighting, or other fixtures to an approved print of OUR DRAWING ONLY, when accompanied by an order, and deposit; see TERMS.
INSTALLATION	Because we have no control over installations other than those made by our studio, under NO CIRCUMSTANCES can we be held responsible for accident, field conditions, dimensional, surface, or other changes.
GUARANTEE	All work is thoroughly inspected before shipment. We will replace or repair at our option= and at no cost=any of our products that have been proven to us as defective in either material or workmanship. A claim for such repair or replacement must be made within a period of three (3) months from the date of shipment. In accepting this material for repair or replacement, it is understood that this is the limit of our responsibility, and that no other claims, as a result of this defect, will be allowed.

Fig. 12-5. An example of a guarantee.

save a lot of time and trouble. All of this might or might not be specified in the code. It takes time to learn these things.

Insurance

It will seldom happen that your homeowner's policy will cover a catastrophe that occurs while you are engaging in a clandestine business activity.

Guarantees

The subject of guarantees is truly a touchy matter. Naturally you will have done your best to make sure that your work will endure. Yet the customer is entitled to some form of written statement that your work will last for a reasonable length of time and will stand up to normal wear and tear.

As an artist, you will probably be affronted by a document full of legalese, but you must realize that there are people out there who make a hobby of taking other people to court. You must try to protect yourself against such people. Figure 12-5 is the type of the guarantee that I use. Show it to your lawyer.

Contracts

All contracts are good until put to the test. It is good to have things spelled out, and especially when you are dealing with businesses or third parties such as architects. If your customer holds his grand opening right on schedule, and the sign isn't there, he has every right to be angry. If there have been two weeks of foul weather when outside work was impossible, whose fault is it?

Contracts will be more or less complex as the situation demands, but it should at least say who does what. For example, who gets (and pays for) the permit? Who climbs the ladder and hangs the sign? Who digs the holes for the posts?

Other terms might include periodic inspections to ensure continuing safety and security. Options might include periodic washing of dirt and grime from the sign and touching up the paint. Continuing contacts with established customers can often lead to new business.

BRANCHING OUT

With all the skill and experience you acquire, and all the tools you have invested in, there will probably be many additional markets that you will want to explore. The progression into other areas is a natural tendency.

A homeowner who has chosen to express some individuality through a carved name board might be a natural candidate for a carved front door (Fig. 12-6). A businessman who has chosen a new

Fig. 12-6. Examples of door carvings.

image through a carved sign might be a natural candidate for a new store front (Fig. 12-7).

Window signs and display pieces (Fig. 12-8) are excellent possibilities once *you* create the demand for them. It is also possible to design and execute entire business interiors using sign carving skills as a foundation upon which to build and expand.

Churches, fraternal organizations, universities, and municipalities all have need of carved plaques and signs (Fig. 12-9). Homeowners sometimes want architectural trims and family crests (Fig. 12-10).

Bars, clubs, and restaurants frequently change hands, and new owners are often anxious to upgrade the atmosphere. Carved signs, pictorials, architectural trims, and panels are natural in such cases (Fig. 12-11). The owners of such businesses know the direct value of such work to their business, and they seldom quibble about the price.

Fig. 12-7. A carved store front.

Fig. 12-8. A window sign and a display piece.

Fig. 12-9. Examples of plaques and signs.

Fig. 12-10. A family crest with architectural trim.

Fig. 12-11. An example of a carved panel.

Fig. 12-12. Carvings for vessels.

Fig. 12-13. Carved furniture.

Fig. 12-14. A carved table and chair.

Fig. 12-15. Boutique furnishings.

Fig. 12-16. Gallery items.

Fig. 12-17. Consignment items.

Boat owners and yachtsmen have always used carvers to beautify their vessels (Fig. 12-12).

Well designed and carefully executed one-of-a-kind furniture pieces (Fig. 12-13) are often regarded as sound investments.

Tables and chairs for tea shops and Wedgewood collector's emporiums (Fig. 12-14) need not be of museum quality or price to be entirely acceptable. The same is true of furnishings for boutiques, funky places, and "atmosphere" restaurants (Fig. 12-15).

Many galleries and shops buy, or take on consignment, small items such as lamps (Fig. 12-16) and boxes (Fig. 12-17). Depending on the location of the shop(s), this can be a lucrative venture.

The foregoing represent only some of the many areas in which to branch out. I hope this short catalog will stimulate your thinking, and you will come up with the one area that is just right for you.

This book is intended to teach fundamentals. The true artist never stops learning and inquiring. The books, catalogs, and sources listed in the appendices all have a wealth of information and ideas to offer. The trick is to appropriate what the others have done. Adapt other things and make them your own. Discard what I or anyone else might say that is not worthwhile. "Whatever things are true, just, pure, lovely, and of good report . . . think on these things."

Appendix A

A Wall-Mounted Sign

Figures A-1 through A-5 illustrate the basic steps in making a wall-mounted sign in cypress wood. A router, incised hand carving, and applique were used in constructing the sign.

As shown in Fig. A-1, the enlarged cartoon has been transferred to heavy brown craft paper and taped to the sign blank. Typing carbon and stylus are used to transfer the drawing to the blank. The cartoon has been cut apart and taped together several times in order to get the goose to "fly."

Figure A-2 shows the router with a rocker soleplate being used to cut an unweighted outline of the goose, using a ¼-inch flat bit. The sharp points in the pinions (center bottom) will have to be refined with a knife.

Hand incising of the letters using a variety of traditional gouges ("fingernail" chisels could also have been used, Fig. A-3). Carved as if for gilding, the deepest part of the letters is just slightly below ⅛ of an inch.

Figure A-4 shows a plywood applique in the shape of a hand plane being cut with a coping saw. Because it will be painted black, no modeling of the surfaces or curves is attempted.

The finished sign, (31 × 32 inches) is shown in Fig. A-5. It was carved on a cypress wood hatch cover without trying to remove the aging and defects in the wood. The peculiar mark below the "S" in "GOOSE" is a small bullet hole.

After the carving was completed, and before the applique and paint were applied, the sign was given two coats of penetrating sealer to keep the black paint from crawling into the wood grain. The sign was then set out on a flat roof to weather and age for three months before final installation.

Fig. A-1. Transfer of the cartoon.

Fig. A-2. Using the router to cut the outline of the goose.

Fig. A-3. Incising the letters with gouges.

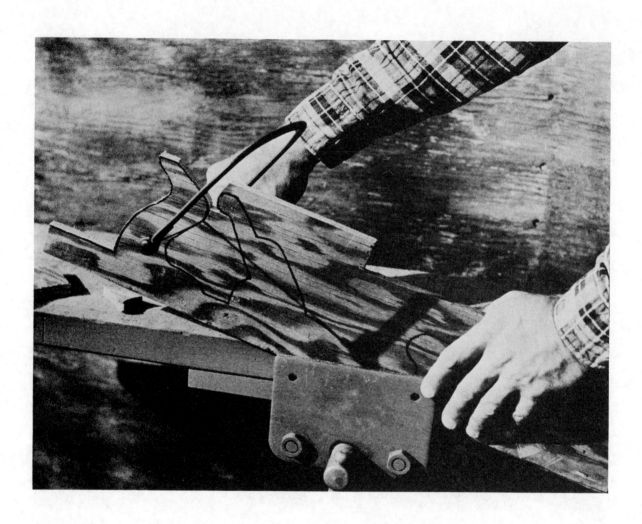

Fig. A-4. A plywood applique.

Fig. A-5. The finished sign.

Appendix B

Sources

General Tools

Silvo Hardware Co.
2205 Richmond Street
Philadelphia, PA 19125

U.S. General
100 Commercial Street
Plainview, NY 11803

Woodcarving Tools

Shopsmith Inc.
Catalog Information
750 Center Drive
Vandalia, OH 45377

Constantine's Inc.
2050 Eastchester Road
Bronx, NY 10461

Craftsman Wood Service Co.
1735 West Cortland Court
Addison, IL 60101

Frog Tool Co.
700 West Jackson Boulevard
Chicago, IL 60606

Garrett Wade Co.
161 Avenue of the Americas
New York, NY 10013

Leichtung, Inc.
4944 Commerce Parkway
Cleveland, OH 44128-5985

Frank Mittermeier, Inc.
3577 East Tremont Avenue
New York, NY 10465

Woodcarver's Supply Co.
3056 Excelsior Boulevard
Minneapolis, MN 55416

Woodcraft Supply Corp.
313 Montvale Avenue
Woburn, MA 01888

Woodworker's Supply of New Mexico
5604 Alameda N.E.
Albuquerque, NM 87113

Plastics

Acme Plastics, Inc.
Browerton Road
West Paterson, NJ 07424

Ain Plastics, Inc.
P.O. Box 151
Mount Vernon, NY 10550

Art Supplies, etc.

Dick Blick, Inc.
Box 512
Henderson, NV 89015

Dick Blick, Inc.
Box 1267
Galesburg, IL 61401

Dick Blick, Inc.
Box 26
Allentown, PA 18105

Arthur Browne' Bro., Inc.
2 West 46th Street
New York, NY 10036

Miscellaneous

Bendix Mouldings, Inc. (precarved wooden moldings)
235 Pegasus Avenue
Northvale, NJ 07647

Dri Industries, Inc. (assorted fastenings, etc.)
11100 Hampshire Avenue South
Bloomington, MN 55438

Greiger's, Inc. (lapidary supplies)
900 South Arroyo Parkway
Pasadena, CA 91109

Industrial Abrasives Co. (sandpaper and abrasive products)
642 North Eighth Street
Reading, PA 19603-9960

Appendix C

Further Reading

Chapelle, H.I. *Boatbuilding*. New York: W. W. Norton Co., Inc., 1941.

A very thorough study of tools, wood, fastenings, and enlarging designs.

Evetts, L.C. *Roman Lettering*. New York: Taplinger Publishing Co., Inc., 1979.

A thorough study of the lettering of the Trajan Column, and Roman lettering in Britain.

Hanna, J.S. *Marine Carving Handbook*. Camden, Maine: International Marine Publishing Co., 1975.

A lightweight book, interesting for its emphasis on carvings related to boats, etc.

Hasluck, P.N. *Manual of Traditional Wood Carving*. New York: Dover Publications, Inc., 1977.

The most useful and comprehensive coverage of the general topic.

Nelms, H. *Thinking with a Pencil*. New York: Barnes & Noble, Division of Harper & Row, 1957.

Quite simply a "must have" for any artist, craftsman, or thinking person. Most recently re-printed by Ten Speed Press.

Rich, J.O. *Materials and Methods of Sculpture*. New York: Oxford University Press, 1947.

Far broader coverage than any sign carver will need, but very good in that it explains how and why as well as what. Fine arts emphasis.

Speltz, A. *Styles of Ornament*. New York: Dover Publications, Inc., 1959.
Reprint of a 1904 German classic. More design ideas than anyone will probably ever use.

Spielman, P. *Making Wood Signs*. New York: Sterling Publishing Co., Inc., 1981.
A great deal of information; photographs of work by East Coast and West Coast masters.

Tschichold, J. *Lettering and Alphabets*. New York: Van Nostrand Reinhold Publishing Co., 1966.
Neither modern nor exciting visually, the introductory chapter says more about good lettering in fewer words than any other book on the subject.

Upton, J. *A Woodcarver's Primer*. New York: Sterling Publishing Co., Inc., 1979.
Admittedly only a primer, but probably the best. Read this one before going on to Hasluck.

Wotzkow, H. *Art of Hand Lettering*. New York: Dover Publications, Inc., 1967.
Much useful information on lettering and layout. The book is written for artists with pen and brush, and some of the material won't apply to carving.

Signcraft Magazine
P.O. Box 06031
Fort Meyers, FL 33906

Signs of the Times Magazine
407 Gilbert Avenue
Cincinnati, OH 45202

Index

Confidence in Public Speaking